Education for Ministry
Reform and Renewal
in Theological Education

George P. Schner, S.J.

Sheed & Ward

©1993 by George P. Schner, S.J.
Sheed & Ward™ is a service of The National Catholic Reporter Publishing Company.

Library of Congress Cataloguing in Publication Data

Schner, George P., 1946-
    Education for ministry : reform and renewal in theological education
/ George P. Schner.
       p.   cm.
    Includes bibliographical references and index.
    ISBN 1-55612-566-6 (pbk.)
    1. Catholic Church--Education--United States. I. Title
BX905.S375   1993
207'.73--dc20   92-32958
                                                        CIP

Published by: Sheed & Ward
                 115 E. Armour Blvd.
                 P.O. Box 419492
                 Kansas City, MO 64141-6492

To order, call: (800) 333-7373

Contents

Preface

AT REGIS COLLEGE MORE THAN EIGHT YEARS AGO, THEN PRESIDENT Jacques Monet, S.J., suggested to me that I write this essay about theological education. He was responding to a reading of the rather terse essay I had written as a result of being part of the Association of Theological Schools of the United States and Canada's Basic Issues Research Program in 1982. Participation in that program was an introduction not only to forms of reflection about theological education but more importantly to a group of Christian scholars whose lively and varied concerns have been an education for me.

At the same time, my professional involvement with the Committee of East Coast Deans of Theologates deepened my understanding and appreciation for educational settings and problems of at least part of the North American Catholic system of preparing candidates for ministry in the Church. A more specialized association was the regular meetings of rectors, deans, and presidents of the Jesuit schools of theology in North America, and these colleagues were an important part of my reflection on the constituent parts of theological education from within my own religious community.

Finally, at the invitation of Barbara Wheeler, I became part of an evaluating team funded by the Lilly Endowment to reflect upon the impact of ATS-sponsored research, with a view to providing a specifically Roman Catholic critique of the literature which had resulted principally from the Basic Issues Research Program. That assignment led me to reflect upon the nearly 20 years I have been a student in, professor of, and administrator for theological education in North America. A great many ideas and persons converged, then, as I consigned thoughts to paper.

In particular, I wish to thank the following whose wisdom aided me significantly in the course of the past few years: Frans Jozef van Beeck, Walter Deller, Joseph DiNoia, Katarina Schuth, Patricia Walter, Barbara Wheeler, and Robert Wister. The faculty and staff of Campion College at the University of Regina provided a most congenial environment in the winter of 1991, during which the major revisions of this work were completed. In particular, I am grateful for the professional expertise of Samira McCarthy, surpassed only by her cordial friendship. A word of special thanks is offered to William Coden for his gracious hospitality on numerous occasions during the writing of this work. I wish to acknowledge the encouragement and financial support of the Lilly Endowment, Inc. for the publication of this work, and thank particularly Mr. Fred Hofheinz for his assistance.

With gratitude for many things over many years, I dedicate this book to a scholar, friend, and companion in the Society of Jesus, Jacques Monet.

Feast of Saint James
25 July 1992

Introduction

QUESTIONS ABOUT EDUCATION FOR CHRISTIAN MINISTRY ARE CUR-
RENTLY the subject of lively debate in both Church and society.
Major constructive proposals have been made from within several
church traditions, and valuable discussions have taken place under
the aegis of the Lilly Endowment and the Association of Theological
Schools. As an introduction to the contents of this book, this introductory chapter does not offer an argument for the importance of
this subject matter or for the attention this essay gives to one specific tradition of Christianity. The topic of education for ministry in
the Roman Catholic tradition might at first sight seem to appeal to a
limited readership. Its importance and effect cannot, however, be
underestimated, and those closely involved with ministerial education will need little persuasion of the value of a careful consideration of the topics contained here. What is about to happen to Catholic ministerial education in North America within the next few
decades will have an effect on every aspect of Catholic life, its role
in the larger world-wide Roman tradition, its relationship with other
traditions, and its credibility and effect in North American culture
and beyond. Such a statement of context for this modest essay is
not for its aggrandizement, but rather to express the passion and
conviction of its author about the importance of the conversation
needed to ensure that education for ministry in the Roman tradition
in North America does not fail to live up to its already praiseworthy
history, its present earnest self-scrutiny, and its vital role in the future of its tradition.

My remarks in this chapter will attend to four preliminary matters so as to aid the reader to understand what follows. First, I will
indicate whom I envision my readership to be, the intent of the style

and content of the work, and therefore some recommendations about how it should be read. Second, since the text does not employ a set of notes to augment the text but only provides a bibliography of sources, I will acknowledge my debts to a variety of sources. Third, there will follow a brief outline of the contents and their logic of organization. Finally, there will be an initial remark about an overarching characteristic of education for ministry necessary to all its parts, namely its scholarly and intellectual character.

I

This book is most obviously intended for theological educators and those who oversee theological institutions, students beginning their education for ministry, and those who have completed it but wish to reflect on what it accomplished and what sort of further education would profit them. Beyond this obvious readership, concerned Catholics generally might find it a satisfying source of insight into how their priests and ministers came to be the way they are, and might spark their own reflection on how important it would be for them to make known their evaluation of ministerial education. As well, just as many Catholic educators have already profited from reflections on ministry produced out of other traditions than their own, so members of other traditions will, I hope, find my remarks similarly helpful. At times the text will be somewhat technical but not, I hope, esoteric for either the general Catholic reader or those from other traditions.

Upon finishing the book, I discovered that it follows quite inadvertently what is known as the adult learning cycle, passing from questions about experience, through conceptualization, to prospects for implementation. With this movement or logic, the essay aims at a certain kind of practicality. It invites not only the criticism of its theoretical stance, but also criticism fashioned through efforts to act upon its suggestions which might prove or disprove its contentions. Perhaps every book invites this two-fold involvement. This book requires it.

Certain decisions had to be made as to vocabulary and examples, both as to their function in the style and content of the work. Chiefly that has meant a conscious choice on my part to discuss ministry, and not priesthood alone, and to address the whole range of institutions from seminaries educating candidates for priesthood only to schools which are not only part of ecumenical consortia but which have highly diverse student bodies and faculties. Some may find this a debilitating choice, or at least one guaranteed to confuse the issue. I am convinced, to the contrary, that unless this diversity of ministries and plurality of institutions is addressed, one cannot say much of value about the revision and renewal of education for ministry in the Roman tradition. To offset the very real confusion this inevitably involves, I trust that my attempts at clarity of thought, precision in vocabulary, and limitation to general principles are successful. To the extent that they are not, I await my critics' improvements.

The subject of education for ministry is purposefully focused within the Roman Catholic tradition, which I most often call the "Roman tradition" so as to indicate that there are other rites within its catholicity, and to highlight indirectly the unique role North Americans have within that tradition. It is a tradition with a distinguished heritage, and the one I consider my Christian home. To discuss theological education without adverting to its locale in specific traditions is to court one of two dangers: to imply that the problems and solutions of one tradition are applicable to all, without remainder; or to verge on offering increasingly vacuous analyses. The large and helpful body of literature produced on the subject in the last two decades has not by and large totally ignored this principle. However, Roman Catholic reflection on education for ministry has not been proportionately as large within the more public Christian world as is its membership or influence. It is intriguing to wonder why they have not produced the books and articles which mark the raising to consciousness of deep-rooted problems. It is not germane here to offer an answer to this question; rather, it is important for what follows to indicate that my own effort is deeply indebted to the cross-tradition discussion of which I have been fortunate to be a part.

The effort I have made both structurally and indirectly to use to advantage the best of materials from many sources on each of the topics in my own essay will, I hope, render my remarks useful beyond my own tradition and experience. I have learned a great deal from so many in other traditions, not just by their written works, but perhaps most especially by the conversations and friendships which make ecumenicity a very living reality for me. The coincidence of my own convictions and intuitive insights with other's, which has often made me feel at home in other traditions, is, however, paralleled by a frustration when the specificities of the Catholic situation are not adverted to. The chapters which follow invite an ecumenical readership, and an ecumenical critique.

The materials used, then, originate within several traditions, and I will now turn to a brief survey of what I have chosen and why.

II

As I have already noted, the text contains not footnotes or endnotes, and for a very specific reason. The argument put forward below, if it can be called that, is not dependent chiefly on the quotation of sources for particular points or the confrontation of one opinion with another. It is dependent upon the understanding of and incorporation of several large and complex analyses of education for ministry, its recent history, present state, its problems, and its theological grounding. It requires an appeal to the whole of those books and articles which will be found in the bibliography at the end of the text, and to the basic points of critique which have become generally accepted.

The bibliography contains a preliminary set of official documents, which is by no means exhaustive as a list of sources. It does indicate those I have directly quoted. There follows a list of books, and then articles, which are the background to my own thinking and which occasionally I quote. The following remarks will alert those familiar with the literature to my intellectual debts and preferences, and will be a short introduction for other readers to the names and numbers of the players.

As to factual information and general interpretation of the Catholic situation, the work of Robert Wuthnow, Katerina Schuth, Joseph White, Thomas Day, and the collection of essays edited by Jay Dolan confirmed and expanded my own experience. A number of articles which appeared in the journal *Theological Education* provide important discussions of particular issues, and I use them throughout to develop contrasts with them and to identify the particularly form of the issues in the Roman tradition. The four major studies which deal with a comprehensive set of issues, two by Edward Farley, one by Charles Wood, and the essay with the joint authorship of Joseph Hough and John Cobb, provide both a general framework of ideas and specific instances of text for analysis. I could say in summation that I am more in agreement with these works than disagreement, though it is the points of contrast which are developed throughout my text. Finally, I am indebted to the theological works on ministry by Thomas O'Meara, George Tavard, Edmund Hill, and Edward Kilmartin for scholarship which preceded, followed, and most often confirmed my intuitions and hopes. My effort has been to apply their insights to the specific case of theological education for ministry without, I hope, endangering the theological and historical integrity of their work. Finally, I am dependent in several ways on the works of George Lindbeck and Frans Jozef van Beeck for several of the large conceptual schemes which run through the various parts of the book.

Two other short notes are necessary concerning my sources. For the section on the identity of the minister, in which I employ psychological principles, I am indebted to conversations and team teaching I have done with my brother Joseph Schner, a clinical psychologist who has made this matter a particular study of his. As well, the work of Lewis Brandt and Don Browning has guided some choices in that section. Second, the material on pedagogy was initially given at a National Catholic Education Association Convention, and subsequently developed into a workshop format. I am grateful to the members of several faculties who participated in such workshops and helped refashion that material.

III

By way of a preview of what is to come, and so as to give the reader a map of the exposition and argument, this section of the introduction will detail the parts and logic of the book. It is divided into three Parts, with an introductory and concluding chapter framing them.

Part I poses three questions about the kind of ministers and priests the present education for ministry provides: are they professional? are they practical? are they devoted? Each characteristic is explored for its particularity in the Roman tradition, and each requires some description, analysis, and critique. If the overall purpose of the institutions in question is to provide the Church with well-educated priests and ministers, then it seems logical to me to begin with a look at them and their effectiveness. These chapters are not factual or statistical accounts, however, but descriptions in aid of discovering principles at work. They should be taken as a whole, providing a composite picture, not of daily routine but of motivations and ideals which are taught in ministerial preparation and revised throughout ministerial activity. If these descriptions and evaluations are to help produce more than ad hoc solutions, they must lead to a theological discussion. This I have attempted in the second cluster of chapters.

Part II explores the notions of ministerial identity and authority, and the encompassing notion of tradition as the context for both. I call these chapters theological ones because they are in search of basic rules, doctrines if you like, which animate these ways of describing theologically the person and work of those who engage in official ministry in the Church. If the chapters of Part I are heuristic to larger descriptions of ministry, so these chapters are preparatory to a more thorough systematic theological study not just of ministry, but of education for ministry. By concluding that education for ministry, understood as the formation of the identity and authority of the minister, is a chief vehicle and embodiment of the tradition, I prepare for the movement to a discussion in Part III of aspects of actual institutions of professional education which engage in this essential activity of "traditioning."

Part III focuses on three aspects of the institution itself: the pedagogy its faculty and students engage in, the shape of the faculty itself, and the curriculum it abides by. By placing pedagogy first, I emphasize that the act of teaching in all its variety is the central focus of the institution. In that chapter and in the remaining two, I do not, however, attempt to prescribe solutions to specific problems, but describe and analyze for the sake of discovering general rules which are or should be at work. The introduction and conclusion are brief and, I hope, to the point, not impeding the reader from either beginning or ending. I will now conclude this introductory chapter with remarks about the scholarly and intellectual character of education for ministry.

IV

A conscious intent of this essay is to discover theological issues about theological education. There are, of course a variety of determinants of the current literature and discussion: the pragmatics of running institutions or servicing a clientele; the latest concerns of the North American academy which dominate the world of scholarly publications and meetings; the thematics of practitioners of forms of analysis and interpretation other than theology itself; the political concerns, both ecclesial and otherwise, of those who reflect on the issues. When the discussion is about theological issues, it tends to be about the theoretical investments of various forms of education for ministry and their relation to the university and its practices. What results are proposals about the nature of Christian belief and the methods of Christian theology.

Roman Catholics have been as busy as others in suggesting new priorities for theological construction. It is not the concern of this essay, however, to chronicle the histories of the competing claims of revisionist methodologies, of the pressing reforms which perspectival theologies are demanding, or the hierarchical efforts at influencing institutions, which have their own methodological presuppositions. Much less is it an effort to chronicle or evaluate the effect that the academic and institutional ferment have had on the daily life and viability of individual schools of theology. Unfortunately, the talk of methodology does not always engage with substantive doctrinal issues, nor has it necessarily had much effect on the workings of theological education itself. I would hazard the guess that such matters of method and criteria are more often taught as ideal constructs than practiced as ways of improving theological education. At their best, they are proposals for enactment and are dependent for their life upon innovative teachers who can do more with them than propose them as alternative theories.

I do not question the importance of such investigations as essential to a truly scholarly and intelligent revision of theological education for ministry. What will give that education its specific character as scholarly and intellectual, however, will not simply be its ability to investigate itself according to the norms of academic and public discourse. These norms cannot be set aside, but it is essential to discover from within Christian ministry itself the kind of requirements appropriate for being an intelligent, even scholarly, minister. Such individuals are not, first and foremost, scholars in the academy but practitioners within the Christian tradition. They will be intelligent and responsible in as much as they are learned members of that tradition. Thus I have not chosen to name a special characteristic of the priest or minister as that of being "scholarly" or "intellectual," but rather I have presumed that the proper understanding of how those characteristics are realized within ministry is to be found in discovering what it means for minister or priest to be professional, practical, and devoted.

Discussion of theological education points to the importance of *tradition* as a theological dynamic, as a set of ecclesial operations, which carries forward the life of the Church. This is only as it should be. Contestation over the character of theological education is a vital instance of a tradition's own self-awareness. Let me propose a comparison. Questions about how best to raise a child are frequent moments of argument and potential estrangement between generations in a family. The opinions of grandparents, particularly as societal changes have become more rapid, can be seen as interference or as efforts at continuity within the family. When children have surpassed their parents in their own education and status in life, what constituted good sense to their parents for introducing them to cultural life within and beyond the family may no longer make good sense to them as they begin the process of introducing their own children to the habits of civilization. Moments of continuity will undoubtedly be found, and oppositions can be occasions for discovering deeper loyalties and common points of insight. The importance of education and its forms of legitimization within a religion are not unlike this example, and common sense gives way to reflective and critical thinking much to the benefit of all.

Part I

Questions About Students

1. Are They Professional?

TO BEGIN A SERIES OF CHAPTERS ABOUT THE GRADUATES OF CATHOLIC theological education for ministry with a discussion of their professional character is admittedly odd. The term "professional" is not the first which comes to mind in naming the sort of individuals who are leaders in the Catholic Church. Some might even object to it as evidence of the increasing desacralization of the priesthood, or as an unwarranted form of ecumenical accommodation to Protestant usage. Just as the term "divinity school" is easily recognized as something other than Catholic, so the notion of being a professional, being part of a profession, is not the spontaneous expression of Catholic sensibilities concerning ministry. However, as the North American Church responded in the last 25 years to the conciliar call for renewal, theological institutions underwent thoroughgoing changes. In developing greater cooperation with Protestant schools, and in entering into conversation with the broader academic and public world, with changes in faculty profile, and particularly with the adoption of procedures of public accreditation and its corresponding vocabulary, Catholic institutions took on self-descriptions and responsibilities that were not always easily in continuity with their recent heritage. Thus, when some institutions adopted the name "school of theology" rather than "seminary," they reflected the beginnings of a far-reaching change in their mission, social and academic locale, and constituency. In such schools, and broadly in the seminary world as well, the professional character of both ordained and non-ordained ministry has become generally taken for granted by educators, and increasingly by the laity they serve. While there may be a general willingness to use the vocabulary when necessary and to assent to a statement of principles concerning professionalism, the actual effect

1

of the notion of ministry as a profession remains problematic both in theory and implementation. This chapter will reflect upon these problems by profiting from the literature on the professional model of ministry which criticizes the results of its adoption in Protestant schools and notes the wide range of criticism about contemporary professionalism in general. The principle contrast will be between the conception of ministry as a profession and a vocation.

The third edition of the American *Program of Priestly Formation*, presently being revised, reflects the contemporary situation when it observes that "the priesthood transcends the character of a profession" yet nonetheless "it requires professional graduate education for its competent exercise in our society." (*Program*, 16) A fruitful ambiguity exists throughout the document's use of the term, since at least three different senses of "professional" can be detected in it: a broad notion of "profession" which is compatible with the notion of "vocation"; the more technical sense which distinguishes a professional from an amateur; and the common-sense usage in which "professional" means "qualified" or "competent" or even simply "well-done." It is a fruitful ambiguity because it permits conversation within a range of opinions, including those who would maintain that ordained ministry in particular cannot be a profession by any standards since it is set apart from other forms of ministry, and with those who hold for both a weak and a strong usage of the term. Moreover, a nuanced usage is consonant with those in contemporary society within various professions who still consider vocational commitment as part of their identity, especially in the helping professions. Thus whatever the *Program* means by "competent exercise," it combines both public competency as profession and ecclesial commitment as vocation. This cautious usage is advantageous to Catholic concerns.

The recent major criticisms of Protestant theological education agree that its tendency to adopt a professional model for ministry has been at the expense of the theological and ecclesial determinants of preparation for ministry. In the Roman tradition, the maintenance of both sets of determinants has been and will continue to be a priority characteristic of its theological education in general. Its institutions did not experience the incursion of nontheological elements in the curriculum with quite the same force as seems to have occurred in some Protestant schools. Thus retrieval is not the key issue, but rather the maintenance of balance between competing requirements through the development and implementation of a *ratio studiorum* which integrates profession and vocation. Those who construe theological and ecclesial control over theological education as essentially repressive and obscurantist will emphasize the public professional criteria, and those who construe those criteria as impediments or interference will emphasize the vocational loyalties required of the students of ministry. As the relatively recent Catholic experience of new forms of theological education is reflected upon, it will be necessary to dispel these two inadequate reactions.

In the first section of this chapter, I will consider the ways in which candidates for both priestly and lay ministry experience the professional model differently, and how both relate to the secular understanding of vocation and profession.

I

To use the terminology of "profession" about those who engage in ministry requires a mediating term, such as counsellor, social activist, administrator, teacher and the like. One is not "professional in general" but in specified ways which are analogous among the professions. Professional criteria can be applied to the priest or lay minister insofar as the individual has become competent in a particular parallel secular profession in addition to liturgical leadership and sacramental ministry. Even in parish ministry, as divestment and diversification of responsibilities has occurred, the priest as amateur "jack-of-all-trades" has given way to an identity with a central religious role accompanied by a more conscious specialization in a professional competence. The obvious difficulty of achieving a balance and integration of these two roles requires clarity about the relation of profession to vocation. The tension between the two is exacerbated in the Roman tradition because of the significant increase in both official and unofficial lay ministry. Priests as well as laity have the need to be properly educated in the relation of Christian beliefs and values to the worldview which undergirds secular scholarship and professions. The matter of "being professional" cannot simply be left to the laity, just as the matter of being an adult believer with theological sophistication cannot be left to the priest. Candidates for ordained ministry might indeed feel excessively frustrated if they are led to believe that they must gain professional competence in each of the wide range of services that an average parish is expected to offer. Or, if their liturgical and spiritual activities are devalued by themselves or their congregation, and they lack expertise in any specialized ministry, their priestly identity and functioning might be severely challenged. Candidates for lay ministry face different problems in appropriating a professional stance in their education. Their identity and functioning is more closely dependent upon their professional qualifications, being the ground upon which they secure a job, continue their development, and have an ecclesial role identity. Thus both clerical and lay ministers in the Roman tradition are driven toward the professional model for different reasons, and need modification or enhancement of vocational identity accordingly.

The sort of incursion the professional model made into theological education and ministry itself in the 20th century was dependent upon broader social developments. In the context of discovering the origins of special purpose religious groups, the sociologist Robert Wuthnow notes the general increase in professionalization among religious workers:

> Tendencies toward professionalization have been prominent in the society at large, and religious workers appear to have been no exception. Thus, the fact that new associations concerned with the interests of church administrators, counsellors, and so on, have come into being reflects broader tendencies toward the founding of such associations as well as a greater degree of specialization among clergy. (Wuthnow, 113)

To be professional in Christian ministry is not to be a member of the group in which members are "ministers by profession," but rather is to be specialized within ministry and perhaps to belong, as well, to a nonecclesial group with cognate interests. The nondenominational or cross-denomination character of these special interest groups is both an advantage and a challenge for the priest or lay minister. On the one hand, the benefits are obvious: enhanced self-identity and group support, clarity of operational goals and criteria within the professional group, "scientific" methodology and development within that specialized ministry, and even the benefits of ecumenical cooperation. The challenges arise from questions about the goals, criteria, principles of operation, and ecclesial context of the residual elements of their identity which are dependent upon the uniquely vocational character of ministry. The social and personal benefits of specialization and its social embodiment are many, and in the face of a confused and confusing corporate experience of ministry, especially of the priestly vocation, it is not surprising that some find greater comfort in affinity with their secular counterparts than with their companions within the Church.

This association with professional groups is a contemporary manifestation of an important tradition of maintaining a middle road between acceptance and repudiation of principles external to Christian self-description. Certain extreme forms of accommodation propose a coincidence of ecclesial with secular worldviews, such that theological education could be entirely normed by standards simply identical with the collection of professions with which it intersects. Certain forms of supernaturalism argue to the contrary that biblical or ecclesiastical norms always stand in firm opposition, if not contradiction, to worldly ways. Most of the Christian traditions avoid such straightforward opposition and struggle to recognize compatible elements in secular theory and practice, with an agenda of transformation or absorption into the religiously-autonomous disciplines and professions. Thus the evaluation of the kinds of education and association which establish the professional character of ministry is tied to a much larger theological question of the relation of the truths and values of autonomous secular thought and practice to Christian doctrine and identity.

The confusion of professional and vocational identity appears to be expressed in Katerina Schuth's findings concerning the self-identity of those preparing for ordained ministry. Though they involve themselves in an inherent tension, they appear to conceive of their future ministry as both liturgical and communal, yet also individualized and specialized. The sacramental leadership requires them to "go it alone," but more specialized ministry would give them the support of a professional association and the more readily accessible criteria of such a profession for knowing if and when they are performing well. Some individuals ultimately find that they can function as "professionals" just as well, and sometimes better, by ceasing public priestly ministry. It is not so much that their priestly ministry is at odds with their professional expertise, but that it becomes irrelevant to the character and success of their specialized ministry. When that success is coupled with an arid experience of liturgical leadership, or one fraught with controversy or ineffectualness, the attraction of the specialized professional ministry is enhanced.

Being a professional, then, can be experienced as not of the essence of priestly ministry, but applicable to the specialized activities of the priest, the "career" aspects of a priest's life. The term "career" can be aptly applied even to the limited options for diocesan priests, such as (parish) financial officer, (canon) lawyer, (seminary) high school teacher or professor, (chancery) administrator, and even (episcopal) chief executive officer. If priests are to be professionals, does it mean principally that after basic theologate training, they should then pursue specialized training in other disciplines or fields of learning to prepare them for specialized ministry? This is usually the case for priests who are members of religious communities and whose very communal identity focuses on specialized ministry. Their liturgical and sacramental leadership is focused essentially within the religious community, and their public ecclesial ministry is in the form of their specialized and professional activities.

The demands of career over vocation can result in an effort to invent a professional status for the pastor. This effort surfaces within theological education in the urge to add to the theologate curriculum introductory studies of just about every sort of specialized professional activity that can be associated with the pastor. This may take the form of an ever-expanding pastoral component to the curriculum, with more and more adjunct faculty to train students in skills which may covertly or openly be seen as more to the point than biblical, historical, or systematic studies. Or the vocational character may exert itself over the professional with an insistence from some students and faculty that courses must first and foremost nourish one's spirituality and personal growth, with knowledge and skills subordinate to this primary aim. It is such contestation that tends to give the terms "pastoral" and "spiritual" their pejorative meaning, or to brand the biblical, historical, and systematic studies as "merely academic." A major concern of Farley's *Theologia* and Wood's *Vision and Discernment* is to name, criticize and redress these tensions. As a dialectic of contesting interests, balancing the demands of vocation and profession can be fruitful, but when either becomes dominantly programmatic to the exclusion of the other, the integrity of the institution and its functioning is threatened. No general rule can be stated for a good balance. Each institution must corporately reflect upon its own ethos, the tendencies of its students and staff, and the character of its intellectual and spiritual tradition. In some cases virtue will tend in one direction or the other, emphasizing career or vocation, with factors such as the age of the students, the training of the professors, and the needs and ethos of the dioceses represented at the school to be taken into consideration.

So far I have directed attention to the candidates for ordained ministry. Different questions about the professional model arise when we consider the growing presence of lay students in Catholic schools of theology and their assumption of various roles in local church life. As lay persons and priests are seen more and more to share the vast majority of possible activities which ministry in the Church entails, the specifically liturgical origin and functions of the priest become the identifying difference between lay and ordained persons. Both groups see themselves and are seen within the Church at large as in need of adequate preparation for ministry: they both require "professional" education in the common sense usage of the term. For lay students, professional education is the principal way in which they can develop their sense of identity in ministry and acquire competence in a specific form of ministry, a career or profession. Similarly, parishes or dioceses will tend to adjudicate whom to hire by considering the preparation of lay persons for specific activities, such as pastoral counsellor, chaplain, liturgical musician, or catechist, as evidenced by courses taken, field education units, and letters of recommendation. Lay ministry does not have an origin and authorization in a liturgical "moment" of ordination. Lay persons must "show proof" of having achieved competence.

Such an emphasis belies the common vocational ground of all forms of ministry which unites rather than separates those in professional preparation, which in fact unites all Christians as "ministers of God's Word and Sacrament" intimately concerned about and responsible to each local church. Thomas O'Meara has provided a comprehensive historical study and constructive proposal in his *Theology of Ministry* which provides a grounding for my remarks here and throughout this essay. Without digressing too far, then, into a theology of ministry, let me simply note that baptism functions as the basic sacramental foundation of the possibility and duty of all forms of ministry by any of the faithful. Similarly, the specific sacramental foundation of diaconate, presbyterate, and episcopate in the threefold sacrament of orders provides the public liturgical moment in which the commissioning for ministry is not only witnessed by the community but recognized as authoritative because of the gift of the Holy Spirit. For both lay and ordained, the *status* that is gained, the "order," is rudimentarily conceived of in a liturgical context. One only need take note of the growing use of some form of liturgical event, as a blessing or missioning of lay students who have completed a graduate professional degree, to see the common sense of the Church at work properly locating the meaning of all forms of ministry. This rootedness in the worshipping community is essential to the Christian notion of ministry of any kind. As lay persons in the Roman tradition continue to assume greater responsibility for professional ministry, there will be a growth in the importance of both Sunday and daily liturgy as the moment of nourishment and recommitment to ministry. The connection between baptism and orders will be strengthened in the celebration of the eucharist as it manifests the multiple forms of participation in leadership, not displacing the priestly or episcopal role, but locating them more visibly within a set of related roles. Incompetent liturgical leadership, uninspired or uninformed preaching, routinized celebration, and lack of appreciation for the diversity of roles impede the realization of the common baptismal call to ministry and the nourishment of all forms of ministry. It is precisely the exercise of the specific ministry of priest and bishop which "stimulates, discerns and orders the charisms of the Spirit as they come to a community." (O'Meara, 185).

It is not only students and educators in theological institutions who encounter the problems and values of the professional model. There is a growing awareness among the faithful generally that priests and laity alike, when they assume roles of authority and responsibility in the community, are subject to standards of competence, just as their secular counterparts are. In recent years there has been an increasing interest within the North American Catholic Church, not for the abandonment of the sacramental and charismatic notion of priesthood, but for its combination with the professional model of ministry for the sake of accountability. This is warranted not only by the increasing complexification of issues, for example in morality and politics, requiring more sophisticated reflection and advice, but also by the increasing acknowledgment of the fallibility of clergy and religious, an ever-present reality but now more openly known and spoken about. As to complex issues, if individuals are to offer their parishioners more than platitudes unrelated to the details of biomedical ethics or social responsibility, and more than mere repetition of doctrines in language quite foreign to contemporary thought, there is needed a kind of initial and ongoing education and formation which begins to sound more like the education of doctors and lawyers. As to fallibility, it is not that the stakes are really any higher than they ever were, since incompetence in the giving of advice and in the prosecution of one's duties has always deserved redress. However, Catholic laity no longer simply endure such incompetence. They expose it, argue against it, even pursue it with court action.

What has changed is not the notion that the priest, by virtue of ordination, is accorded a special place in the community, but rather the rules by which the fulfillment of that role is judged. The recent rise in instances of accusation and prosecution of priests for various forms of illegal or professionally inappropriate behavior should be read not only as the recognition of instances of morally questionable acts, but also as recognition of professional incompetency. The distinction O'Meara notes between specific ministries and modes of living (O'Meara, 167), and the tangle of problems which results from the confusion of these two, is helpful here. As the distinction between clerics and laity becomes more ideological and less reflective of actual Church life, the acceptability of the received ecclesiastical or clerical (quasi-monastic) lifestyle as the norm for effective professional ministry will be increasingly questioned. This will mean that certain ways of living and inveterate incompetencies which were simply overlooked will not be tolerated, and other styles of life and talents will be seen as compatible with, if not necessary, for professional ministry. It is therefore insufficient, if not simply odd, to wonder whether such problems result from lack of personal vocational integrity, let alone faulty ordination procedures. There are complex social structures and theological self-descriptions undergoing deep changes. Only a covert voluntarism, individualism, or magical sense of sacraments would see the meaning of such problems as simply located in the individual or his sacramental status. Moreover, when such failures are construed as a lack of adherence to professional standards, however problematic their definition is, and are combined with the increase of other problems such as alcoholism, burnout, and clerical authoritarianism, or with the rise in requests for laicization, all among recent graduates, it becomes clear that what needs to be questioned is the adequacy of the education they received. While institutions are not legally or morally responsible for the actions of their graduates, they are responsible to reflect upon their progress and problems after completion of their formal education.

These negative indicators, and the more positive ones of the desire by nonordained ministers for a vocational rootedness of their ministerial activities and the recognition by priests of the value of specialized ministry, all point to the difficult and changing interplay between notions of ministry as both vocation and profession. Professional competence as the result of education is held in tension with vocational commitment as the result of discernment and spiritual fulfillment through the grace of God. Both notions deserve analysis and criticism. I will begin with the notion of ministry as a profession.

II

The professional model is not without its difficulties when used to characterize Christian ministry, as Jackson Carroll has explored in an article entitled "The Professional Model of Ministry—Is It Worth Saving?" Jackson questions not only the model itself but also the notions it depends on, namely the nature and use of clerical authority, its aim of shaping the understanding and judgments of others, and the identity of the practitioners of Christian ministry who exercise such authority within the community. These theological notions will receive a systematic consideration in Part II of this essay, though they are obviously inseparable from the three characteristics being explored in Part I. For these present chapters, however, I encourage the reader to reflect upon his or her experience of Catholic ministry through the use of my three large questions. My review and criticism of the pertinent literature is meant to be a stimulus to that reflection, and an expansion of it so as to profit from the serious reflection already undertaken, particularly in the other Christian traditions.

Let me begin, then, with Carroll's distinction of two types of ministerial authority and the basic definition of authority he presumes:

> By authority I mean legitimate power. To exercise authority is to influence, direct, coordinate or otherwise guide the thought and behavior of persons and groups in ways that are considered legitimate by those persons and/or groups. (Carroll, 1985, 7)

There are two quite different warrants for the exercise of such authority by the minister: the individual has either a unique relationship to God through personal charism or ordained status, or has professional expertise based upon personal talents which have been educated or trained for use in institutional roles. Both warrants require the community of believers to recognize and accept the individual, and for the individual to have some notion of the community and its members as a group. Depending upon which warrant for authority predominates, there results a different emphasis in the operative model of ministry: minister as representative of God or minister as professional. In a subsequent book entitled *As One With Authority: Reflective Leadership in Ministry,* Carroll distinguishes ultimate and penultimate bases for ministerial authority. From the human side, the Christian minister as

> leader is granted authority to lead because she or he is believed
> to protect, interpret, and represent the group's core values and
> beliefs and contribute to their realization. (Carroll, 1991, 43)

From the transcendent side, Christians grant authority to scripture, tradition, and to their ministerial leaders because they believe ultimately "that these authorities are grounded in God and God's purposes for the world." (Carroll, 1991, 43) The two basic forms this ultimate foundation takes are "the authority as representative of the sacred and the authority of expertise." (Carroll, 1991, 45) The community's self-understanding and the ministers' sense of whom they work with and for parallel these two basic forms of the ministers' identity, being more often discovered in how they spontaneously act than in their expressed self-definitions. While in the daily life of contemporary Christian communities both forms of authority and identity are inseparably operative, each community and its tradition will explain their interrelation in keeping with their own history and theology.

The possibility, particularly in the Roman tradition, of using the professional model emerges in the mid-20th century. Though O'Meara does not use the term "professional," his analysis of the demise of the last phase in the history of the metamorphosis of ministry, which phase he calls "the romanticization of ministry," and the emergence of a new phase, corresponds to the origins of the professionalization of ministry. (O'Meara, 95-133) In each of its historical manifestations, Catholic ministry has not been an either/or matter, but a symbiosis of the sacramental, vocational, ultimately charismatic foundation with the outward, ecclesial form of actual service it engages in. O'Meara's insightful choice of women religious in North America as the vanguard of a new manifestation of ministry (O'Meara, 126-127), with their emphasis on education and health care, confirms the professional model as an essential element of the emerging shape of a new stage of Catholic ministry. The descriptive study by Patricia Byrne in *Transforming Parish Ministry* (Dolan, 111-200) details how insight into the importance of gaining professional qualifications not only enhanced women's ministry in North America, but resulted in an important challenge to and revision of their style of life, the theology of their vocation, and perhaps was ultimately a factor in the diminishment of the size of their communities. A large portion of ministerial activities was taken out of the sphere of religious life into the life of the faithful. Becoming a professional in one's ministry was partly responsible for liberating individuals to engage in ministry in forms of life other than religious and clerical ones. Similar effects could be detailed as the results of the professionalization of priestly ministry as well. (Dolan, 54-78).

For the Roman tradition in North America, then, the adoption of the professional model has the quite positive effect of aiding in a transformation of ministry. Carroll's suggestion, then, that the adoption of an emphasis on ministry as a profession was partially an effort to address a crisis of identity and confidence among the clergy in face of modern secular society would be only partially true for Catholics. Becoming professionals was seen not as a substitute but as an enhancement and strengthening of the ecclesial mission received in the seminary and religious life. The extremes of near substitution of profession for vocation, especially when it meant the adoption of some form of "humanistic religion," as exhibited in the study of Sherryl Kleinman, stand more as warnings to Catholics than descriptions of the actual process of their professionalization of ministry. In the seminary world itself, the incursion of professional concerns and standards was somewhat slower and less substantial than in the Protestant, and even now while Catholics would not underestimate their value or importance, they do not accord them a simple priority. Whether it is curriculum revision, the hiring of competent faculty and staff, the assessment of candidates' acceptability for ordination, or the attitudes and reactions of pastor and congregation, it is not secular professional criteria which are primary. Doctrinally, Catholics still live out a deep belief in the charismatic, vocational, sacramental character of ministry. Institutionally, there is still a common, even international, world of reflection and revision which guides the inner self-regulation of schools of theology, providing criteria and models suitable to the local Church's needs for credibility, but which are not simply subsumed into the secular world of professional standards. At times this oversight is burdensome and restrictive, unresponsive to or ignorant of the local church. Nonetheless, it is the forum in which the dialectic of vocational and professional concerns must be played out.

A moment of contemporary tension in the integration of vocation and the profession for Roman Catholics results from the longstanding tradition of training their priests in personal piety made effective though private and liturgical exercises, and through communal living, as was done from the establishment of the seminary after the Council of Trent. While this element of formation in clerical piety is founded on a theology of vocation and ministry as the work of the living presence of the Holy Spirit, it can degenerate into various preoccupations deleterious to preparation for ministry when that living presence of the Spirit is limited to only certain ecclesiastical styles of life and spiritualities. This disproportionate attention to personal and spiritual formation need not take on the form of a retrograde movement to reestablish the piety of the Curé of Ars, but is also evident in the enchantment with techniques and practices of much psychologized spirituality. It would, of course, be naive to presume that intellectual and pastoral competence were uniformly achieved in former efforts in seminary education. Whatever knowledge and skills were required consisted principally of acquaintance with basic doctrinal theology, more recently with biblical criticism and historical knowledge, and basic technical expertise in interpreting church law and administering the sacraments. Of course this was a general ideal, and it might be wondered how much typical Catholic clergy knew, in a thoughtful way, about Christian doctrine or the subtleties of liturgical leadership, and just how sophisticated their spiritual development was. However, the benefits of adoption of the best features of the professional model in Catholic theological education for ministry would be lessened if being a professional was inadvertently limited to matters of spiritual and psychological finesse, in the name of preserving the notion of ministry as vocation.

When we consider, then, the five criticisms of the professional model of ministry which Carroll chooses to address, there are important differences from the Catholic perspective. His criticisms of the model are the following:

   i) it perpetuates the notion of a need for distinctive expertise and education;

   ii) it causes difficulty for churches who cannot afford such ministers;

   iii) it creates a dependent laity;

   iv) it focuses on functional competence to the exclusion of the theological and sacramental dimensions of ministry;

   v) it ignores the vocational character of ministry. (summarized from Carroll, 1985, 9-10)

For anyone knowledgeable of the Roman Catholic situation in North America, if not the world, such a list would not be the criticisms of the professional model from within the actual situation we live in.

As to the first criticism, the distinctiveness of clergy education has always been prized and has been insisted upon again recently, being an essential part of the very notion of presbyteral formation and not the result of adherence to a professional model. Those who criticize this very distinctiveness would not compromise a belief in rigorous, scholarly education, but would question whether such an education is possible in anything but a pluralistic academic situation which included a multifaceted student body and nuanced curriculum. The distinctiveness is not to be taken away but to be shared with a greater variety of individuals preparing for a greater diversity of ministries. The Catholic solution seems to be taking the form of preserving the identity of presbyteral education but doing so while incorporating the theological education for other ministries. This has two important results: it ensures the specificity of the priest while including the element of collaboration; and it ensures that others are educated into the same kind of competence generally as presbyteral candidates.

Collaborative education is important not only for the candidates for priesthood, but also for the men and women preparing for other forms of ministry in the Roman tradition. Experience continues to teach us about this rather new situation, but it is clear that the self-identity of anyone preparing for ministry might be malformed in contexts where the whole gamut of Church ministries is not evident. Thus as to the third criticism, it must be remembered that the education and empowerment of a once dependent and obedient laity has been raised only recently to the level of a very urgent *desideratum* in Catholic culture. In fact, many would question the very appropriateness of the vocabulary of "lay" and "cleric," and the inadequate theology of ministry which it perpetuates. (O'Meara, 143-146) Critique of the present state of the faithful does not appeal to the inadequacy of a professional model for ministry which casts them in a dependent role, but to the failure to implement the rejuvenation of the Church envisioned by Vatican II. In particular, the development of a nonhierarchical model of the varieties of vocation in the Church necessitates a thorough reconsideration of the relation of various types of ministry, without loss of the determinative character of the presbyteral vocation and profession as such. Collaboration has already had significant results in the development of spirituality and social conscience among the faithful, and has provided for a more adequate administration of services in the parish and diocese. The school of theology must take a leading role in furthering preparation for this sort of collaborative ministry.

In fact, professional (read "adequate and equal to the clergy") education for ministry of any kind in the Catholic Church is becoming normal and normative throughout North America. That is not to say that there are not those who would prefer the Catholic world to return to the clear lines and practices of the 1950s. Chief among the nostalgic desires would be for the former clarity of roles and expectations, not in itself an unreasonable request. Oddly enough, the very independence of thinking, the possibility to voice criticism, and the opportunity to exercise influence which these nostalgic Catholics have, is in contradiction to the ecclesial ethos they wish to retrieve.

As to the second difficulty which follows from adherence to a professional model, namely financial problems associated with employing adequately educated ministers, it is clearly an issue when it comes to the hiring of ministers other than priests. The shape of parish finances throughout North America is undergoing significant change as it comes to terms with the necessity to pay all ministers a just wage for their work, or with having the parish remain satisfied with volunteer efforts. Thomas Day's *Why Catholics Can't Sing,* a book at times contentious, often insightful, and invariably humorous, ably points out in the area of liturgical music the complex of problems which face North American Catholic parishes which want to improve this and any other area of their life. Professional standards, not to mention good taste, good sense, and good theology have not been the steady diet of these communities. Presbyteral leadership will have to include education of the congregation to discover that it deserves better service in many areas. As to the effect on finances concerning priests, two activities associated with being a professional will require financial support formerly unheard of: sabbatical leaves and continuing education. A serious investment in professional self-development for the priest has begun to involve both diocese and parish in new forms of personnel management and the concomitant financial planning. The financial demands of the professional model for ministry, rather than being a liability in the Catholic world, are an occasion for facing several important choices: will parishes take diversity of ministry seriously enough to pay for it, and will well-trained professionals be able to win support for the arduous task of raising the standard of Catholic sensibility in many areas, art, music and liturgy in particular? Theological schools have multiple responsibilities in assessing and fostering this situation, with much to be learned from the Protestant traditions. As will become clear in a later chapter, however, there are institutional problems which will result from expecting too much by way of comprehensive educational programs from the already overextended faculties of many schools of theology.

As to the last two criticisms of the professional model, they are not material to the Catholic situation: we have not lost our emphasis on the theological, sacramental, and vocational aspects of the Catholic priesthood, however much they are in need of redefinition and implementation. What is most urgent is the discovery of how non-ordained ministry (a problematic notion in itself) can be understood theologically in relation to sacrament and vocation. It might be argued, as O'Meara does throughout *Theology of Ministry*, that in losing sight of certain essentials of Christian ministry in general, the Roman tradition has in fact severely hampered authentic ministry, priestly and otherwise. Conversely, it might be said of any tradition that, no matter how much they may have set aside the sacramental understanding of ministry, the Spirit has not entirely failed to be at work in and through their ministers.

For some time now, priests, sisters, and the Catholic faithful generally have successfully combined a commitment to ministry with expertise in various secular professions. During that same period of development, basic education for ministry has to some degree been also conceived in terms of the professional model. As well, we can note that the very movements which urge those dependent upon doctors and lawyers, for example, to be more critical and less accepting of the service they receive from such individuals, are being paralleled by the movements which have begun to urge parishioners to be wary of blind acceptance of Father's advice or leadership. Increasingly, the Catholic faithful are understanding their ministers to be professionals, and these individuals must exercise their authority and act out their identities in an atmosphere tinged with suspicion about the professional's expertise.

In order to evaluate the adaptability of the professional model to preparation for ministry itself, to the program of study in schools of theology and seminaries, I will begin by considering the list of characteristics of the professional model, which Carroll borrows from the sociologist Wilber Moore:

a) it is a full-time occupation set apart from the amateur;
b) it has a sense of calling, according to enduring norms;
c) it sets one apart from laity, in a formal organization;
d) it involves esoteric knowledge and skills;
e) it has a service orientation;
f) it enjoys an autonomy restrained by responsibility. (summarized from Carroll, 1985, 10)

Even if one grants that these characteristics would be varyingly present on a scale of intensity, it seems evident that much of Roman Catholic ministry, though more particularly ordained ministry, would score high in each category. According to such a list, then, it is clearly compatible with the professional model. As Carroll himself observes, these characteristics do not alone determine what we today call a profession, and the concern for such activities as the regulation of entry to the profession, the definition of standards of practice, and self-regulation can overshadow and even displace the comprehensive sense of any profession as a vocation with a concomitant social and cultural status. The manner in which professions have become increasingly technical and distanced from common understanding, sometimes summed up by noting their dependence upon "technical rationality" (Carroll, 1985, 30ff) introduces a note of caution. Well into the 20th century, professions were accorded respect, deference, social and cultural status in a more unquestioning way. Since the 19th century, they have gradually been transformed into occupational groups educated in professional schools and dependent on technical language and procedures somewhat remote from a broad base of liberal education. As "professional" became synonymous with "specialist" and "expensive," its more immediate association with "trustworthy" and "devoted" became challenged. When applied to the case of Christian ministry, it is more than the question of changing terminology or countering prevailing attitudes. The perception of the authority and identity of those engaged in ministry, and the manner in which such agency is received by the community, is in the process of undergoing more than a cosmetic change in the Catholic world, and the issues of professionalism are central to it.

We should not be ignorant of the critique of the professions by their own members, but we must forward a theological critique based upon the doctrines which shape the Christian way of life, and the Catholic tradition of embodying that way of life. Thus, it is vital to read the exploration of the history and implications of the incursion of the professional model in the Protestant world as developed by Farley in *Theologia*, by Hough/Cobb in *Christian Identity*, and by Wood in *Vision and Discernment*, to mention only three major studies. To what extent did the Roman Catholic education of priests become part of this situation? What kind of history of changes of identity did Catholic priests undergo? Even a cursory review of the evidence presented in *The Diocesan Seminary in the United States* (White, 237-264; 360-387) shows remarkable continuity from the 19th century to the present in the basic curriculum of education for ministry. When coupled with the use of standard textbooks, the relatively uniform graduate preparation of new faculty, and the lack of substantial impact by the changing pastoral situation on the life of the seminary, this continuity guaranteed a minimal incursion of both the encyclopedic movement and the professionalization of which Farley and others are justly critical. For a fuller analysis, a historical and theological study of curriculums, textbooks, and faculty composition would be required. The causes which have brought about a closer alignment of Catholic institutions with the typical divisions of theological study within the academy and with the aims of the professional model were not so much direct change through legislation (though the *Plan of Priestly Formation* ultimately uses such categories and terminology) but indirect change through the use of a broader range of texts, diversification of faculty membership, and greater ecumenical cooperation. The beneficial results are obvious, especially where carefully supervised field education and internship programs have improved the student's preparation for effective ministry, and where greater participation in the secular academy has combined with the *ressourcement* of European theology prior to the Second Vatican Council to deepen the scholarly work of seminary faculties. Nonetheless, the integration of speculative with practical wisdom remain a serious *desideratum*, and many of the criticisms of theological education in Farley, Hough/Cobb, and Wood do indeed apply to North American Catholic schools of theology. The chapter on curriculum in Part Three will consider these matters in greater detail.

To sum up, then, seminaries until quite recently remained organized and inspired by a *ratio studiorum* quite different from those elements of an emerging contemporary understanding of a profession rooted in technical rationality. Chief among the characteristics of that rationale was the emphasis on the core of the curriculum as doctrinal and systematic theology and on the development of a personal relationship to God. Even upon accepting the procedures of accreditation that made both seminaries and schools of theology more broadly accountable, there was no concomitant loss of the internal logic in such institutions. As noted above, even the present *ratio studiorum* as presented in the third revision of the *Plan of Priestly Formation* subordinates the professional model to other requirements. However poorly that theology might have been taught or how inadequate the spiritual direction provided, at least the ideal was still structurally determinative. To be more specific about its deficiencies, let me note that there is a significant difference between having a curriculum which prescribes learning a great deal of information about doctrinal and systematic theology but which does not teach students how to think theologically in their ministry, integrating that theological knowledge with biblical, historical, and pastoral learning. They do not become practical professionals simply through amassing information. Similarly, a proliferation of courses in pastoral techniques does not necessarily educate students in practical wisdom and adaptability. As to the improvement and augmentation of spiritual formation, if it is forming individuals in an inappropriate style of life for contemporary ministry or is permeated by principles and techniques at odds with sound theology, then it is obviously not fulfilling its vital function. Thus, though the Catholic situation may have in principle preserved central features in its theological education for ministry which offset the deleterious effects of the professional model and its alliance with the encyclopedic pattern, nonetheless it still confronts the basic issues of integration of studies, preparation of practical theologians, and formation of an effective style of life for future ministers. It may not have become a professional education determined by technical rationality, but it had not necessarily avoided equally grave problems. The extent to which, factually speaking, Catholic students of ministry consider themselves professionals, have adopted that identity for themselves, or are taught to do so directly or indirectly, is probably small. Whether they ought to, or will be forced to, is the question for the future. In light of both the contemporary secular attitudes of the faithful and the growing incorporation of diverse ministries in the Roman tradition in North America, it seems that the adoption of a modified professional model is not only inevitable, but might actually have beneficial results. What is needed is a more conscious theological reflection on that model by educators and practitioners alike.

Carroll adverts to the existence of two sorts of criticism beyond sociological or intraprofessional concern. First, there is a variety of criticisms which theology itself would make, the focus being on matters of relationships and self-definition, of authority and identity. The professional model could foster a notion of ministry based upon the isolation of the minister from the faithful and the characterization of ministers as clerical experts and the faithful as lay dependent amateurs. Such a definition must be challenged by a theology of the church and its ministry which articulates the singleness of mission, the necessary commonality of tasks and the requirements of collaboration. If nothing else, the reduction in numbers of candidates for priestly ministry and the concomitant rise in a wide variety of persons seeking adequate education to assume ministerial roles in the Roman tradition has raised to prominence the need for theological scholarship concerning the entire question of ministry and for a raising of awareness and sophistication about ministry among the faithful. Moreover, to bring the scholarly theological literature on ministry to bear on the daily administrative tasks which actually shape a theological school will require a special kind of administrator and faculty member whom I am not sure has as yet been adequately fostered.

Carroll also considers a third form of critique of the professional model, which he calls theological-pedagogical, giving attention particularly to Farley's work which ranges far beyond a criticism of the professional model alone. The Catholic adoption of the four-fold structure of theological curriculum and the division of faculty and courses into departments bring us well within that study. The submission of issues of theological methodology and substance, of particular items of doctrinal theology, but especially of historical and biblical study, to the criteria and trends of the academy has also become typical. And the administrative structures and procedures are increasingly those of the secular university or professional school, particularly since Catholic schools are members of ATS. Since the incursion of field education and an emphasis on the acquisition of skills have been less disruptive, and since the wholesale loss of theology as the chief determinant of the curriculum has not been the case, schools in the Roman tradition fall somewhat outside his study. More importantly, as to the pedagogical effects, it must be remembered that Roman Catholic schools still function within a worldwide ecclesial community which has considerable concern for inner Church identity, and even control, of methods, content, standards, and institutional structure. The simple existence of authoritative Vatican documents legislating every aspect of Catholic seminaries, however generally, establishes a unique milieu for pedagogical questions. It would be impossible to find a Catholic school of theology, even when it is associated in an ecumenical consortium or federation, which is not aware of and concerned for its Catholic identity. I do not think it untrue to observe that unlike the situation to which Farley's critique is addressed, the situation for Catholics has the advantage of a homogeneity in North America which is bureaucratically subjected to regular exchange of information and various levels of critical inquiry. In a certain sense there is a large hidden literature parallel to Farley's two books, and much of the ATS literature on theological education, which has consumed a great deal of the time and energy of the faculty and staff of Catholic seminaries, and involved levels of episcopal reflection as well. Though the comment is not meant to encourage some sort of "separatism" concerning theological-pedagogical critique of the professional model, it might be observed that perhaps the paucity of Catholic participation in a broader assessment of theological education is the result of these more internally focused efforts.

In any event, to bring a critique of the professional model and its implications to bear on the daily life of a school of theology requires not only reflective analysis but commitment to practical solutions. The prospects would include comprehensive discussion of curriculum and pedagogy, the assessment of the effectiveness of the academic, formational, and spiritual components of any program of study, and perhaps most important of all a growth in a collaborative model of education which would bring positive results out of a shrinking seminary world with its financial and staffing problems.

In summary, Carroll notes a convergence of criticism of the professional model which results from all three forms of critique, sociological, theological, and theological-pedagogical. As applied to the Catholic situation in North America, his criticism requires additional specification and certain cautions, but is nonetheless apt. This is particularly so because of the strong connection between ministry and vocation which has been operative in the Roman tradition.

III

In conversation with Jackson Carroll's proposal for rethinking the professional model of ministry, I have developed observations concerning the use of the model in the Roman tradition and the special difficulties which arise there. In particular, if the model is to be useful for theological education, it must provide for the needs of a more collaborative ministry and for the foundation of the identity of the minister in a sense of vocation. The model's strength is its emphasis on competence; its weakness is its general dependence upon the normativity of technical rationality and the social embodiment of the exercise of that rationality, which works against both the collaborative and the vocational character of Christian ministry.

The revision of the professional model for use in understanding the nature of the preparation for Christian ministry need not be simply patient upon the public and secular refashioning of it. Collaboration and vocation are two strong ecclesial, theological, and spiritual realities which authorize the modification of the model. Both notions require forms of thought and action which are not entirely compatible with those which the phrase "technical rationality" refers to. In the second part of this book, I will consider the theological basis for a revision of theological education which would enhance collaborative ministry and take into account the demands of ministry as a vocation. Before doing so, I wish to consider two other notions, practicality and devotion as elements of ministerial identity, whose inner sense and dynamics exercise a series of controls on the professional model. They too will raise other notions like collaboration and vocation, but are themselves at once broader and deeper characteristics of ministry, ministers, and the education they require.

I turn first to the requirements for authentic Christian practice. The refashioning of theological education to ensure that it is "professional" requires attention to its goal of developing "reflective practitioners for whom it is the practice of Christians which should be the constant reference point for all teaching." (Hough/Cobb, 32) This quote from *Christian Identity* by Joseph Hough and John Cobb introduces another more lengthy proposal which will be my partner in conversation in the next chapter.

2. Are They Practical?

CONCERN FOR THE PROFESSIONAL CHARACTER OF MINISTRY in the North American Catholic Church must be held in tension with an equally primary concern for the adequacy of that professionalism to the actual needs of the community. What constitutes *appropriate* professionalism is more than a matter of attention to public standards in secular professions or the politics of the academy, intellectual or otherwise. If being professional means gaining a specialized competence beyond theological education and the ordination or appointment to ministry, then the standards appropriate to the professions, however much in need of improvement, obviously apply to the minister as well. What we have just been considering, however, was the manner in which ministry itself is a profession, and how preparation for it needs to be professional education. In this chapter I am proposing that the quality of being practical, understood as meaning not merely up to date or popular, is an essential qualification of being professional. Simply put, the question to ask is whether the graduates of our institutions of theological education know the what, when, and how of enacting their vocations as Christian ministers. To borrow a phrase from some of the pastoral literature, are they "reflective practitioners," or, to quote R. Scott Appleby's summation of the expectations of contemporary Catholic parishioners, do they function with a "persuasive professionalism?" (Dolan, 107)

I have chosen the term *practical* rather than *pastoral* in order to place my discussion outside the still troublesome opposition of pastoral and *academic*, the one or the other being used as a pejorative term. They are not terms denoting simple alternatives, unless they are simply rendered into redefined catchwords. What I intend to imply by my choice is a judgment that to be practical the contemporary minister must be both pastoral and academic. Not only must the learning of pastoral competence be academically rigorous but the academic competence must be focused on subject matters inextricable from pastoral responsibility, and therefore from Christian life as a whole. The education and ensuing ministry must also give evidence that scholarly, intellectual expertise is itself a pastoral responsibility just as much as finesse in attitudes and sensitivities. As in any profession, mirroring the common sense life that it gives technical structure to, the actual *praxis* of a profession is a unity of theoretical and practical. This opposition of practical and theoretical has had its own history both outside of and within theological education, and I should note that I am not taking a side in that set of oppositions either. Wood has offered a succinct and pertinent set of remarks on this opposition (Wood, chapter IV) with which I am in agreement. Instead of pursuing either the pastoral/academic or the practical/theoretical alternatives, I am proposing that the application of the criterion "are they practical?" be put in dialogue with the criteria "are they professional?" and (in Chapter Four) "are they devoted?" Moreover, I will continue to relate these three characteristics of ministry and the theological education for it to specific theological matters in preparation for Part II. As with the previous chapter, this one will continue the conversation with the recent literature on the subject, to which I now turn.

I

Christian Identity and Theological Education, written jointly by Joseph Hough and John Cobb, names its purpose as follows: ". . . the clarification of Christian identity as the basis for Christian practice" (Hough/Cobb, 18) with the qualification that "the history of what God has done in the world is intrinsic to that self-definition." (Hough/Cobb, 17) Without both these elements, ministry within the Church could indeed be understood through an amalgam of models taken from other professions. The introduction of an essentially theological question as the basis of what constitutes practicality sets the discussion off in the right direction. The further determination that the "horizon of inquiry" will be the "world historical approach" (Hough/Cobb, 19,20) introduces criteria which will remain in an uneasy tension with the former two elements throughout their proposal. It will encourage a revision of theological education into a preparation for addressing the pressing issues which that world historical situation presents, requiring study and practice in the nature and context of those pressing issues. There seems to be a considerable presumption that students, or even the Church at large, already possesses an adequate grasp of Christian identity and of "the history of what God has done," such that study and practice in these matters is functionally secondary. Moreover, it seems that the contemporary issues exercise a critical function in determining what will remain of traditional understandings of the other two notions. Thus, this set of pressing issues as the task of ministry constitutes the definition of "being practical," and shapes Hough/Cobb's criticism of Farley's proposal in *Theologia.* In particular, they consider his proposal to be too abstract and to lack a teleological focus for theological education. They propose to give substance to Farley's call for a return of *theologia* as the material unity of theological education, while maintaining the proper teleology of that education, namely preparation of leaders for the Church. The substance of *theologia* will be provided by discovering the contemporary identity of Christians in and through the "global context," the "historical horizons of the world." (Hough/Cobb, 4) Neither objection ultimately holds against Farley's proposal, and ironically the same problems could be said to beset *Christian Identity* as well. The remainder of this section of Chapter Three will consider the objection of abstractness, and the next section will consider the question of teleology in theological education.

Hough/Cobb suggests that the abstract and formal character of Farley's account of the habit of *theologia* does not necessarily help faculties searching to renew their curriculum or other institutional particulars. Preparation for such renewal might well take the form of a consideration of the historical and theoretical investments which authorize the present state of affairs, as is contained in Farley's *Theologia.* Hough and Cobb understand, no doubt, that a discussion of the origins of modern Protestant theological education in the 19th century, as a response to the Enlightenment, requires not only historical study but also philosophical investigation of the nature of cognition and of theories of religion, and of hermeneutic and social scientific theory as well. Proposals for renewal which consist of alternate descriptions of rationality and methodology, are principally in conversation with the world of university scholarship and research. Rethinking theological education in these cases focuses on rethinking thinking, and all the ways in which thinking becomes embodied. This project continues in Farley's second book on the subject, *The Fragility of Knowledge,* where he does address indirectly

Hough/Cobb's objections. He gives considerably greater detail as to what *theologia* is and how it shapes theological study as a whole, and he makes clear that ministerial education does indeed have a teleology. He does not lessen, however, his criticism of the displacement of theology by pastoral skills:

> What is disastrous is the idea that clergy education is simply professional training focused on ministerial skills, for that idea allows the distinctive professional aspect of clergy education to displace rather than to shape and supplement, and to be shaped and supplemented by, the structure of theological study. (Farley, 1988, 177)

As well, in his proposed structure for theological study, Farley addresses the worry that *theologia* is too much focused on the personal and ecclesial life of the Christian, and not directed toward the world. Unfortunately, the cluster of issues which represents the global context or the world historical approach, a cluster of the basic forms of human suffering in their contemporary guise, seems ultimately to replace the content of *theologia* essential to Farley's proposal.

It is more important to explore the abstract character of Farley's *Theologia* as it results from the lack of specification of the object of theological habits, perhaps in consequence of his preoccupation with explaining what the theological habit is as a human activity, thereby furthering the longstanding discussion of theological method which so preoccupies contemporary theology. His particular philosophical bent is towards phenomenology, and what is offered by way of suggestions for procedures could profitably be compared to a number of other such proposals based in other philosophical systems. It need not necessarily follow that a revision of theological education through a retrieval of theological habits as a focus of that education should avoid, let alone deny, the object of those habits being God, God's acts and our relation to God. However, the retrieval of *habitus* from the complex of notions used by Aquinas, for example, requires for its intelligibility also retrieving *habitus* as dependent upon its object for specification and development. It is not completely retrieved by a translation into a set of various human operations which can be explicated by phenomenological method or some other cognitional theory. To quote only a brief passage from Aquinas about the nature of theology:

> That God is the subject of this science should be maintained.
> For a subject is to a science as an object is to a psychological

power or training (*habitum*) Now that properly is designated
the object which expresses the special term why anything is
related to the power or training (*habitum*) in question. . . .
(Aquinas, 25, 27 [Ia.I,7])

The integrity of the training (*habitus*) and its consequent functioning
as a form of knowing or doing is determined by its object. Habits
are not self-contained operations, but are intentional, other-oriented
activities. What orders theology as a form of knowledge is its object, God. It should also be noted in the passage that *habitum,* translated as "training," can have a social and external existence as well
as an internal, personal one. A dichotomy between them, let alone a
preference for the "interior" or "subjective," would not have occurred to Aquinas.

Does the object of theological knowledge also order theological study, and if so, how? There are two ways in which to explore
an answer to this question, one by focusing on the person who, so to
speak, enacts the theological habit, and another by contrasting God
as object of that habit with its other possible objects. I will use two
further quotations from Aquinas to indicate briefly the direction of
discussion of these two points, as required by a retrieval of the notion of *habitus*. First, as to the functioning of the theologically-
habituated individual (the appropriately-trained practical minister,
one might say), Aquinas observes:

Since having a formed judgment characterizes the wise person,
so there are two kinds of wisdom according to the two ways of
passing judgment. This may be arrived at from a bent that
way, as when a person who possesses the habit (*habitum*) of a
virtue rightly commits himself to what should be done in con-
sonance with it, because he is already in sympathy with it;
hence Aristotle remarks that the virtuous man himself sets the
measure and standard for human acts. Alternatively the judgment may be arrived at through a cognitive process, as when a
person soundly instructed in moral science can appreciate the
activity of virtues he does not himself possess. (Aquinas, 23,
25 [Ia.I,6])

Concerning theology, Aquinas considers the first way of judging to
be the gift of the Holy Spirit, and the second the result of study.
Both sorts of judgment are learned and practiced within the social
context of a specific local church, initially through family life and
rudimentary education, and possibly in formal theological education.
As many authors have noted, this ability to judge wisely should be

common to all believers and is not the determining characteristic of the leader in the Church, though there is a hope that the candidate for ministry has some of that basic disposition as a wise Christian. Its development in professional education goes toward the second sort of judgment through which the candidate for ministry learns how to value and foster those "virtues," as Aquinas calls them, which abound in the community but which might not be among his or her own Christian gifts or talents. In any tradition which maintains the leadership role of the minister in the service of Word and Sacrament, this notion of acting according to a theological habit, and the announcement of "judgement" could be developed at length into one way of understanding how *theologia* is also the wellspring of liturgical leadership and priesthood in particular. Beyond being able to live a sound Christian life oneself, and to lead others to do so, the Christian minister is required to announce God's judgement, God's point of view so to speak, in an authoritative and efficacious way. To paraphrase, then, it could be said that the truly practical Christian ministers are those who can act in accordance with the appropriate habits because of their personal appropriation of them, and through formal education, by the broadening and deepening of those habits for their own good and for recognition of them in others. In either case, the habit is determined, formed, and maintained by its engagement with its proper object.

This need not turn the theological habit into abstract thinking, since the Christian God is quite concrete, the story of divine agency quite specific. Moreover, the introduction of the proper object of *theologia* need not obfuscate the context of theological judgment in the Church and the world, with all the specificity of issues within those contexts which require the application of sound judgment. That only occurs in the degree to which the God of the Bible is replaced by the God of philosophy, and human suffering is thought not to be of concern to God. Nor does it need to entirely ignore the modern preoccupation with the implications of the structure and limits of human knowing. Aquinas was not ignorant of these factors, but in being pre-modern, he is also somewhat post-modern. Thus, as to whether the habit of theology should be determined by God as its object or by other matters, I quote a sentence from Aquinas' prologue to his systematic exposition of theology:

> We have considered how newcomers to this teaching are greatly hindered by various writings on the subject, partly because of the swarm of pointless questions, articles, and argu-

ments, partly because essential information is given according
to the requirements of textual commentary or the occasions of
academic debate, not to a sound educational method, partly because repetitiousness has bred boredom and muddle in their
thinking. (Aquinas, 3)

There are places and times, of course, for textual commentary and
disputation, as Aquinas' *Sentences* and various disputations themselves give evidence. And there is a distinction between the manner
of exposition in a text, and the lively work of the teacher in leading
the student in the formation of knowledge and skills. Aquinas tells
us he is committed to avoiding what will confuse the student and
hinder the appropriation of the proper object of theological study,
and therefore the successful development of the theological habit.
Even the diversity of the Scriptures themselves are seen to be secondary to the singularity of their sharing in "the same formal objective meaning," (Aquinas, 13, 15 [Ia. I,3]) namely, God whom they
reveal.

Hough/Cobb objects to Farley's proposal because concern for
theological methodology is not an adequate beginning for the revision of theological education, "substituting an academic concern
about a particular way of approaching the understanding of faith for
the faith itself." (Hough/Cobb, 4) While sharing their concern about
the deflection of attention resulting from a discussion of methodology abstracted from the contexts of the mission of the Church, I
have noted that lack of attention both to the object of the habit of
Christian theology and to the identity of the theologically adept, as
those who possess clarity of judgment about that object and its en-
tailments, are equally if not more serious contemporary problems.
Their positive suggestion at first seems consonant with my concerns:

What is needed today as a basis for reforming theological education is a strong conviction about who we are as a Christian
people. It is true that no such assertions will command universal assent. Indeed, a quest for total agreement is a hopeless
one. The hope instead is that the discussion precipitated by
concrete proposals will lead to conclusions that will motivate
action. That is not impossible. (Hough/Cobb, 4)

The shaping of that identity must not, they suggest, limit itself
to the "personal and ecclesial life as distinct from the historical horizons of the world God loves." (Hough/Cobb, 4) In this preference
they follow the same general requirement which Farley adheres to,

namely a reconstruction not from an essentially doctrinal or intra-ecclesial perspective, but with an eye to demands beyond the concerns of the church leader as manager (concerned with internal church order) or as therapist (concerned with personal Christian development). They have made Christian identity the key determining factor of their proposal, with the key theological category for determining that identity being "mission." The caution expressed by Hough/Cobb about education for managerial or therapeutic competence does not seem to be essentially a matter of suspicion about interference in education because of church polity or a matter of a pragmatic assessment of what will sell in the educational marketplace. Theirs is not a strategic or reactive definition. Rather, they are recapturing an emphasis within the tradition of Christian education, and fashioning a statement about it in terms of the requirements of the new enlightenment of the global context or world historical perspective and its agenda.

In fact, it might be argued that the issues of the world which function as determinants of identity are not, strictly speaking, external to the Church at all, but are drawn into its own perimeters to be, first, redefined and then attended to in an appropriate Christian fashion. The Christian's identity, as established and nourished by worship, issues in both teaching and witness as inseparable moments of the mission which follows upon acknowledgement of Christ as risen Lord. The alternative would be to first locate and appropriate issues of human suffering and be immersed in them such that they begin to define Christian identity and mission. In terms of education, ministerial preparation would consist in the experience of human suffering, laboring with it such that the application of the agenda and methods of the various human sciences, of social and political analysis, becomes the principle vehicle for becoming a competent, practical minister. Thus, just as the European Enlightenment exercised far-reaching influence on the actual shape of the Church and on the forms of its inner life and its own self-description, so what I am calling the new enlightenment of "global context" or "world horizon," is now to do the same. Not that the agenda of the prior enlightenment has been thoroughly attended to. Though Hough/Cobb may wish to counter Farley's discussion of the history of method with one of institutions, roles, and issues, they agree with Farley that there is still a need even to address the residue of the 18th and 19th century critique of religion. The received Christian identity is itself an ingredient in the problem, both fostering various kinds of human suffering and impeding an adequate vision of ecclesial complicity and ineptitude. There seems to be a great confidence that attention to the issues, aided by nontheological and nonecclesial perspectives, will liberate Christian charity. Christian identity is not essentially a matter of faith seeking its self-understanding and enactment, but a matter of understanding the world situation in order to shape what faith should and should not think of itself and do by way of ministry. Practicality for both Farley and Hough/Cobb is dependent upon identity, and it is not unhelpful to agree that ministerial identity is characterized by a set of hermeneutical modes called "theology" (Farley) or that the minister's mission responds to a set of issues called "global context" (Hough/Cobb). The relation of both habits and mission to their object and their sustaining form of life is my concern. The redefinition of methods, procedures, operations, what have you will be debilitating without attention to the object, in Aquinas' sense, of those habits, and the revitalization of the Church's mission, central as it was to the Second Vatican Council and the whole renewal of the Roman tradition, will be fragmenting, polarizing, and even secularizing in the pejorative sense if it compromises its foundation in worship.

"Method" and "mission" are not simply opposite possibilities when choosing a focus for the revision of education for ministry by the reshaping of the minister's identity. However, they are opposites in the effect they might have on such revision, mission having a centrifugal force and method a centripetal one. If rediscovering the "proper" mission of the Church through a critique of traditional attitudes and activities is to reshape the curriculum and life of a theological school, it might do so by diversifying the curriculum away from a central core of establishing identity (perhaps by presupposing it), by diversifying tasks, subject matters, and methods through giving a priority to context and perspective in all its diversity and directness. Such a proposal seems to conceive of the theological school to be more like a congregation than anything else: a healthy, vital congregation experiences its worship of God to inevitably direct it to witness in speech and action in a diversity of perspectives and concrete purposes. Education within the congregation enacting its mission requires the leadership and enabling direction of various sorts of ministers. Their education in turn must be in more than the practicalities of multiple facets of evangelical and charitable works. That is the gist of the beginning of Farley's critique of the secularization of theological education. Emphasis on the need to be effective in one's mission, combined with serious attention to the Enlightenment critique of religion, produced an education for ministry more aptly normed by secular social sciences. In such a *ratio studiorum*, becoming practical ministers consists in the accretion of as many perspectives and skills as possible.

To take the other proposal, then, if rediscovering method through a similar critique of received paradigms is to reshape the curriculum and life of the school, it does so by moving inward towards the identity of individuals, even to the character of specific intellectual activities of those individuals, though not necessarily ignoring the corporate identity and effect of theological scholars within Church and society. It need not be intellectual methods alone, it might be concern with spiritual practices or psychological abilities, or even the dynamics of the school community itself. Such a proposal seems to conceive of the theological school more like an academic department for the study of Christianity or a monastery. In the first construct at its worst, refashioning methodology collapses into an endless process of preparations which do not engage subject matter or alter pedagogy. At its best, it brings about new and insightful rereadings of the traditional *loci* of a discipline or science. It might be wondered, of course, whether the new in methods which is ultimately significant is discovered as a byproduct of attempts at new readings, not of attempts at discovering new methods. More comprehensively, it must be asked whether the practicality of the minister is chiefly the practicality of the academic scholar. In the second construct, if the methods thought to be in need of revision are the spiritual, psychological, or social dynamics of the members of the school of theology, at best it imitates the moments of rejuvenation in religious life throughout the history of Christianity, with charismatic leaders needed to bring about the changes. At its worst, it degenerates into what the academic responsibles in the institution pejoratively call "navel gazing." Just as competent scholarship is not essentially the appropriate practicality for the minister, so also spiritual maturity is not the essence of ministerial practicality.

Neither Hough/Cobb nor Farley authorize such a misuse of their central insights which opportunistic interpreters might engage in. Given the best interpretations and implementations, revivals in method and mission can hardly be gainsaid. They both have a primary function as correctives, as is obvious from the nature of the literature of which these two specific proposals are part. They are correctives of the situation as it stands, and correctives of one another. While there are undoubtedly many other refinements possible to Farley's rediscovery of *theologia,* I have only suggested one. The ramifications of allowing the object of theological habits to determine those habits could be discussed further in terms of the priority and normativity of the Scriptures in giving access to that object, and the consequent construct of the nature of the Church and its mission. Of particular use for such a development are several recent essays by Lindbeck which concretize his work on the nature of religion and doctrine and address the interrelation of the Church's self-description and mission with its use of the Scriptures. (Lindbeck, 1988a, 1989a, 1989b)

Let me regain the train of thought of this chapter: the question before us concerns the practicality of Christian ministers. Two major proposals for the revision of theological education envision what that practicality is and how to provide for it in opposing ways. I have suggested that both might profit from attention to the classical priority of the object of theological study and of the inner dynamic of the Christian community itself as essential to the renewal of both methods or mission. The general question remains however: even with the correctives I have suggested (and others might be added) do Hough/Cobb and Farley lead us any closer to a notion of Christian practicality that will help specify the kind of professionalism appropriate to ministry, and the sort of revision necessary for its theological education, particularly in the Roman tradition? What is at stake, of course, is the practicality of Christians generally, a matter inseparable from the practicality of ordained and specialized ministry. Our concern here is the specific difference, the defining sort of practicality needed by ministers in the Roman tradition, not because of their specialized roles, but in their ecclesial roles as priest, bishop, or lay minister. I take it as axiomatic that the matter of both greatest import and greatest practicality is the ability to bring a traditioning, authentic notion of God and God's acts to bear on the decisions to be made in the local churches, ultimately in communion with the Church as a whole. The retrieval of theology as habitual knowledge as suggested by Farley is invaluable, but greater agility in theological method *per se*, independent of doctrinal determinations, is not the kind of practicality the minister urgently needs. Hough/Cobb's insistence upon the urgent issues of human suffering is equally invaluable, but fragmentation of the theological curriculum through the dominance of perspectival "theology of . . ." and the limitation rather than expansion of study of the tradition would be unfortunate. In both cases the student would be deprived of the essential knowledge and facility with the kind of practicality which is constitutive of their profession. It involves the ability to bring the profession to the threshold of confession and witness, with the realization that at the core of their ministry to be professional is to be able to lead the community in their confession of faith and witness to God in authentic and appropriate ways which are inherently "practical." This requires what seems quite new, but which is really quite traditional, namely the notion that Christian doctrine states the most practical of rules for Christian living. When the self-involving implications of "I believe . . ." are reduced to intellectual requirements and not life-forming responsibilities, substitutes for Christian doctrine (and for the Scripture text which contains and thus authorizes those doctrines), such as the refinement of theological methods or the demands of issue-oriented strategies, become increasingly attractive.

A second more specialized question asks: with what sort of practicality as a guiding principle has the Roman tradition in North America responded in its revision of theological education? The answer is complex, the evidence being found in unspoken and unquestioned foundations underlying the obvious factors in educational reform, rethinking both the *ratio studiorum* of theological institutions, the identity of the community and its ministers within the Roman tradition, and rearticulation of the mission of the Church. Being left unquestioned and presupposed has not been a good thing, fostering as it does both a false security and even an indifference in face of the urgency to provide truly practical ministers for the Church. Factually, it is clear that there has been considerable salutary scrutiny of every aspect of theological institutions of late, involving no doubt some wasted energy and much anxiety in some quarters. Theologically, there has been a considerable increase in teaching and learning about the new shape of ministry in the Roman tradition in the Western world, some of it in the form of books and articles, some through workshops and new or revised courses in programs of study. There have been several revisions in the United States alone of the *ratio studiorum* of theological education approved by the national conference of bishops, and considerable official documentation about specific issues in social teaching, morality, and worship. In addition, there has been considerable sociological and statistical investigation of the actual state of ministry in general, of the profiles of seminarians and priests, and of parish life. A calculation of the investment of time, energy, and money, and a listing of the tangible results, literary and otherwise, would give impressive evidence of Roman Catholic activity concerned with theological and institutional reflection on identity and mission for practical purposes. However, the issues of continuing revision are not principally that of regaining the priority of theology in the curriculum or instilling convictions about the need to manifest faith in works. That is not to suggest either that the practice of theology which has priority is actually educating ministers to be practical, or that the sense of mission being instilled in them will result in the most appropriate forms of evangelization for the contemporary world.

Farley and Hough/Cobb could have an important role in the reformation of Roman Catholic education for ministry, however, through providing insight into two matters fundamental to the maintenance of the theological focus of that education and the revival of a missionary spirit among North American Catholics. Farley, in conjunction with the shift in conceptions suggested by Lindbeck, could provide an important alternative to the tendency in some quarters to maintain a notion of doctrine as propositional, principally requiring intellectual assent. They would also provide a much needed challenge to the opposite tendency to disregard doctrine in favor of perspectival theologies and the ever-increasing fragmentation of belief into *ad hoc* solutions for particular needs. If ministry as a profession is to take its cue from the requirements of being practical in one's ministry, then students in preparation for the whole range of Catholic ministries must learn how to bring the reality of God and God's acts to bear directly on the everyday life of believers, bringing doctrine alive as rules for life, and the wisdom of the tradition as insight into contemporary problems. Professional expertise in specialized ministries looks to this rudimentary practicality for a limiting norm, though it has an eye on the insight and functioning of its secular counterparts.

Hough/Cobb can be profitably read by Catholics for the straightforward way in which it proposes a critique of Church practice which internally does not fully practice what it preaches, and thereby may lose sight of its mission. There are urgent concerns within the Roman tradition, evident in everyday events, which require the kind of refashioning of ministerial practicality that we are considering. Unless these problems are attended to, the broader mission of the tradition to the suffering of the world will be severely hampered and whatever priority theology may have in Roman Catholic ministry will be eclipsed. Though others might name them differently, I think that three ecclesial issues have come to the fore throughout all of the recent scrutiny and revision. First, there is the need for the redefinition of priestly identity and ministry, its theology and practice, with the inseparable issue of the role of lay ministry, both issues requiring attention to the changing role of women in the tradition. Second, there are many questions concerning the embodiment and exercise of authority in the Church, both universally and locally. And, third, there are concerns for the preservation of Catholic identity through the maintenance and development of the tradition, both in contrast to and cooperation with other denominations and other religions. Greater collaboration, more effective leadership, and ecumenical sensitivity as elements of the mission of the Roman tradition in setting its own house in order are as much in need of development through the implementation of sound doctrinal rules as are the many forms of witness which constitute the mission of the church to the world.

Needless to say, the efforts at tackling these issues generate reactionary and reductive responses of both a regressive, nostalgic sort and a functionalist, accommodationist sort. When issues of authority and traditioning are raised, it is often presumed that one must take one of two sides, which at their worst require mindless repetition of the past or plunge one headlong into fascination with the latest possibilities for adaptation to contemporary issues. Traces of these trends are to be found not simply in speculative literature, but in the actual administration of the local churches and in the piety of Catholics at large. Spirituality and liturgy are two areas which especially exhibit the more bizarre instances of reaction or accommodation.

A consideration of the first objection which *Identity* has offered to Farley's proposal, namely that it is abstract, does not require denying that the issues of the *ratio studiorum* and of Christian identity are vital. Rather, in relating both issues to the search for practicality in ministry, I have suggested that a retrieval of the objective reference of *habitus* is necessary for addressing the matter of abstractness, and names the chief determinant of both the rationale for study and the identity and appropriate authority of the minister. Further, the recognition of a revised specification of Christian identity as inseparable from a renewed vision of the mission of the church both to its own members and to the world could coincide with this intentionality of theology understood as a collection of habits which are both speculative and practical.

II

Hough and Cobb's second objection to Farley concerns the need for a teleological unity for the education of those preparing for leadership in the Church:

> . . . the unity of their special education, whether or not it includes anything other than *theologia,* will be teleological, that is, it will be guided by the aim of providing the special education appropriate to church leaders. (Hough/Cobb, 5)

As I have noted above, in his second work, *The Fragility of Knowledge,* Farley prefers to consider this teleology ("the aim to prepare a certain kind of church leadership") under the rubric of a specification of the mode of theological understanding called vocation, and ministerial vocation as one variant within that mode. (Farley, 1988, 160-162; 169; 177) As an answer to Hough/Cobb's objection, it still maintains the priority of *theologia* and the subordination of any teleology to the structure of theological study itself. Anyone who engages in theological study must learn about a variety of modes of interpretation and of the application of faith in life situations. Thus vocation is not limited to clerical vocation, and theological study cannot be ordered exclusively to a vocational situation or goal, clerical or otherwise. Whether one adopts Farley's choice of hermeneutical and phenomenological vocabulary to describe these activities, his insistence is a salutary one, especially in the Roman tradition. A broadening of the actual base of those who study and teach theology, especially as a profession, and the consequent reconception of its procedures and preoccupations as not solely determined by the necessities of clerical leadership ensure the preservation of the longstanding tradition of the Church at large, but also highlight the inspiration of much Roman Catholic theology, namely that the study of it for its own sake is an inner moment of the life of faith. That such study tended until very recently to be chiefly the province of clerics, and therefore of men, indeed needs redress, but a clerical, eventually functionalist, paradigm did not entirely suffocate the larger contemplative and speculative workings of Catholic theology. The inner logic of a curriculum as preparation for ministry cannot determine the logic of theological study *per se,* and in this I find myself in agreement with Farley. However, my purpose in adverting to this second objection is not to justify Farley, but to follow out the path that Hough/Cobb suggests, so as to explore what they consider the particular purposefulness of ministerial education.

They begin their exploration of the specification of that teleology by describing the history of the various ministerial "characters" who have exercised leadership in the American Church. This device of locating types or characters is a useful means to giving clarity to elements of change and to demarcating periods of development. The characterization of 18th-century ministers as apprentices to teaching pastors has some resemblance to the Catholic situation presented in Joseph White's recent history of diocesan seminaries. (White, 27-164) The practice of beginning one's ministry as an associate subordinate to a pastor, combined with the general dependence even of pastors upon the local bishop, was the Catholic equivalent. If one were to fill out the picture of the 19th-century pioneering priests, it would require attention to their missionary character, their dependence upon European-inspired training and practice, and the late 19th-century attempts to forge a more indigenous clergy. This early history would show some differences in Canada between the French and English, Lower and Upper Canada, the established eastern provinces and the western territories. By the third decade of the 20th century, the priesthood had become established in what R. Scott Appleby names the "ombudsman" role, which required of the priest an ubiquitous functional presence in the parish. (Dolan, 3-107)

Between the 1930s and the 1970s Appleby traces the gradual displacement of the ombudsman by the "orchestra leader." The former was required to carry out a myriad of duties in the parish, all of which required differing kinds of expertise and personal skills. The training such priests received, Appleby suggests, was woefully inadequate to such demands. One might suppose that the years of "apprenticeship" under a seasoned pastor functioned to provide the environment, given the best of circumstances, for learning what to do. The seminary had provided a quasi-monastic spiritual life and some basic intellectual development, while the first years in a parish were to provide the on-the-job training. The period between 1930 and 1970 saw a gradual realization that priestly ministry could take on the pressing intellectual, social, and political issues of the day, and do so in new collaborative efforts with Catholic laity and with socially active individuals in other traditions and faiths. In this period not only priests, but men and women religious especially, pursued academic qualifications to enable them to function effectively in many new, professionally-oriented ministries. Appleby sums up the situation as follows:

> The large majority of American Catholic priests did not leave
> the parish at all in this period. But in ministering to their
> parish communities many sought to combine the effective pas-
> toral presence of the ombudsman with the newly earned
> sophistication about modern existence that came with profes-
> sionalization. (Dolan, 70)

In this context, we can combine Hough/Cobb's discussion of the
characters of manager and therapist in the Protestant world with
Appleby's analysis of the specialization that prepared for the emergence of the orchestra leader role. However, this interpretation of
practicality in terms of specialized ministry which is somehow
"combined" with general pastoral ministry drew attention away from
an arduous task which it does not seem was undertaken entirely successfully. I am adverting to the lack of liturgical and theological
professionalism which encountered the rapid and thoroughgoing
changes required by the reforming documents and disciplinary
changes of the Second Vatican Council. Those charged with the
everyday implementation of the Council lacked, not entirely through
their own fault, the kind of practicality necessary. The question
some 25 years later is still whether the schools of theology are pro-
ducing ministers prepared for the elementary sorts of practicality required in community leadership in liturgy and theology first and
foremost.

Katarina Schuth's study of American schools of theology provides a wealth of information to ponder. Regardless of what they may
be taught about the priesthood, students in Catholic theologates conceive of their future ministry as involving administration of a parish
(even though they do not anticipate such work with enthusiasm). Sum-
marizing the work of Hemrick and Hoge, Schuth notes that only a
small portion of students see counselling as their most essential future
role, though the preference for one-on-one ministry is clear. Hesitancy
about institutional responsibility is not surprising either among the
young or in an era when such leadership is so publicly scrutinized and
often found wanting. And preference for more intimate ministry might
even be a sign of a sincere desire for the affirmation of faith, though it
may well be symptomatic of contemporary needs for instant gratifica-
tion in one's life and career. Beyond the recounting of attitudes and
the marshalling of figures, Schuth reflects on their significance and the
criteria of response of theologate personnel in the formation, and reformation, of students' attitude towards future ministry:

> Of fundamental concern is whether attitudes and orientations toward different types of ministry are compatible with the anticipated needs of the Church. (Schuth, 131)

And again:

> The faculties of theologates see it as a crucial part of their task to present an understanding of the needs of the Church that will help students reflect on the most appropriate role for themselves once they are ordained. (Schuth, 132)

Such concerns on the part of educators are, I think, pointing beyond the issue of specialization, in which practicality is more easily identified, towards a fundamental conception of ministry in the Catholic tradition which will name the kind of capacity for practicality which basic education for ministry should develop. The responses to the Hemrick and Hoge study confirm this: students see their ministry principally as liturgical and sacramental, involving teaching and preaching, which are among the well-established roles and duties of the priest. Not only the *Plan of Priestly Formation*, but the catalogues of Roman Catholic professional schools of theology as well would mirror the same basic identity of the minister, whether presbyteral or lay. There is little doubt that liturgical, sacramental, catechetical, and educational needs are the vital needs of the contemporary parish community. Just who is and is not to engage in specific ministries, just what the manner and priority of implementing them should be, and judging their soundness according to theological principles are not peripheral questions, mere accidental matters. They are the issues I have identified as the very ones challenging the new minister to act in a practical and professional manner. The presumed identity of minister and community, or the proposed revision of that identity, is the key to recognition and reconception of the practicality necessary to the contemporary minister, and I now turn to Hough/Cobb's discussion of it.

III

Christian Identity presents it as axiomatic that Church organizations possess authenticity and unity only when they are expressions of the Church's theological understanding of itself. Leadership in the Church is charged with "guiding the church in developing its own theological identity so that its organizations will be authentic expressions of that identity." (Hough/Cobb, 19) Hence for the school of theology "the understanding of what it is to be a Christian community in the world will be the aim of its research and pedagogy." (Hough/Cobb, 19) The proper implementation of these principles will produce a description of (or prescription for) the Church which attends to both external and internal matters. Concerning the external, the horizon of theological inquiry should be a world-historical approach to understanding the Church. As well as grounding itself in Israel's witness to God's activity in the world, the world-historical horizon requires Christian theology to attend to Islam and Eastern religions with an openness to the expansion of Christian identity through what Hough/Cobb considers to be the broader history of God's activity through the great sages and spiritual giants of China and India; these can become part of the internal history of a religion centered in Jesus Christ, just as Plato and Seneca did. By means of conversation with other religions, and through successful adaptation to cultures beyond the European and North American, Christianity might become a true "world" religion. Such a basic requirement need not be foreign to the Roman tradition, which makes claims to being a universal Church, though its present struggle is to become a truly local Church as well. These matters are often dealt with in terms of ecclesiastical authority and style of life, and not as theological problems. Hough/Cobb ever so briefly adverts to the concept of revelation necessary to its notion of a world-historical horizon. It requires a relinquishing of exclusivist claims concerning God's activity, for the reason of "the innumerable sins of the churches" in persecuting other religions. (Hough/Cobb, 21) Revision of the appeal to revelation in establishing the Church's self-understanding is dependent upon reconsideration of whether that appeal does follow the basic doctrines of Christian belief, and part of that assessment is observing the appeal in action.

As to internal history and identity, one can easily agree with Hough/Cobb that the act central to the Church is the celebration and renewal of the memory of Jesus. The particular emphasis on memory in *Identity*, however, tends not to speak of Jesus as present and operative in the Holy Spirit, though such a notion is hardly contradicted by the text. For example, the section on worship as essential to images of the Church is clear about the intentional character, the other-directedness, of worship, going so far as to say that in worship "God is met ever anew." (Hough/Cobb, 75) And the role of Jesus as mediator is not absent. However, throughout the text refer-

ence to the memory of Jesus lays emphasis on the task of the Church
to keep it alive, seemingly indicating that it is not alive of itself, that
is to say, that the risen Jesus is present, active, and in conversation
with the Church. Similarly, prayer is defined as "the deepest and
most pervasive expression of care," (Hough/Cobb, 53) and the kind
of care the Church is to provide is

> to the needs to which other institutions expect the church to
> offer the primary ministry: the need to worship, to meditate,
> and to pray; the need for meaning in life's major transitions
> and crises; and the need for guidance in determining convic-
> tions, commitments, and vision. (Hough/Cobb, 52)

A certain Protestant emphasis on the role of preaching over sacraments, of hermeneutical issues over ascetical practice, underlies this
particular vision of Christian identity, its practicalities, and the preparation for its exercise. Yet the quotation seems to belie this very
emphasis, and Christians of various traditions might question
whether the work of the Church is determined by what "other institutions" expect of it, and what the implications might be of being
the purveyor of meaning and conviction *to* life, than being a way of
life itself. Though the comparison may seem somewhat irreverent, I
suggest there is a significant difference between the attitudes and
actions of the entrepreneur who sells goods for consumption, and the
consumer who buys and uses them. Christianity is not, of course, a
commodity for sale and consumption. Talk of satisfying needs for
meaning, convictions, commitments, and vision as determined by
other institutions is, however, in keeping with the prior principle of
the world historical horizon, from which will proceed the critique of
Church practice and the reshaping of the notion of Church life and
ministry in accord with modern consciousness and conscience.

A reverse order for discovering the Church's identity would
begin with worship and prayer as the primary category. It presumes
that in such activities an encounter with Christ shapes and determines the life of individual and community, one of the chief characteristics of that "new life" being Christian charity. The forms of
charity follow from the living relationship with Christ through the
empowerment by the gifts of the Holy Spirit, such that how the
Church chooses to enact its love of neighbor is not restricted by
limited resources or by the expectations of other institutions, but is
internally given, commanded in fact, by the complex of Christian
experiences, and sometimes brings about humanly unexpected

events, even miracles, we might say, because it flows from the life of God, not from the Church's own efforts to "keep alive" the memory of Jesus.

Such a notion of the Church and its mission is rooted in a theological understanding which encompasses the *memoria Christi* in the *memoria Dei*, beyond the life of Jesus into the life of the Trinity, which is itself the agent for both establishing and understanding the life of Christ and the Church (Kilmartin). As with the ground of ministerial professionalism, so also with ministerial practicality, a foundation is to be found in participation in the missions of the triune God, Creator, Savior, and Sanctifier. One can agree with Hough/Cobb in its observations that "addressing the urgent issues of faith" is more important than questions of methodology, but one need not follow them in interpreting these issues to be the determinants of the shape of theological education. Caution is needed, lest this point be misinterpreted, and the careful distinctions suggested by Schubert Ogden are particularly helpful here. (Browning, 21-36) If one is looking for *theological* foundations for revisions of theological education, that is not to say that one denies or ignores the arena within which Christian ministry is exercised. However, a distinction between historical, practical, and systematic theological study allows us to distinguish, as does Ogden, between the different ways in which attention to our heritage and attention to the Christian desiderata for action in face of actual, concrete evil and human suffering are determinative. If the theological self-understanding of the Church is to provide the unity and shape of its mission, then understanding why and in what ways that self-understanding is biblical, historical, ethical, systematic, and pastoral is as essential as knowing the pressing issues of the day. (Wood, 37-55)

From a Catholic perspective, it must be observed that liturgical studies and ascetical theology, what we more typically call spirituality now, are regularly not among the general categories of theological study which the mainly Protestant literature on theological education considers. In particular, ascetical theology is perhaps not so much a subject for study, as an activity to be engaged in. Its popularity among students in schools of theology is not only due to the ways in which it addresses the aridity of modern culture. It also tends to take as programmatic the character of theological learning (if not of all learning) as formation of habits and therefore as formation of one's person. When wrested from the sometimes reductive hands of psychologists and popularizers, it can be more than a faddish distraction and be pursued in concert with both doctrinal and fundamental theology, aiding the former to maintain its rooting in the mystery of God and preventing the latter from collapsing entirely into prevailing cultural demands.

In relation to the present issue of practicality in ministry, it is systematic theology in its constructive work, poised between doctrinal and fundamental theology, and dependent upon the other areas of theological study, which requires discussion. More will be said about this in the chapter on curriculum. For the present, it is sufficient to note that the efforts of professional theological education to form practical ministers, when understood as the formation of habits, has a special unity in the subject matter and procedures of systematic theology. Hough/Cobb is correct in wanting greater specificity of Farley's *theologia*. I would suggest, however, that the specificity comes not from the context of Christian ministry and its very real and urgent demands, but from the spectrum of doctrinal requirements which systematic theology considers beyond, but not without, the question of validity and truth which Ogden names as the core of systematics.

In this light, the shape of my agreement and of disagreement with the remainder of the text of *Christian Identity* can be described. Two examples concerning the challenges to the maintenance and faithful development of Christian identity will suffice, the problem of distortion and the need for a unifying image or ideology. First, that there are distortions of Christian identity cannot be gainsaid, and that anti-semitism and misogyny are chief instances of these distortions are indisputable. Beyond the obvious suggestion that there might be other such distortions, racism being primary among them, the question should be posed as to whether the issue of distortions might not be usefully analyzed in relation to distortions of the Church's relation to God, active and present, such that these distortions of relation to neighbor might be comprehensible and remediable upon specifically doctrinal grounds. In fact, a case can be made that many secular concerns for inadequate social, political, or economic relations have remote origins in basic Christian doctrines.

At somewhat greater length, as the second chapter proceeds, Hough/Cobb investigates distortions due to the impact of the Enlightenment on Protestant Christianity, as to the adoption of its tenets within Christianity and the forms of resistance to it (which also have a quite striking history within Catholic Christianity). These remarks take their place among current preoccupations with post-modern alternatives to established ways of dealing with the long list of problematic Enlightenment notions and results. A pervasive concern of the text, however, is what might be called the new Enlightenment, variously called "global awareness" or "the world historical approach." Just as with the complex shift of intellectual, political, and social factors in the 18th century, so with the new and not altogether clear shifts of the late 20th century, demands are placed upon the Christian self-identity and its enactment. As in the 18th and 19th centuries, a full range of intellectual, spiritual, and ethical responses are being made, some having to do with perspectival theologies, revisionist and accommodationist theologies, or theologies of retrieval and consolidation. Whatever form of "enlightenment" it may be, and in whatever era it originates, Christian theology's concern with it as a critic of its own internal distortions cannot displace the role of critique which the internal doctrinal rules of worship, conduct, and creed exercise simply by their maintenance of Christian identity. A major difference in appreciation and use of these intra-ecclesial means of critique would be possible if Hough/Cobb had not conceived the results of the work of tradition as distortive, and in need of externally originating criticism, but as preservative, illuminating, and self-critical. Retrieving the role of tradition and doctrine can be significantly aided by the analysis and proposal which Lindbeck has offered, and which others are beginning to develop.

The second example I wish to consider is the preoccupation in the third chapter of *Christian Identity* with normative images of the Church. The choice of "images" as the pivot between the description of historical shape and distortion, and prospects for the reformation of theological education for the Church is in keeping with the priority of practical over historical or systematic theology. What is needed are ideals to be held out, as it were, in front of those engaged in ministry, such that they can compare the actual with the ideal and come to decisions about what to do to bring about the kind of Church the images project. The collection of images is a mixture of things: the Church as human, caring, evangelistic; as for the world, for the poor, for all peoples, and for women; as integrating, repentant, virtuous, worshiping. Strictly speaking, none of these are "images" of the Church, though they could be turned into them. The New Testament provides a sourcebook of such images: the mystical body of Christ, the new Israel, the gathering of disciples and friends, God's household, and perhaps by extension, shining lights, clay pots, and earthly tents. Numerous individuals and their stories are recalled as types of the Church, and the "praxis" of the early church required a whole narrative forming a complex image of the Church in *The Acts of the Apostles*. Moreover, the great tradition itself poses images, such as Jesus's mother Mary. Images and narrative go hand in hand, with the result that the Church is not so much a doctrine itself, as the ever shifting context of the application of such rules of life.

It is tempting to look for an inner logic to this complex ideology. Images or models of the Church could be organized and tested as to their biblical origins, their historical context, their credibility in a secular culture, or their effectiveness in fostering pastoral works. However, as Wood suggests (Wood, 50-54), systematic theology has the task of integrating these forms of theological study, with the understanding and integration of doctrines being at the heart of systematic theology. Doctrines can be considered the most practical of Christian rules, which are themselves the statements not only of the historical past and the operative present as authentic and authoritative, but as the operational initiatives of practicalities which shape the task of witness as projective. Thus doctrines of creation and the fall, of salvation and grace, of sacraments and moral life seem to underlie the movement in the Hough/Cobb images from theological anthropology, through soteriology, to ecclesiology. No doubt the images presented could have such doctrinal foundations. The question is whether in contrast to an issue-driven curriculum, a doctrine-driven curriculum could be as practical through a more conscious and systematic theological norming. This is not a mere matter of speculation; meeting such a requirement has consistently been one major ingredient in the effort of Roman Catholic revisions of the seminary curriculum.

To be highly commended, then, is the search for a manner in which to highlight the practicality of the Christian minister without repeating the unsatisfactory efforts tried in some quarters whereby a substitution of theological study with the methods and ideologies of other disciplines and sciences was thought to be the best solution. What Hough/Cobb is concerned about in the term "practical" is echoed in Catholic situations where the term "pastoral" is forwarded as naming the panacea for all the problems of theological education. Make the education pastoral, and we will produce competent and successful ministers, ordained and otherwise. As with being practical, so with being pastoral: doctrinal clarity, as well as historical accuracy and contextual inventiveness are of the essence in resolving some of the arguments about the revision of theological education, especially as it challenges naive notions of both practicality and pastoral finesse.

IV

This chapter has taken the characteristic of practicality as its focus, and the proposal in Hough/Cobb has been investigated for its applicability to the Catholic situation. Being practical or pastoral is hardly a novel concern and White's history of the diocesan seminary gives ample evidence of the struggle in the last two centuries of the American Catholic Church to ensure that its priests were aptly prepared to minister in a manner appropriate to the ethos of the local Church. This was not an easy or always successful task, and the recent study headed by Jay Dolan augments the story of this struggle by considering the change involved not only for priests, but for religious and laity as well.

Though it is only one of the possible contexts for the exercise of ministry in the Catholic Church, the parish is, as it were, the crossroads in which many forms of ministry come to bear on one another and on the faithful in general. Schools, institutes of learning or social action, retreat houses, and monasteries are also the locales of the everyday experience of ministry. Reflection on the character of practicality and pastoral effectiveness could be conducted in these settings, and the revisions of theological education they have required be evaluated. The documents of various religious communities which tend to staff such works would be the texts to consider. Most communities have engaged in vigorous revision of their apostolic commitments, abandoning some activities and reshaping most in response to the general call for *aggiornamento* from the Second Vatican Council. Diocesan offices, in which the ministry of administration generally and the work of marriage tribunals in particular is undertaken, have been served by the revision of canon law. It both recognized already operative changes and initiated others, based upon a renewed theology in general and revisions of ecclesiastical authority.

The parish, however, does not have a rule of life, as does the religious community, or a manual of procedures like *Robert's Rules of Order*, though perhaps a case could be made that canon law gives it a kind of rudimentary order. At least, at first sight it doesn't. However, two sorts of order seem to be essential to it, not only theoretically but in the practicalities of its everyday life. The first is the liturgical and sacramental order that the liturgical year provides, and the order of activities which the preparation for and celebration of the sacraments require. Into this ordered life enters the concrete needs of the community centered around the worship of God and the service of neighbor. The second evidence of order is in the roles assumed and activities performed by those who function officially as the ministers of the community, maintaining and executing that liturgical and sacramental order, and all the teaching and preparation which it involves. The actual shape of a given parish will reflect the abilities, preferences, training as well as incompetence, prejudice, and ignorance of its team of ministers. Whatever the specialized training of individuals may be, particularly their participation in professional competencies as counsellors, administrators, educators, musicians, and the like, there remains the need for an underlying order of worship and communion which founds the service of neighbor. Of course, as a general principle this order takes on quite different concrete manifestations, and the parish of the 1940s is not that of the 1980s. (Dolan, 283-306)

It must be asked, though, whether there is a foundational preparation for a generalized ministry for that team of ministers which underlies all specialized education, whether for the works of a given religious community, for administrative or legal work, or for specializations within a diocese or parish. In other forms of professional education, the answer seems obvious: after a general introduction to medicine, law, or music, one can pursue a specialization. In the case of theological education, it may be necessary to rediscover parish leadership as sharing a general preparation with any form of ministry, yet being a kind of specialization itself.

I will consider only one specific Catholic publication which attempts to review and give a prospect of clerical leadership on the parish level, *A Shepherd's Care: Reflections on the Changing Role of Pastor*. While it begins with the caveat that it "is not a technical, sociological essay" nor "a theological and scriptural study" (*A Shepherd's Care*, 3), its descriptive and analytic efforts make use of a variety of other studies, and are a good instance of the presuppositions which inform the Catholic understanding of an essential form of leadership, that of the pastor. My summary and observations will follow the text's exposition of the three traditional categories of activity the pastor engages in: leadership, teaching, and pastoral care.

Leadership as a general category is further divided into consideration of the demands of spiritual, communal, and administrative guidance. All three have been marked in the last 20 years by engagement in activities of renewal, reassessment, and innovation. In each area the pastor has been required to accommodate to dramatic changes in the fabric of Catholic parish life. Liturgical renewal itself has required careful theological reflection and theater skills. Demographic changes in the parish population and greater involvement in social action have called for skills in community organization as well as practical theological acuity. And the institutional changes in the relation of parishes to diocesan committees and the development of more complex teams of parish administration have required pastors to be attentive to managerial skills and collaborative techniques.

Similarly in the leadership that is the teaching responsibility of the pastor, the liturgy itself as an occasion for formation of the faithful, particularly in the homily, has received much needed attention. Even more complex development has taken place in the areas of catechetics, social justice ministry, and educational ministry which have required collaboration with experts in these areas, or further education for the priest himself so as to engage in such work effectively.

As for pastoral care beyond these two specific types of leadership, one only need name the complexity of medical problems which now rise during hospital visitation, the legal and political finesse required in caring for the group rather than the individual alone, and the sensitivity and insight needed to adjust to quickly-changing cultural mixes in any given parish. The committee of writers of this document sums up the matter as follows:

> This historical review has led the Committee on Priestly Life and Ministry to conclude that the contemporary pastorate has become a "specialized ministry." Because of the unique demands made on the pastor, because of the variety and cluster of skills required to do his ministry effectively, the pastorate is not just a generic priestly function. (*A Shepherd's Care*, 15)

If this is indeed the case, then the task of the renewal of Catholic theological education will have to sort out those elements of such an education which belong in a foundational way to any individual preparing for a ministerial role in the Church, and those which constitute the specialized preparation for specific ministries, even that of pastor. If, as the document suggests, such specialized preparation is actually only being provided through workshops or extended seminars of an auxiliary nature, then the question arises of how much curricula in general are addressing such needs for preparing the pastor. Nor will it be as simple as sorting out specialized courses which are additional to the basic curriculum.

It is striking to me that in the section on "Changing Spirituality and Morale" the facets of a pastor's spirituality which the text discusses are those of the faithful as well, even if the pastor's vocation in Christian life is the special gift of leadership, most especially in the sacramental and liturgical life of the community. The four "styles" of pastoring which the document identifies would have parallel emphases in the spirituality of leadership, clerical or lay. Each style emphasizes one aspect of the full work of the pastor: preacher and teacher of the word; leader of worship; builder of community; steward of the community's goods. The responsibilites are not unique to the pastor, much less totally unique to the presbyter. They are expressions of the common call and commissioning by which Baptism establishes every Christian as a disciple. So, without wishing to be facetious, perhaps there is a simple way to begin addressing a challenge the Committee puts as follows: "to speak of a unique and distinctive "spirituality of the pastor" is to speak about a book yet to be written." (*A Shepherd's Care*, 27) The power of reading and praying the Scriptures, the celebration of the Eucharist and the other sacraments, communal prayer, comforting the faithful, giving witness to the unbeliever, caring for the poor and oppressed—all these are common works of discipleship for both presbyter and faithful.

The concern in a document like *A Shepherd's Care* for the spirituality of the priest, and by extension for that of his co-workers and parishioners, is typical of the Roman Catholic perspective on ministerial identity and authority. I began this first section by considering the least typical of characteristics of ministry within the Roman tradition, professionalism. In turn, the qualifications of the priest or minister as professional seemed to require specification of the kind of practicality appropriate to Christian ministry. While profiting from both texts by Farley and from the Hough/Cobb text, I have proposed that the practicality underlying specialized ministry as well as the rudimentary internal leadership of the community in worship and witness, should be conceived in terms of competence in the application of the rules of life, doctrinal rules in effect, which constitute the steadfastness of the community's traditioning. Those habits of life, whose subject is the believing community and whose objective focus is the living God, are the most essential of habits necessary for practical ministry. Familiarity with God has long been thought to be a major criterion of adequacy for ministry in the

Church. To revision such a criterion for the end of the 20th century will require holding spiritual maturity in close connection with professional and practical expertise. That is the subject of my next chapter.

3. Are They Devoted?

IN ADDITION TO BEING PROFESSIONAL AND PRACTICAL, THOSE WHO engage in ministry are expected to be individuals distinguished in their exercise of the Christian way of life. Terms such as holiness, virtue, piety, devotion, spirituality, closeness to God, and sanctity designate in different traditions the characteristics and activities which the Christian faithful expect of those who are called to ministry. In Roman Catholicism in particular, the emphasis on ministry as a vocation, as a response to a call from God, in combination with the sacramental and devotional ethos of Catholics, account for the shape of the present day institutional commitment to spiritual formation as an essential component of preparation for ministry. It is valued as a desirable characteristic of our leadership, admitting of many varieties for many missions, and articulated in a critical theological literature and its debates.

Though spirituality is part of our general piety, seen by other Christians as a typical and valuable preoccupation of Catholics, nonetheless it has its problems. They range from the superstition that practices can turn into to the invasion of psychological jargon and schemas which can displace its Christian content. Among the Catholic faithful there is often less interest in doctrinal or biblical study than in the enneagram, Jungian archetypes, journaling and many other similar techniques, just as devotions to the Infant of Prague, the Sacred Heart, or Our Lady of Perpetual Help tended in the past to displace the Eucharistic liturgy and the study of the Bible. The imagination is among Catholicism's valuable assets, but also has potential for disarray and distraction. Thus, in any given seminary or school of theology, it would not be hard to find individuals who would champion spiritual preparation generally and probably a specific form of it as the key element, perhaps the only really important element in education for ministry. They often have a few choice words for the incursion of other demands upon what they consider the primary one. This is not altogether unexpected since the appeal to spiritual formation draws together convictions and interests both from within the Church and from secular culture at large. The contemporary emphasis is not merely an accidental one nor simply a continuance of the longstanding importance of spirituality in Catholic seminaries from their foundation after the Council of Trent. Its present forms and purposes clearly reflect the present state of contemporary culture and Christianity.

Leaders in the community are expected not only to have a developed spirituality of their own, but also to be able generally or as specialists to direct the faithful in their own spiritual development. As to its general characteristics, like other areas of renewal since Vatican II, spirituality is now more attentive to its biblical foundations and its action-oriented character, the former in keeping with a more ecumenical theology, and the latter because of the increased awareness of social responsibility. As to its incorporation in education for ministry, emphasis on the vocational character of ministry intensifies the importance of spirituality as a preparation for ordination or appointment (a parallel to the exercises of the catechumenate) and as the shape of the "new life" of the minister (a parallel to the mystagogy for the newly baptized). Finally, as to its relation with theological study, the Catholic conception of theology and of theological education in general still maintains at least conceptually the tradition of faith seeking understanding, of a rootedness in prayer and liturgy, however scientific, speculative, or apologetic it has become in its conversation with social sciences, philosophy, or contemporary culture. This theoretical companionship can not always be found actualized, of course, in specific situations.

Spiritual formation is experiencing its own form of contemporary scrutiny and revision along with formation for practicality and professionalism. Some sense of a need for competence analogous to professionalism was no doubt present in previous centuries, though it developed in North America with a very specific meaning and content in this century and, as we have seen, is being questioned currently for its appropriateness in theological education. Similarly with the demands for forming students to be practical, they too were surely present from the beginning, but have required specific curricular changes in recent decades as Roman Catholic theology generally treated biblical, historical, and pastoral theology as important elements of theological education in their own right rather than mere adjuncts to systematic theology. What has been felt more keenly, perhaps, has been the demand by educators and the desire among students for an education into a ministry marked by greater attention to specialization beyond scholarly and liturgical competence. Practicality, therefore, has quite evidently taken on new forms within ministry and the preparation for it.

In this chapter I wish to reflect upon some of the criticism of spiritual formation as a chief factor in theological education for ministry. As with practicality and professionalism, some forms of spirituality are problematic, others are neglected, and in general an emphasis on spirituality can become disproportionate, though for reasons quite proportionate to the present state of theological study, Church life, and academic practice. As a resource for the Church as a whole, Catholic experience with spiritual formation can be a valuable ecumenical contribution to the general revision of theological education, but that is not to say that it need not be revised or that it cannot learn from the Protestant theological and pastoral hesitation about it.

I

As with professionalism and practicality, so also spirituality comes to the fore when times of change or crisis highlight the inadequacy of former routines. This was true of the time of the origin of seminaries and is so in the present day. Beyond the Tridentine establishment of the institutional shape of priestly education, the inauguration of Sulpician, Vincentian, and Eudist seminaries in the 17th century added what the conciliar decree did not provide for, namely, a spirituality of the priesthood rooted in a theology of the personal, even ontological, relation between the priest and Christ, the ascetical practices appropriate to it, and a companion theology of the Church defining the role of the priest and his ecclesiastical duties. (White, 1-23; Ciuba) Many such seminaries were initially "houses of formation" which did not provide the academic component, but depended upon a university or similar institution which offered a course of theological study. One might add from the previous century the foundation of the Society of Jesus by Ignatius of Loyola and the order of studies he prescribed for Jesuits, though

Jesuit theological education did not become as vital a force in the renewal of the education of priests as did the others, particularly in North America. Benedictines, Franciscans, and Dominicans also contributed in varying degrees with their own distinctive views of spiritual formation, especially when they established seminaries for the training of others beyond their own members.

All of these traditions within Roman Catholicism are distinguished by their adherence to practices beyond the common liturgical life of Catholics. Such practices as discovered by a charismatic founder or group become articulated in seminal texts, usually short and seemingly simple expositions of the life of Christ, methods of prayer, anecdotes or wise sayings, or the narrative of experience. These texts are not strictly rules or constitutions such as the founders of religious orders ultimately devise for the good order and governance of their members. However, they function as guidelines which, in the hands of the subtle interpreter or spiritual director, can be used to form the personal habits of individuals in conformity to a particular emphasis or insight into human relationships with God, emphasizing certain aspects of Christ's life, and fostering participation in one or other work of the multifaceted mission of the Church.

Such spiritualities are specified by reference to their founders, Ignatius or Dominic for example, or for their special concern with simplicity of life, contemplative withdrawal, education, or social action. What the spirituality consisted in was shown by pointing to the members of the communities formed by that particular living out of the Gospel and the specific mission. A complex interweaving of habits of thought, action, and speech marked the group, its routines, its spontaneity, its everyday life and its saintly heroes. Only recently has it become necessary, when the members of a theological school, for example, have not also been simultaneously members of a religious community, to ask how it is that the school is Jesuit or Dominican, for example. And in the diocesan seminary, as collaboration in education with the laity developed, there emerged a need to specify the spirituality of a diocesan priest in contrast to both religious priests and lay ministers. While these situations are intensified by the newness in the Catholic world of collaborative education for ministry (ecumenically and coeducationally) and by the radical secularity of contemporary culture, they are by no means without precedent. The struggle in the second half of the 19th century to provide for the preparation of priests spiritually and otherwise to be indigenously apt priests in North America might offer insights into the present situation.

More strikingly, however, has been the growing experience of formation staff who discover, as do their colleagues on the academic staff, the lack of Catholic ethos which many of the otherwise earnest students exhibit, at least in comparison with candidates for ministry who grew up in the 1940s and 50s. Spiritual formation in the graduate professional school may have to begin with a kind of remedial work which gives some of the basic foundations for Christian spiritual life before it can begin the task of aiding students to develop a spirituality appropriate to their particular form of ministry. This situation is also exacerbated by the lack of experience of good liturgical celebration which can be generally expected among North American Catholics. Certain longstanding habits of worship and their contemporary manifestations militate against the formation of a sound spiritual life among the faithful at large.

The six metamorphoses of ministry which O'Meara uses to organize the last 2,000 years of Christian ministry have their equivalent spiritualities. (O'Meara, 95-133) Until recently, it would not have been thought necessary, or perhaps even possible, to isolate out such a thing as spirituality from the complex of theology and life. Texts which we now regard as the classics of Western spirituality were more generally part of an organic whole. In that respect, the contemporary situation allows a more direct consideration because spirituality is so often found in specialized texts or activities. The remarks of this chapter, then, can merely allude to the task of providing the historical roots and an analytic description of the contemporary situation, which are preparatory to addressing the question at hand: how does a theological school attend to the spiritual formation of its students for ministry? That question itself depends upon a prior one: is there a spirituality uniquely appropriate to the vocation of priest and lay minister? Or, to put it another way, is there a spirituality for ministry apart from those developed in and for specialized forms of Christian life or mission in the Church? The answer seems deceptively simple.

As I have considered in the previous two chapters, so also here in the case of spirituality, the identity and mission of those specially chosen for ministry along with all of the faithful have a common ground in their participation in the mission of both Word and Spirit through baptism. This common spirituality can be observed in the lives of the principle figures of both Old and New Testaments as those who exemplify in a normative fashion what roles of leadership and ministry require. In fact, much of the renewal of religious communities that Vatican II inaugurated consisted of a retrieval of the originating charism of founders and their founding ministries through a renewal of their Scriptural inspiration. Similarly, the renewal of diocesan priestly life which various documents of Vatican II envisage requires a similar return to a study and use of the Bible as foundational. If there is a spirituality of ministry in general, then it must be formulated out of both the example and the self-articulation of the first disciples and witnesses of the Lord's own ministry. (O'Meara, 47-94) This is simply the same reading that the charismatic initiators of specialized spiritualities engaged in. It might prove helpful to the discussion of what is appropriate priestly spirituality to reconsider the use of the term "evangelical" to denote not principally a monastic way of life, but a theology and practice of discipleship consonant with the baptismal call to witness and service as derived from the New Testament. Such a liberation of ministry and ministers to imitate the broad range of archetypal discipleship seems very much needed in face of the challenge to be professional and practical, whatever one's ministerial status. Moreover, the development of contemporary forms of spirituality, and the formation appropriate to foster them, must admit of a certain freedom based upon a Christian belief in the living presence of the Risen Lord, of the Holy Spirit.

Now, this rudimentary scriptural spirituality might never exist on its own, but may always be mediated through persons and groups who by their very engagement with the Christian life tend to give it a specificity appropriate to their personalities and locales. Like subcultures, spiritualities, or more concretely those who try to live according to them, form groups and associations, adopt distinctive language forms and habits of life, and as such are the concrete manifestation of Christian culture as it devolves into its particular embodiments. The challenge is to maintain this diversity in a unity, and this is especially true in developing a spirituality for priestly ministry and a spirituality for the pastor in particular who has always had, but perhaps has more urgently now, the task of fostering unity rather than uniformity, of encouraging initiative and self-appropriation rather than silent and often inauthentic obedience. Perhaps the most apt avenue of exploration would be a spirituality in continuity with that of the faithful as a whole, but with attention to the role of the one who presides at the worship of the assembly, oversees its education and prompts its works of charity. Being able to differentiate this rudimentary responsibility from the more specialized tasks of the pastor would alleviate much confusion in the forms of theological education which impose the requirements for preparation for pastoring on everyone preparing for ministry, priestly or otherwise.

As with the professional and practical qualities of the priest and minister, so also their spiritual qualities are being discussed in many traditions. As an acute observer of Catholic life as well as other traditions, George Lindbeck has offered a set of reflections on "Spiritual Formation and Theological Education." His remarks cut across the particularities of Christian traditions and place the issues of spiritual formation within the larger context of the genetic, personal, and cultural factors determining contemporary notions of spirituality in relation to theology and theological education. His remarks are distinctly pertinent to the review of the Catholic situation I have just offered, though it is important to recall that he offers them as non-theological remarks. I shall only briefly make use of them as a basis for theological implications, leaving a fuller development for the next section. Let me quote his conclusions directly:

> First, special ministerial spiritual formation should be avoided whenever possible because of the dangers of clerical elitism (even "we are anti-elitists" can function as a divisive boast). Second, in the present situation when both socialization and personally-committed internalization of communal traditions is weak, it may nevertheless be desirable for spiritual formation to be a programmatic part of seminary life. Third, this is difficult. Theology and spirituality have for long been so thoroughly separated that spiritual formation . . . is in danger of being an orphan, an erratic block, within the seminary. Fourth, changes in the regnant view of science, of both *Natur und Geisteswissenschaften,* give some hope for the future. To the degree attention to spiritual maturity is methodologically incorporated into the normative descriptions of a religion, the actual processes of theological education will encourage interest in spiritual formation rather than indifference or opposition as at present. (Lindbeck, 1988b, 30)

The first conclusion may seem, at first sight, contradictory to received Catholic opinion, if not contradictory to the very existence of the Catholic seminary or school of theology. However, as I have begun to suggest and will continue to develop, ensuring that the students preparing for ministry of all kinds acquire habits properly called Christian spirituality should be increasingly rooted in a liturgical spirituality common to all the faithful, and the specialization of such habits should build upon this common foundation. This is not merely a matter of expediency, so as to avoid clerical elitism. It is based upon a theological reason which roots all ministry in a common call, a common life, a common worship which itself argues against elitism of any form, clerical, spiritual, intellectual or otherwise. Lindbeck's second conclusion reflects the current experience of many Catholics, and his third and fourth conclusion broadens the discussion of institutional, curricular, and pedagogical matters into a discussion about the relation of spirituality and theology, and into the nature of doctrine and religions themselves. As I have already indicated in the introduction, his remarks on these matters can be exceptionally insightful for Catholics. It will be necessary to offer some tradition-specific remarks about spiritual formation in dialogue with Lindbeck. To do so I now turn, as in previous chapters, to conversation with some of the literature on the matter from outside the Catholic tradition.

II

As Schuth's study documents, the present operation of Catholic schools of theology and seminaries gives evidence not only of general agreement on the importance of spiritual formation as chief among the purposes of theological education but also of commonality in practices: pre-seminary preparation, preliminary screening of candidates, spiritual direction, retreats, confidential evaluation of individuals, use of psychological therapy when necessary, courses and workshops, a rich liturgical and sacramental life, and a regimen of daily living. Nonetheless, there are those who do ask: to what effect all this attention to spiritual direction and formation in its many forms? Does it accomplish what it sets out to do, particularly as it is aided by modern psychological sophistication and the recent burgeoning publication of both classical and contemporary spiritual writings? The rate of retention of young priests who have benefited from the reform of North American seminaries, and the more intangible track record of lay people, has yet to be chronicled, but there is sufficient evidence that newly-ordained priests still leave active ministry, well-trained lay persons abandon their efforts to pursue ministry, and both groups experience various forms of dysfunction from burnout to despondency. Religious communities engage in an analogous scrutiny of their own formational procedures in the face of a seeming lack of success in forming their members for long and effective ministry. Of course, perseverance in a vocation is not guaranteed by any form of spiritual, professional, or practical formation, nor does such instruction limit the surprises that a living relationship with God and the Church will bring.

Others would wonder what a renewed emphasis on this aspect of seminary training has done to the intellectual character of seminary life and teaching. It is not always the case that there is a harmonious relation between members of the faculty charged with formational duties of a spiritual nature and those chiefly concerned with academic formation. Conflicting claims on the time and energy of students, and more importantly, conflicting theologies at work in the spiritual and intellectual regimens of the program of preparation are confusing if not detrimental. The ideal, of course, is a harmony of parts. In addition to questions about whether this or that aspect of such formation is appropriate and effective, about how to integrate it within the program as a whole, and about why this renewed emphasis has appeared at this time, there are also questions about whether its principle paradigms are adequate to Christian belief.

J. Douglas Hall, in his essay "Theological Education as Character Formation?" offers various cautions about the use of the term *spiritual* and the whole notion of *character formation*, particularly because of its association with the narcissism of contemporary North American culture. The emphasis on the need for character formation presumes a lack of spirituality or character in theological education, observes Hall. This need not be an indication of institutions simply failing to provide what is necessary. Beyond structural, curricular, and circumstantial causes to account for this apparent lack, there is the disjunction of doctrinal, historical, and exegetic from spiritual insight in Christian theology, unknown to the early Church and not entirely present in medieval and reformation theology and Church life. The dissociation of theology and spirituality, of the scholarly adept from the spiritually mature, gradually developed in the modern period of Christian theology, aided by the division and specialization of the studies and fields which comprise it, and in Catholicism by the distance between theology and worship. The evidence for this dissociation could be found, for example, in a study of the rise of historical critical methods in biblical studies, or in the dominance of philosophical systems in doctrinal study, whether for integralist or modernist purposes, or ultimately in the secularization of pastoral studies. To the degree to which theological study in general distances itself from the liturgical and moral life of the community, the more problematic becomes the question of whether theological education includes, or even requires, spiritual foundations and formative exercises. When the distance is great enough, there can even develop a contestation of loyalties through parallel but unrelating worlds of discourse, spirituality on one side and academic theology on the other. I would interpret the work of Farley on habit, Lindbeck on the nature of religion and doctrine, and Hall on formation as converging in their attention to the root causes of this "lack" of spirituality.

In his article, Hall valuably suggests that we need not only to diagnose the malaise before prescribing a cure, but to consider whether much of the proposed cure is part of the problem. His immediate concern is with the implications of construing the matter as character formation, but any number of other schemes might come under scrutiny. What is needed, he suggests, is a reassertion of the priority of grace, of the action of Christ in shaping one's life, and of the exercise of the freedom of the Spirit as the appropriate notions with which to name the dynamics in Christian life which are determinative prior to any efforts on our own part. Suspicion of the inward and mystical, and caution about the abilities of unaided nature, are often associated with certain doctrinal and ascetical preferences within specific Protestant traditions, and can function as a corrective to opposing tendencies. A Pelagian or mechanistic notion of spiritual development, confident in our own efforts at Christian personal development, is of course more consonant with the contemporary preoccupation with the self, with psychological schemes for self-actualization and control, and the dominance of metaphors of interiority for understanding reality. The Roman tradition more recently has attempted to join liberal Protestant theological notions with its spiritual heritage, with ambiguous results. The criticism of such efforts within the Catholic world is often confused because much of it construes the situation in terms of obedience to ecclesiastical authority or a very limited retrieval of the tradition, rather than questioning the doctrinal preferences at work.

The established practice in both diocesan and religious seminaries is to use the demands of community living, personal prayer, and liturgical celebration as the principle means of shaping the spiritual habits of students. Such practices are firmly based upon a doctrine of the priority of grace over nature, and of nature cooperative with grace. Such formation is embodied not only in the forms of prayer and the interiority which they require, but in the attitudes and actions necessary for living with others and carrying out one's community responsibilities as the realization of a common mission which animates the group. Such communities thrive on the outward directedness of their members, on the orientation of their lives towards their particular ministry. This spirituality at work in the structures and activities of the community as a group is a necessary dialectical companion to, and perhaps a corrective for, the personal and inward activities often emphasized in contemporary schools of spirituality. Thus Hall's suspicion of some forms of spiritual formation as yet another form of contemporary narcissism encourages the development within theological education of communal and public forms of habit formation, which are hardly foreign to the Roman tradition.

The reformulation of spiritual formation as learning how to live as a disciple ensures that what is prescribed by way of educational procedures will embody the general rule of the priority of grace over nature, and will address the tendency towards self-preoccupation inherited from contemporary culture (and often clothed in theological terminology). Such formation is focused on the other to whom the disciple is oriented, the Lord; its objective is the development of a relationship; its end therefore transcends the process itself; it must necessarily attend to the present-day community of believers; and it encompasses the very process of theological education itself. All five aspects indicate how, if discipleship is used as the chief metaphor for spiritual formation, it would counter the by now oft-repeated troubles of individualist, functionalist, elitist and secularist tendencies in spirituality. On the constructive side, discipleship as paradigm encourages whatever is done by way of formation to be aimed at receiving one's identity through a relationship—with the Lord and in the community. Such a formation transcends the institutional process itself because the focus rests ultimately on God who effects the transformation of men and women into ministers of Word and Sacrament within the community, but it also encompasses the educational process because study, worship, and imitation in action are already the activities of discipleship, in fact indispensable activities. Such formation could establish and foster the basis for collaboration between laity and clergy, perhaps even the dispersal of the distinction between them, and provide for the recognition and development of distinct kinds of ministry. The Catholic tradition could adapt such a paradigm, provided it did not engender a spiritual passivity (which has deep roots in the Roman tradition) or a disparagement of the valuable insights which result from the study and exercise of theologically and psychologically sound spiritual practices.

Hall completes his article by specifying three spiritual qualities essential to discipleship: covenental commitment, discerning discipline, and apostolic responsibility. They obviously name habits for all Christians, and I am tempted, in keeping with Hall's reminder about the priority of grace over nature and his caution about self-oriented language and activity, to wonder how they relate to the three theological virtues of faith, hope, and love, habits shaping self-identity, knowledge, and action. All three virtues emphasize the graciousness of God, and all three orient the individual beyond the self, to God and to the Church in the world. They remind us of the radical priority of God's acts which make possible discipleship: commitment is rooted in conversion and reconciliation; discipline is rooted in healing and illumination; and responsibility must first learn the acceptance of suffering if it is to be more than self-assertion. Such remarks pass over familiar territory, but perhaps it is helpful to retrieve contemporary spirituality from what sometimes seems to be a plethora of schemes, techniques, perspectives, and esoterica of various sorts, and return it to conversation with primary theological topics.

Covenantal commitment, though not the usual vocabulary of Catholic formation, does capture in a phrase what spiritual formation is after: appropriation, assimilation, and internalization of the faith tradition which makes possible and nourishes personal commitment and the realization of particular God-given gifts and vocations. The candidate for ministry is prepared by entering deeper into the tradition he or she is to lead, has an inevitably limited experience broadened for the sake of more comprehensive understanding, and discovers inventiveness and adaptability within an established context. Such an emphasis relativizes other commitments, whether to a specific institution, program of study, group of scholars, or interest group. It also encourages a balance between the confidence which comes from learning and the Christian humility necessary to discipleship. Hall's reference to the potential danger of turning intellectual labor as a form of Christian obedience into pietistic anti-intellectualism clearly has its more typically Roman Catholic embodiments, integralist reductionism of spirituality measured by ecclesiastical obedience, and modernist selective spirituality measured by an appeal to the democracy of feeling or "experience" and the goal of human self-fulfillment. It always remains troublesome to accept the fact that Christian spiritual maturity is ultimately a gift from God requiring suffering.

The second quality Hall discusses is discerning discipleship, given by him an admittedly Protestant definition as discernment of the living Word of God as the ever new source of Christian life. This activity, this habit, is precisely what theology is, in all its parts and throughout the Church. It has both a general and technical sense, then, since discipleship and the task of theological thinking is both a general activity of Christians, and a special gift which enables some to pursue theology more rigorously and more authoritatively. When leadership in the community is conceived as principally discipleship, as a heightened and more self-consciously dedicated and self-critical following, then discernment as a leading notion in understanding preparation for leadership is not so much what sets the priest and lay minister apart, but what unites them with the rest of the community and specifies the fundamental duty they have to intellectual, liturgical, and moral acuity. They may not be perfect, most of them may not be geniuses, and they may experience their fair share of doubts and frustrations, but such elements of their leadership are ingredients of any disciple's life, as Mark's account of the first disciples gives ample evidence.

In contemporary Catholic usage, the term discernment has passed from being a technical term within a highly sophisticated spiritual ascesis to becoming an all-purpose term which often conveys less rather than more clarity about what it consists in. Just about anything passes for discernment among some, and it often exhibits preoccupations which can be troublesome. Two phrases sum up the tendencies: "discerning the signs of the times," and "discerning spirits." Neither are inappropriate usages of the term, but both, when isolated from the other, and especially when detached from "discerning the Word of God" can too easily lapse into a discernment at the service of generalized humanitarian social criticism and action, or programs of self-improvement at their best, syncretistic spiritualism at their worst. Like the rhetoric associated with professionalism and practicality, the persuasive talk about spiritual formation which trades upon the culturally popular concerns about social and psychological dynamics is simply doing its job well.

Catching the attention of would-be disciples by going in the door of natural religiosity in order to come out into the realm of Christian discourse and action is hardly a 20th century invention. Moreover, social concern and personal fulfillment, despite the trendy vocabulary, are longstanding goals and desires of Christian preaching and practice. What is troublesome is the tendency to shed Christian particularity in order to engage in them, or even to submit Christian discipleship to norms incompatible with Christian doctrine, for the sake of a wholehearted attention to either the signs of the times or the needs of self-fulfillment. On the one hand, lack of knowledge about, or even disparagement of, the profound resources of the tradition plagues the attempts of the faithful in general in their very serious and earnest attempts to be socially and personally responsible. On the other hand, the accommodationist agenda, whether pursued unreflectively or purposefully, is often countered in the Roman tradition with an appeal to ecclesiastical authority as the source of ensuring fidelity to the tradition. This constitutes a serious misconception of the nature of discipleship, whose defining element is that discernment of the living Word of God which Hall emphasizes, not ecclesiastical obedience. Discerning the living Word of God need not collapse into exercises of prayer and meditation, but needs to infuse the intellectual rigor with which the scriptures, the history of doctrine, the experiments in practical application are studied, evaluated, enacted. The disciplined discernment of a Christian disciple need not adopt the canons of rationality which dissociate learning from wisdom, the technical and calculative thought which ignores the material and spiritual transcendence of all reality, or the humanitarian respect and responsibility for creation rather than obedience to the rigors of God's love for humanity and the world.

The third quality which Hall considers is apostolic responsibility. Being apostolic, evangelical, mission-oriented, socially concerned—each tradition has its own particular term—belongs to discipleship, and theological education for ministry aims at equipping one for service. The importance of practice, of course, can be emphasized at the risk of losing the intellectual and spiritual dimensions of discipleship, but then the same risk of imbalance haunts the other two as well. Many of Hall's final remarks as he engages the problems of professionalism and practicality recall the discussion I have already presented. He is quite forceful in insisting that discipleship is a centrifugal force, and he quotes Gordon Kaufman with approval:

> Devotion to God, loyalty *to God* . . . cannot be contented with any sort of private pietism or parochial concern for particular traditions and communities. It demands reflection on and action to bring about a *metanoia* in human life as a whole, for God is here understood as that ecological reality behind and in and working through all of life and history, and the service of God can consist thus only in universally oriented vision and work. . . . (Hall, 76-77)

Such a conclusion advocating responsibility could be adequately served by a deist notion of God and the rhetoric of secular humanism. Hall quotes the passage with approval, but remarks just prior to it that this particular concern for the world ought to flow from a discipleship rooted in "devotion to the God revealed in the crucified one." The extension of Christian responsibility to a universal vision that takes on the agenda of any number of contemporary social concerns, whether ecological, political, economic, or social, is hardly foreign to recent Catholic concerns and controversies. It is Kaufman's reference to "private pietism or parochial concerns" which gives me pause, and may be a more telling phrase than the appeal to a theme of global responsibility in alerting the reader to the ingredient of natural religiosity.

The question may be put in the negative, namely, can one really be professional, practical, and devoted if one retains the tradition specific character, and even the specifically Christian character, of one's ministry? Or the question can be put positively, that is, do the demands of a global perspective or world historical horizon require an increasing detachment from tradition-specific, or specifically Christian, articulations of doctrine? The theological issue is whether discipleship as responsibility can be fostered in students of ministry through formation which attends to the requirements of both person and tradition precisely as required by the logic of Christian doctrine and practice. Personal piety and facility with the practices of one's tradition need not necessarily cause a narrowness in either the conception or enactment of Christian responsibility. In fact, the preparation of individuals to be leaders in the community requires that their spiritual formation be broad enough to ensure sympathy and understanding for the great variety of ways in which the Spirit draws the Christian faithful to live out their love of God. And Christian responsibility increasingly requires knowledge of and appreciation for the other great religions of the world and their followers' dedication to the transcendent they call God. The priest or minister need not personally find great enthusiasm for each and every manifestation of Christian responsibility, but such individuals must be able to recognize the gifts of the Spirit and shepherd those who are called to live according to them. This is an ability essential for the kind of practicality the Christian minister must exercise, and is one gained not simply by study but by prayer.

Anyone who has attempted to assess the suitability of students for ministry knows that identifying, let alone measuring, such things as commitment, discernment, and responsibility are tasks accomplished indirectly, by way of impressions, through the telling of stories about students and by offering perspectival evaluations. And anyone who has engaged in curriculum revision, or in assessment of the content of specific courses or activities related to spiritual formation, knows the dangers of settling too easily for satisfying one's academic or administrative conscience with trendy solutions, no matter how topical or earnest they may be. Discussion of spiritual formation can tend to resolve itself into rhetorical flourishes and exhortations with little practical impact or resolution of specific problems. In a manner analogous to professional or practical capabilities, spiritual maturity conceived of as a Christian habit essential to formal ministry in the Church does not have single corresponding doctrines or beliefs, or a narrow group of exercises guaranteed to produce such habits in the student. As I will discuss in the chapter on pedagogy, becoming professional, practical, and spiritually mature is more aptly thought of as learning to be a member of a particular culture, a particular way of life, in which one has a certain role and tasks in keeping with one's identity and its relationship with others.

III

An effort to search for the general rules underlying education for ministry resolves itself into a theological discussion. And any theological discussion will depend for its integrity and logic upon a constellation of basic doctrines which are themselves a redescription of the Christian faith guiding a particular community of the contemporary Church and its relationships with human culture and history. Throughout this and the previous two chapters, the term *ministry* has been used to hold together a great many activities which Christians engage in as forms of discipleship. Understanding these activities requires understanding how they manifest a specific relationship with Christ and with the Christian tradition and its community, through which individuals receive their ecclesial identity and authority, and simultaneously develop their personal identity. Just as the shape of theological education depends upon presuppositions about ministry, so also a general presupposition about ministry admits of further specifications foundational to it.

If the variety of purposes and dynamics in theological education for ministry are to have unity and integrity within a given institution, then some agreement about common theological presuppositions will be needed as criteria for sorting out what does and does not belong, and how various parts and activities are related to one another. How do psychological development and socialization in the community, personal and public forms of piety, training in skills and developing scholarly insight, promotion of basic human qualities and receptivity to the work of grace—how do these *desiderata* find their appropriate forms of coordination and subordination? Several levels of reflection move us from the immediate implementation of courses, procedures, and other kinds of institutionalization, through documents and discussions of principle, to the mission statements expressing the founding vision of a school, to the living fabric of the religious community or diocese which gives its stamp to the specialized work of a school of theology.

Efforts to assess and renew the basic orientation of all forms of ministry in the Catholic tradition began in this century in many disconnected and seemingly remote efforts, all of which can now be seen to have their culmination and coordination in the Second Vatican Council and its implementation. The pastoral intent of the Council and its interpretation tend to encourage a reading of its documents for their efforts to bring Roman Catholicism into dialogue with contemporary culture, and to reorient its mission, liturgy, and theology to serve that dialogue. Equally important to the meaning and effect of the Council was its efforts to recover and promote essential features of the Christian tradition which had been obscured in recent forms of Catholic life, particularly some held in common with Protestant traditions, which were to become more intentional dialogue partners in the post-conciliar period. The renewal of education for ministry received its theological mandate in three documents addressing religious, clergy, and laity, and I wish to focus on a particular appeal common to all three.

Speaking of religious life, *Perfectae Caritatis* offers a basic rule for renewal in its second paragraph: "Since the fundamental norm of the religious life is a following of Christ as proposed by the gospel, such is to be regarded by all communities as their supreme law." In the last chapter of the Council's document, *Dei Verbum*, in paragraph 25, the education of the clergy is given a task in keeping with the exposition in the rest of the document of the nature of revelation and the reassertion of the priority of the Scriptures: "Therefore, all the clergy must hold fast to the sacred scriptures through diligent sacred reading and careful study. . . ." And, in the document *Apostolicam Actuositatem*, paragraph 4, the Council states that "the success of the lay apostolate depends upon the laity's living union with Christ." Though there are undoubtedly other common threads in these and other documents of the Council which are a source for explicitizing the common foundation in education for ministry for priests, religious, and laity, multiple reasons converge for me in the preference for a Christocentric foundation, such as the documents themselves suggest. The other possible constellations of rules might take God transcendent, the Church, the Holy Spirit, human nature, or the structure of human society and its cultures as pivotal. Whatever the choice, the responsibility remains to do two things: ensure that the other doctrinal areas are attended to for the sake of the integrity of the faith, and relate the concrete measures needed to achieve an education to the leading doctrine and its particular constellation in a manner that is coherent and appropriate to the contemporary Church.

The task of this last section of the first Part is to offer a few initial remarks about education for ministry which takes a theology of the person and work of Christ as foundational. This is not the place to advance a complex theory about ministry. I am indebted to the work of O'Meara, Tavard, Hill, and others, as I have indicated in the introductory chapter. The present theological and ecclesiastical discussion of ministry is full of vested interests with claims and counterclaims to ideological critique. If the meaning of professional, practical, and spiritual as adjectives to specify the character of contemporary ministry is unsettled, equally so is the meaning of ministry itself as the end or goal of a particular form of theological study. The theological task is to look for and articulate the common essence which appears through the multifaceted history of the Church and can function as a summation of what has been done and as an ideal for testing out contemporary efforts. Elsewhere I have made an attempt to lay out some possibilities for discovering the general rules that underlie formation for ministry. (Schner, G., 1986) I still find the same major concerns pertinent.

First, the primary focus for defining ministry is the person and work of Christ. Even if one takes the analysis of the work of the Church suggested by George Tavard, for example, as having a four-fold structure of mediation, proclamation, service and education, all four, and any number of other possible general terms to conceptualize Christian ministry would have to submit to the question: are they established by participation in the mission of Christ as self-manifestation of God and savior of us all? As was the case for Christ himself, the embodiment of God's word and work is in human structures, and the inevitable selectivity and particularity of such structures accounts for the varying dominance of preferences for mediation or proclamation by some traditions, and for social action service or education by others. Such preferences are obviously not exclusive ones, just as terms like imitation, conversion, collaboration, or friendship can also indicate the complex of activities that being conformed to Christ in the Church for the continuance of his mission requires.

Second, acceptance of Christ as Lord for whose sake and in conformity with whom the Christian minister is drawn into roles of service and leadership involves the everyday task of learning and engaging in ruled behavior, in the shaping of experience and action in conformity with habits which are themselves the structure of human participation in Christ's mission. These habits can be understood as rooted in the gifts of the Holy Spirit, in grace, in the empowerment of human beings to act in and effect the world in co-operation with God. This requires adopting the Christian story not simply as something to be known, but something to be lived. As James Ross has put it succinctly:

> Yet anyone who knows the Christian or Jewish religion will recognize instantly that bible stories, credal teaching, stories of saints and all the religious talk (even sermons when properly done) are designated to modulate one's conception of oneself and of one's relationship to other people, to modulate one's judgments about the physical world, about the goals and values of life and one's judgments about God (who is to be encountered through faith, in obedience to moral law and in the pursuit of holiness). The discourse is inherently action-

oriented, response, self-construal and judgment-oriented. (Ross, 167)

Third, this development of habits is through the adoption of an ideology set forth in a logic of ideals, not abstractly, but in the logic of a story into which the Christian minister is invited to enter. I use the term ideology advisedly, not in its pejorative sense deriving from Marx, but in a positive sense indicating the necessary way in which a logic of ideals, originally rooted in actual life can become independent of that origin and remain heuristic for other ages and places as an invitation to reshape the present in accordance with, in this case, a transcendent and divine understanding of reality. This requires two major activities, that of developing a sense of other persons as God sees them and of the contemporary human situation and its cultural forms as both liberating and limiting of human potential and divine intervention. Education for ministry will take on the tasks of developing self-knowledge and social awareness, using both a hermeneutic of the religious dimension of experience and a hermeneutic of human social structures, each giving evidence of sin and grace.

These are three of the more basic characteristics of a spirituality for ministry which might ground a basic discussion of being professional and practical, as well. As I indicated in the beginning of this chapter, this evangelical spirituality will inevitably appear in a variety of forms, as faith engages culture, and the Church renews itself not by finding a new Lord, but by bringing the Good News of that same Lord to the actual world it inhabits. The dynamic which O'Meara explores, from Jesus' being and doing, through the gift of the Spirit, to the primal ministry of Christians in the first decades after the Resurrection leads to the long history of concrete manifestations of ministry and ministers over nearly 2,000 years. (O'Meara, 26-94) Part of the extraordinary risk which God has taken in involving humanity in the "coming of God's Kingdom" is the possibility that ministry itself adopt forms and self-descriptions which will impede or obscure that very invitation to participation. In the three chapters of Part I, I have attempted to engage that possibility through posing three questions for reflection about what goes on in education for ministry, and in ministry itself, particularly as manifest in the Roman tradition. I indicated in the introductory chapter that the reader's own reflection on their experience of Catholic ministry would be necessary to supplement, and perhaps correct, my generalizations. And the exercise has tried to be particularistic, yet ecumenical. The reflection could be significantly longer and more detailed, and I anticipate a lively discussion to ensue. At this point in the text, however, it is necessary to move from reflection and question to the presentation of theological concepts.

Part II

Theological Grounding

4. Identity in Ministry

IDENTITY, AUTHORITY, AND TRADITION, THE SUBJECTS OF THE next two chapters, are not uniquely Christian theological terms or issues, nor do they specify aspects unique to education for Christian ministry. They are constants of any human society, are given specificity through cultural diversity, and enter into the theory and practice of both general education and the specialized education of professions, skills, and arts. They are terms, however, which indicate pressing problems for both the exercise of Catholic ministry today and education for it. As the literature I have considered in the first part of this essay suggests, they are terms locating problematic areas for many Christian traditions, as perennial issues with a particular contemporary face.

Discovering what determinate character they have in Christian self-understanding and life, and how they can express fundamental theological issues for theological education, is itself a theological task. Identity and authority will admit of a quite different discussion than the notion of tradition, and though these introductory remarks can be applied to the study of all three terms, I will preface further cautions at the beginning of the next chapter concerning the study of the notion of tradition.

I

While identity and authority are terms necessary for the discussion of both God and the Christian in the doctrines of creation, salvation, and sanctification, they have an equal importance in theological anthropology and the theology of the Church and its pastoral particulars. In a fully developed ecclesiology, these terms cannot but be used in harmony with other doctrinal areas upon which it depends. However, in more popular discourse it is not infrequent that ecclesiology is at the service of the maintenance and stability of the established ecclesiastical order, or of ideology critique and apologetic theology in conversation with contemporary culture. In the former case, ahistorical and integralist claims are made about the Church, its ministers, and its organizational structure which are not in keeping with the rules of sound doctrine, and in the later case the application of principles from the psychological and social sciences, or modern forms of criticism, can produce functionalist solutions for the evaluation of old manifestations and the construction of new forms. More drastically, when matters of identity and authority are consigned to the area of ecclesiastical polity, and determined by the current contestation of bureaucratic with populist concerns, it is not surprising that one or other side of what should be a dialectic of positions becomes unyielding to the inevitable passage to a higher and more integrated moment. That is not to suggest that strong oppositions and the rhetoric which carries them are not necessary. The truth they manifest, however, is inevitably partial and is self-fulfilled only through integration and reconciliation.

The following two chapters are not intended as thorough expositions of a theology of ministerial identity and authority, and much less are they adequate to the elusive and complex theological notion of tradition. I do intend, however, to resist locating these matters in anything other than a broad theological context in order to invite others to do what I will merely outline here: develop a theological understanding more directly in conversation with the educational process itself. In a time of rapid change in both the shape of institutions and in the demands of scholarly work, there is an understandable tendency to allow administrators, or even circumstances themselves, to make the decisions about what will happen in matters of curriculum and program requirements. In the Roman tradition these matters are also often conveniently left to episcopal bodies and the documents they produce. The matter of theological harmony and grounding seems to be readily accomplished through descriptive and prescriptive documents whose regulations and norms are used to ensure that actual institutions and programs are appropriate to the tradition's self-understanding. This is by no means an unfortunate procedure, particularly for a Christian tradition which is and has been a worldwide tradition, albeit more recently attentive to the ill effects of uniformity and the evangelical values of adapting to the local Church community's cultural diversity.

Documents and other forms of scrutiny and approval are stabilizing, even comforting, given the actual confusion and disheartening divisions which can appear when members of a faculty actually talk to one another about the theological principles which motivate them individually and corporately. Equally attractive is the appeal to such documents as warrants for what goes on in a given institution when it is questioned by various groups critical of the *status quo* in theological education, from anywhere on a continuum of reasons from reactionary nostalgia, through honest dissatisfaction, to idealistic insistence for instant change. It is an unwieldy process to involve an entire faculty, let alone members of the community at large, in the various aspects of revision. The inability of members of the diverse scholarly specialties which make up a theological faculty to converse in a common language about common goals and objectives is taken for granted by most of the recent studies of theological education. Radical suggestions about involving congregations in the actual shaping of the means of preparation for ministry beyond field education practicums are only beginning to be tried. These studies have proposed a variety of solutions to the problem: a new curriculum which reassigns priorities, a new theory of theological knowledge, a new arrangement of theoretical and practical elements. As insightful as these studies are, the problem remains that specific faculties in specific institutions, with quite specific ecclesiastical histories and investments, must get down to the business of carrying on a reconstructive conversation and making corporate decisions which are then carried through and evaluated. This will require a subtlety of reflection which will distinguish between operant principles and declared ones, and make good use of the various proposals of the recent years.

An essential ingredient in such a process is a discussion of theological principles, of basic credal and doctrinal matters, as they authorize the conversations and enliven the actual educational efforts. This is not something that can be handed over to administrators to settle or which a general consent to a regulatory document accomplishes. It cannot be simply taken for granted that a faculty will easily possess a common theological vision and commitment, and in some cases even acceptance of rudimentary doctrinal rules may be in question. These difficulties are most evident in situations in which worship itself in the theological institution becomes the contested issue, visibly manifesting discord rather than a harmony of spiritual gifts.

Whether from reading texts or observing activities, it is easily evident that identity and authority are not settled notions in contemporary Catholic life. Along with tradition, these notions cannot be investigated in the present circumstances of Roman Catholicism without consideration of those terms and issues which are in dialectical relation with them. I have, however, chosen these three as having a logical and existential priority over others, construing the present situation as one in which we are in a moment of reconstruction, passing from one coherent manifestation of identity and authority within the tradition to another. This choice presupposes truths not only from the human sciences, but from philosophical and theological reflection as well, about what can be known and how we know it, about human nature and society, about the transcendent and its existence as known from Christian revelation, and about God's relations internally and toward us. It is my intention that the choice of authority, identity, and tradition as primary terms should not initially or unreflectively embody a preference for a particular theory of ecclesiastical structure. There are undoubted tendencies to read too quickly into such terms particular interpretations or embodiments of identity, authority, and tradition. In fact, it might be said that at times the present Roman Catholic Church seems to have altogether too much identity and authority.

More frequently perhaps, Catholics, and particularly students of ministry, hear terms like pluralism, diversity, relevance, collaboration, innovation, and the like as naming the leading edge of faithful discipleship, and conversations tend toward statements like the following. Ministerial identity, especially priestly identity, is in crisis; what is required is a diversification of identity and the displacement of the regnant model for roles more in keeping with contemporary society and its actual effective social relations. As a matter of fact, as Dolan, White, and others have shown, what is being experienced in this crisis of identity is a heightened form of the development of what has been a continuously evolving social role. As for authority, it has been so identified with an inherently inadequate hierarchical and patriarchal order within the Roman Catholic tradition, or at least has been so misused, that it is falsifying, ineffective or at least mistrusted, and now functions as an impediment to Church order and mission. Collaborative ministry, a consensus model of decision making, and a more congregational church order are to be preferred. As for tradition, it is a term to refer to what is limiting or obscuring, deadening, even oppressive; experience rather than structure is to be consulted, innovation is the more proper vehicle for religious vitality, and a radical rereading of historical forms and practices is essential to authenticity. Whether from liberationist, feminist, existentialist, or revisionist perspectives, notions like identity, authority, and tradition are initially to be the subjects of ideology critique before they can be theological topics which might admit of radicalization, redefinition, or rescue.

It would not only be foolish but unchristian to fail to engage in the dialectical exchange from which a new understanding and manifestation of identity and authority will issue. That exchange is itself the work of tradition. And both identity and authority have, within Christian self-description, an inherently dialectical character, in relation to God and to the community. It is particularly urgent for theological education to name and appropriate the way in which it engages in some of the most vital acts of the tradition, specifically as it is about the business of forming the identity of those who lead and who themselves will be instruments for the formation of the faithful as a whole. And because it is about the business of forming leaders who exercise proclamatory and sacramental, pastoral and intellectual authority in the community, it cannot avoid asking what sort of authority it prepares individuals to exercise. The moment of critique is as important as the moments of establishment and preservation within the maintenance of the tradition. This lays a responsibility on educational institutions to assess the authenticity and effectiveness of their efforts at forming individuals for critical thinking as much as for conforming thinking.

To these general cautions I will add one further introductory remark. Throughout the discussion of professionalism, practicality, and spiritual maturity, I tried to elicit not historical or pragmatic considerations alone, but also theological issues which seem to me to be the foundation of the similarities and differences between the preparation for ministry particular to the Roman tradition and that of other Christian traditions. In this central section of my essay, I wish to bring those theological concerns together, not from within a fully constructed ecclesiology, but from the area of theological study which considers the broad range of elements and procedures which every area of theological construction uses. And to repeat a point of importance, I take as the backdrop of my efforts the educational enterprise of preparation for ministry, rather than a disembodied discussion of theological method. Much like the theological matters raised by the use of Scripture as normative in theological construction (and hence in theological education), so the formation of Christian identity, the character and exercise of Christian authority, and the nature, purpose, and function of tradition as a conceptualization of an essential element of Christian life and Church order requires theological clarification outside established ecclesiologies, since these notions are not parts of or results of such constructions, but elements which precede them. Elsewhere in an admittedly terse and abstract fashion I have tried to give the general outlines of an incipient vision of elements and procedures involved in theological study and, therefore, in the educational process as a whole. (Schner, G., 1985) It came from my efforts to develop a course of introduction to theology in the Roman Catholic tradition which would hold together a number of things. It would not be a course of fundamental or foundational theology in which, for example, a transcendental anthropology, whether individualist or otherwise, would justify theological method and be the basis for a revision of Christian doctrines themselves. Rather, it was to be a discussion of authority in its various forms (Scripture, tradition, institutions and their polity, or other sciences and social movements) as warrants and occasions for theological argument, for the education toward an identity within ministry, and as such was an initiating exercise in becoming inventive within the tradition. Such an introduction to theology in all its parts, and therefore an introduction within preparation for ministry, requires simultaneous attention to the constellation of doctrines as themselves foundational, as well as to the basic elements and options within philosophical, scriptural, and experiential materials which are the stuff of theological construction, and which can become operative in ministry. It is out of this context that I offer the following remarks in this chapter on identity and authority, and about tradition in the next.

II

Three related efforts to address the crisis do so by emphasizing one or other element of ministerial identity. Let me propose three types of individual, leaving the reader to provide concrete examples from experience. A first type tends to foster maintenance of a form of spirituality, pastoral practice, and style of life, which O'Meara has called the romanticization of ministry. (O'Meara, 122-128) The more difficult it becomes to maintain and exercise ministerial identity and authority in the Roman tradition, the greater is the appeal to solutions through spiritual strength and finesse, often as opposed to doctrinal or moral acuteness which are thought of as the domain of the church scholar or lawyer, and which are overshadowed by the appeal of encounter with God in prayer and simple good works. Or it might be manifested through the reassertion of an ecclesiastical style of life and ministry which grew to prominence in the late 19th and early 20th centuries, and went unquestioned until well into the 1950's. Whether in its older forms or presented in modern guise, it is intriguing to see the return of an identity for the minister analogous to the proposal by Pius XI in 1929 of St. John Mary Vianney as the model priest. A second type can be seen in those who take absorption in practical activities as the sign of fulfillment of the ministerial identity, often to the detriment of collaboration with others or to the interior life which would require leisure as well as labor. Models for this identity would be more contemporary figures who would be more likely to be found in front page newspaper stories than in the calendar of 19th century saints. A third type pursues specialization in ministry through the secular professions, and the heroes of this resolution of the crisis are those who eschew the clerical (in a pejorative sense) style of life for a more egalitarian conformity with the faithful generally. These three types may not exist in such clear form except in rare cases, but they are examples of solutions which take one of the three characteristics of ministry and the minister discussed in Part I in isolation from the others in order to achieve an identity.

Perhaps the great majority of presently active ministers and priests simply do not reflect on these matters, and belong to a type we might name according to their typical experience of ministry and theories about it: bewilderment. They are quite simply confused, not because of lack of ability, but because they are participating in this "crisis" of identity in their everyday work. My purpose in proposing this typology is not to make a sociological claim based upon research in the field. Whatever the proportion of individuals or mix of types, one with another, it is clear that theological institutions can adopt the agenda of one of the first three types, but not of the last. Intentionally or unwittingly the faculty, programs, and style of an institution can propose a model of identity for its students which takes as central the spiritual, practical, or professional character of the minister in whatever variation and relatedness to the others.

They hardly would present the model of bewilderment as the ideal. These preferences are perhaps inevitable, but I am suggesting that the greater the balance and harmony among them, the more thoroughly competent the student will become, learning to avoid the inherent distortions of ministry which one or other imbalance leads to. Strangely enough, while the preparation for religious order priests has been made to conform more closely with diocesan preparation in some respects, the tendency in diocesan preparation to advocate one particular characteristic would seem to lead students toward the ministry of religious orders without the communal way of life to support it.

Without attempting here to sort out the complex of factors presently at work, it is a fact that the multifaceted crisis which constitutes the present state of Roman Catholic ministry in North America, if not elsewhere as well, urges the issue of identity upon us with questions that focus it beyond terms of either introspection or practicalities: why are there fewer and fewer individuals who wish to take on the identity of priest (at least among those able to do so), but more and more of the faithful who want to take on other sorts of pastoral identities, and would even consider priestly identity if it were open to them? Why is there a disjunction between what students of ministry do and say in school, and what they do and say in the first years of their ministry? Why are those already well established in priestly and lay ministerial identity experiencing various forms of dysfunction, and is the incidence of it any greater than in previous ages of the Church? What can be learned from the phenomenon of "temporary" vocations to ministry? How are we to recognize the authentic forms of reconciliation and mediation which will resolve the oppositions and incongruities? To some, these new forms seem either too little, or too much, in terms of their own positions on matters of identity and authority in ministry. What is essential is the discovery of those forms of mediation, forms of identity and authority as essential mediating structures, which can give shape to the faith at the heart of the Christian and Catholic handing on of the tradition.

Investigating the situation presented in the preceding list of questions through the vocabulary, principles, and methods of psychology and sociology yields valuable information and interpretations, as the recent surveys and analyses of Roman Catholic priests and seminaries have shown. When coupled with the recent histories of Catholic seminaries and models of priesthood and ministry, these materials provide a sophisticated picture of the present state of affairs. Assessment of their content from a theological perspective will require some time, but a consideration of the six summary issues with which Katerina Schuth concludes her comprehensive study leads me to conclude that theological consideration of identity and authority in ministry is vital. (Schuth, 213-219) Of the six summary issues Schuth presents, those of staffing and planning at theologates are obviously comprehensive, yet ultimately must look to theological convictions which underlie mission statements and the deployment of resources which they authorize. As to the two issues of changing contexts of ministry and changing Church membership, they are both the cause of the revisioning and the crucible in which the newly formed are tested. The challenge remains to resist merely pragmatic solutions on the basis of efficiency or any other accommodating principle. It is Schuth's remaining two issues, the fostering of vocations and the evaluation of models of ministerial preparation which seem to me to be closest to the heart of the problems and most directly related to theological questions about identity and authority. Theological analysis and ecclesiastical decisions about these two issues will require guidance from doctrinal principles, knowledge of the tradition, and evaluation of the experience of contemporary Christians' spiritual and pastoral insight. These are not necessarily in opposition to, but certainly cannot be substituted with, statistical, psychological, or sociological analyses. Ignorance of what one is actually reflecting upon, and of the human dynamics and operations involved, is disastrous for theological work, and obviously so for ecclesiastical administration. Schemes of interpretation and their principles make possible the rational appropriation of everyday life, including God's presence to that life, rendering it amenable to redescription.

Much of what we say about identity will depend upon the conceptual language, both of common sense and of scholarly investigation, which provides a theory about human identity. The technical vocabulary of various psychologies has found its way into the discourse of common sense such that a theological discussion of individual and social factors in identity cannot escape involvement with complex theories, whether recognized as such or not. Moreover, however much there is an asymmetry between natural religiosity and positive religion, in favor of the historical and revelatory, the notions of grace transformative of nature, and nature cooperative with grace, are the doctrinal warrants for the following brief remarks which are reminders of some well-established interpretations of human identity.

I will give particular attention, first, to the insights of scientific psychology, though other sciences and philosophies could be profitably consulted. Then I will consider an instance in contemporary literature which portrays some of these general principles through specific characters and plot. In both cases, identity is treated as a single stage in a continuum of development, and like every other stage it is one that has inherent possibilities for bringing forward former moments of inadequate growth and for being itself an unsuccessfully negotiated stage. In a more positive vein, the achievement of an identity by the minister might be conceived of with the aid of cultural anthropology and its notion of a liminal state, a rite of passage, which marks the transition into a new identity and place in a society. Of course, the dynamics at work are more complex than even just two or three disciplines and sciences can determine. The next two sections, then, are merely facets of a rather large investigation.

III

Asking questions about identity is both as commonplace and as odd as shaking hands. We do it all the time, but we seldom reflect upon it. Telling someone who I am is as simple as stating my name, and as elusive and complex as trying to write my autobiography. Identity is something I have before I know it, and yet something I never really know or possess until I die, for I am always in the process of inventing it. Identity is something I *am* rather than *have*, and yet it is essentially a socially constructed reality. Such has been the case with human identity since animals had rational souls, but our contemporary world is interested in personal identity in its own peculiar fashion. In fact, as philosophical and cultural analysis has developed in the last few decades, it has become increasingly evident that Western civilization is in the process of reconsidering the legacy of the modern preoccupation with the self, its identity, rational autonomy, and will to objectivity and domination. Consideration of identity, then, is somewhat complicated by an important shift taking place as the hermeneutic of it in sciences and disciplines moves away from the modern agenda of subjectivity and individualism. In a more technical philosophical essay, I would consider the many converging influences that have brought about this shift. To be preoccupied with identity is to be preoccupied with an interpretation of identity and with the social, cultural, linguistic context which originates and fosters that particular interpretation. If identity is elusive in an ontological sense, if I may use that term, it is experienced as all the more elusive a moment in times of cultural change when the matrix for providing the interpretation necessary for having an identity is itself in flux. This is yet again complicated by the fact that the Roman tradition, as perhaps Christianity at large, is attempting to refashion its cultural and symbolic matrix in its effort to live its faith in God within the contemporary world. Postmodern thought requires quite different preoccupations, and the metaphor of the self within, and the values associated with individual assertion of autonomy are highly contested.

Beyond this initial observation concerning the elusive and complex character of identity, my second remark concerns its developmental character. Identity is constantly in the process of being formed in unnoticed but vital and indispensable ways at each stage of human life, as various developmental psychologies schematically describe for us. The notion of stages of development is hardly a new discovery of the 19th century, though experimental and depth psychology have mapped out personal growth with great detail. Without exception, this development is experienced as a *struggle*; it is problematic, for there is no perfect negotiation of our passage from infancy to the final stages of adulthood. What is often not discussed is the heuristic notion of full, sound, or authentic human being which provides some notion of teleology and order to the stages themselves. The current prominence of various forms of ideology critique (as old as Kant at least, though more often invoked with the trio of names—Marx, Nietzsche, and Freud), has found its way into a questioning of the foundations of psychology and psychoanalysis themselves. (Brandt, Browning)

The development of identity is not merely temporal, however; it is dialectically progressive, each new moment being built upon the accomplishment of the preceding stages, incorporating and furthering them. The success of each stage is dependent upon the success and maturity of those preceding. To use Erikson's terminology, one's identity is based upon the resolution of the earlier moments of trust, autonomy, initiative, and industry which chronologically precede it. For example, if one only partially achieves initiative, one might find it hard to function in groups, and might expect others to initiate contacts and projects. A striking example of the result of this truncated development is encountered today in individuals who are the adult children of alcoholics and in the related problem of codependence. A person who has grown up in the family of addicted parents generally has had great difficulty negotiating the stages of basic trust, autonomy and initiative. Such a person may find expression of feelings in any spontaneous and free fashion to be most difficult. Autonomy is severely hampered by codependence on the parents. Initiative is almost nonexistent because of the fear of rejection, discovery, and reprisal that accompany any such expressions of individuality. While such behavior is dysfunctional for any adult, it is exacerbated for persons who because of their professional or social responsibilities are called to exercise a great deal of trust, autonomy, initiative, and industry on behalf of the community. Another important example is that of foreclosure. Rather than inability to alter an already established identity or truncated development, an individual may have foreclosed on an otherwise normal process of development and taken on the identity desired by parents or another influential person. This too-eager resolution makes the authentic exercise of former stages equally difficult, and prepares for a return to the problems of identity when the following stages are to be negotiated. (Schner, J.)

Just as it depends upon previous stages, so development does not stop at identity, as we follow Erikson's schema. Intimacy, generativity and integrity follow upon the passage through the stage of identity formation. It is important to pause here and remind ourselves that a concern for identity is a focus on only one point in a continuum of development, one which has both a before and an after. Concern about the identity of priest and minister as a clue to the revision of theological education must acknowledge its dependence upon prior stages and be attentive to the further stages which are prepared for by the formation of identity. Schuth's analysis and evaluation of the two models of formation operative in theologates today, that of integration and of identification, offer conclusions which are consonant with these psychological observations. (Schuth, 147-155)

As has already been implied, in addition to its being developmental, identity has an inherently relational character. It is known only indirectly, in terms of relationships of interdependence. I come to know other persons by observing how they act, and I come to know my own self through reflection upon and articulation of my own awareness of how I live, and through the multiple ways in which other persons, and even objects to which I have given order, can reflect back to me just who I am. For both psychology and philosophy, identity is known through behavior broadly conceived. This sometimes means that I discover, develop, and renegotiate my identity only consequent upon recounting stories about how I have acted and what I have felt. Moreover, personal identity is known through an understanding of the specific social relations which both confine and actualize the individual, providing the context in which to enact personal identity. Identity must offer an individual both the attributes of continuity and differentiation. It must be a unifying force in the day-to-day experience of the self, and also chronologically over the years of a person's life. At the same time, this identity must be distinct and unique from other identities. Failure to achieve identity gives a striking example of this need for continuity. Here one can think of individuals who are so fragmented that they cannot maintain long-term personal relationships or job commitments. In other cases, continuity or differentiation is maintained to the exclusion of development, as in the case of individuals who cling to roles or relationships despite failure or inadequacy, or individuals who are so differentiated that they become eccentric.

One further observation should be made. Issues of identity, psychologically speaking, are those generally associated with adolescence. Failure to negotiate successfully the formation of an identity returns to haunt every succeeding stage of development. As well, there is plenty of evidence that students in preparation for ministry or entering religious life actually do return to the stage of adolescence in significant ways in the course of the reshaping of their already-established identities in order to become members of religious and ecclesiastical families which offer them new identities or at least modifications of their already operative ones. Does it make sense to ask whether there can be a kind of corporate return to adolescence upon the part of an entire social group, if indeed it is struggling to reform, reshape, even redefine both the group and its individuals' identities? Teachers and spiritual directors in Roman Catholic schools of theology and seminaries can easily testify to the very real existence of this return to adolescence, and to the honest struggles of men and women who undertake the reshaping of their identities in order to take on ministerial roles.

III

Elusive, developmental, dialectical, and relational are the four characteristics I located from a psychological perspective on human identity. Personal stories, rendered into case histories, were essential to the discovery of these structures, and the full investigation of them requires discovering the social structures which authorize and maintain the embodiment of them. The study of biological factors augments the psychological and social categories of interpretation. And a philosophical investigation looks to the family resemblance across cultures and histories for comprehensive categories of discovery and explanation. Literature and art, just as much as the rest, are a valuable mirror in which to discover ourselves, and there is a small but significant body of novels, plays, poems, and autobiographical accounts by and about priests and religious in various ages of the Church which add another world of interpretation and portrayal of just what ministerial and priestly identity is about. William James, for example, knew very well that such accounts were a valuable resource in his invention of a psychology of religious experience.

I have chosen a recent play by the British playwright David Hare as merely one instance offering some striking examples of the struggle for priestly identity in the contemporary Church. The play tells the story of four Anglican priests working within inner-city London. Each is struggling with what it means to be a believer and a priest. In turn, each of them is affected by his relationships with other priests, bishops, members of the parish, friends and family members. The comparisons with the Roman tradition are obvious, and though the characters are specifically male and priests, it is not difficult to imagine them as salient examples of individual types within many forms of ministry. It would be wise, of course, not to presume that the challenges for males in ministry are simply the same as those for females.

Not surprisingly, Hare chooses to have each priest reveal his identity in explicit self-reflection in moments of prayer. This is an important reminder that while psychologies, or any other kind of study, might consider the transcendent dimension as it enters into the understanding of the formation and maintenance of identity, they do so only with an acceptance of that dimension as hypothetical. Literature, however, has the advantage of being able to place that suspension of judgment over everything it invents, not singling out the transcendent. Within the world it invents, God and the realities of religious belief can have full and active parts of the construction of identities.

One character Hare presents has achieved a priestly identity with a settled, self-evident center, both in relation to God, to himself, and to his parishioners. His name is Donald Bacon, known to his friends as Streaky. He loves ministering to his people. It is his life. However, the generous and winning simplicity with which he conducts his ministry is at the expense of insight into the bewilderment of others, particularly his friend and pastor Lionel. His settled sense of himself also does not admit of the risk involved in helping Lionel when his tenure as pastor is threatened, because Streaky fears he might lose his job, too. In prayer he describes himself in this way:

> . . . blissfully happy. Can't help it. Love the job. Love my work. Look at other people in total bewilderment. . . . Why can't people enjoy what they have? . . . Lord, I have no theology. Can't do it. By my bed, there's a pile of paperbacks called *The Meaning of Meaning,* and *How to Ask Why.* They've been there for years. The whole thing's so clear. He's there. In people's happiness. . . . Or the love of my friends. The whole thing's so simple. Infinitely loving. Why do people find it so hard? (Hare, 63)

The process of ongoing but not yet achieved identity development is typified by Lionel, the main character of the play. He is the pastor of the inner-city parish, experiencing a struggle to refashion his priestly identity and the ministry which will flow from it. Essential to that identity is his sense of God, of God's absence, to be precise. At the beginning of the play he prays:

> God. Where are you? I wish you would talk to me. God. It isn't just me. There's a general feeling. This is what people are saying in the parish. They want to know where you are. The joke wears thin. You must see that. You never say anything. All right, people expect that, it's understood. But people also think, I didn't realize when he said *nothing,* he really did mean absolutely nothing at all. You see, I tell you, it's this perpetual absence—yes?—this not being here—it's that—I mean, let's be honest—it's just beginning to get some of us down. You know? Is that unreasonable? There are an awful lot of people in a very bad way. And they need something besides silence. God. Do you understand? (Hare, 1)

The sense of the absence of God is as important to understanding Lionel's search for identity as are the breakdown of his familial and professional relations, and his rejection of an imposition of identity by his bishop. The Right Reverend Charlie Allen would like to impose an identity on Lionel. He warns him that he is not fulfilling his duties. Priestly identity for the bishop appears to consist in a *persona* through whom the priest ministers to people by keeping them "happy." He begins with an observation about the Anglican communion, but it could be applied to the Roman tradition in a lesser degree. He tells Lionel:

> Start talking to our members and you'll find we hold a thousand different views. Only one thing unites us. The administration of the Sacrament. Finally that's what you're there for. As a priest you have only one duty. That's to put on a show.

> Give communion. Hold services. Offer the full liturgy. And look cheerful as you do it. . . . Please fulfill your job description. Keep everyone happy. (Hare, 3-4)

Lionel is unable to do as the bishop requests, and as the play unfolds Lionel comes to a better understanding of who he is, though at great cost. In the process he loses his parish, his wife, and his friends in order to attain a new identity. The process is by no means a simple success, and the quite tangible suffering involved is not simply due to his own ineptitude.

Another member of the parish team, Tony, is an example of a foreclosed identity, although it is not the one that the bishop recommends either. His intimate relationship with the woman Frances must be "cleared out of the way" if he is to get on with the job, and ultimately the bewildered Lionel must also be gotten rid of. Tony mistakes a kind of fundamentalism for his priestly identity and goes about trying to destroy the uncertain Lionel, and his parishioners, in the process of enacting his identity. For Tony ministry is simple. It means controlling and shaping other people through intimidation:

> You know I'm damned if I get this. I'm damned if I know what the hell's going on. . . . It's only a year or two since I was a student. I was a completely different person. . . . I was easy-going. . . . But now . . . I can actually feel my sense of humour departing. It's gone. I mean, can you tell me, is anything *right* with the Church? I mean, is the big joke that having lived and died on the Cross, Jesus would bequeath us— what?—total confusion, a host of good intentions, and an en-

dlessly revolving [duplicating] machine? Is he really entrust-
ing his divine Mission to people like the Reverend Donald
Bacon, universally known as *Streaky*? . . . We are individuals.
We have souls. Christ didn't come to sit on a committee. He
didn't come to do social work. He came to preach repentance.
And to offer everyone the chance of redemption. In their in-
nermost being. (Hare, 21-22)

Throughout the play, Tony's identification with an ideology he mistakes for the Gospel deepens until he is possessed with it, and with
the power that it gives him to have Lionel removed from the parish
so that he can set up his own model of ministry and thus save his
parishioners, whether they wish to be saved or not.

Finally, there is the priest called Harry, in whom the theme of
the relation of public and private in the life and work of the minister
is played out. In response to his friend Ewan he offers a quick theology of his ministry:

I am the vessel. I am only the channel through which God's
love can pass. That makes me, as a person, totally irrelevant.
As a person, nobody should even be conscious I'm there. If I
do something which is in any sense worrying . . . if I upset my
communicants in any way, then the focus is moved. From the
Lord Jesus. On to his minister. And that is not where the
focus belongs. (Hare, 24)

Even when he encounters his blackmailer, a newspaper reporter,
Harry interprets his predicament from a strong basis of personal and
professional identity:

I'm clear eyed. I think I am. There is people as they are. And
there is people as they could be. The priest's job is to try and
yank the two a little closer. It takes a good deal of time.

People have souls. That man from the newspaper. He has. In a
dirty corner of his heart. You have to believe that. I have to re-
member. It's my duty. But it's also my duty to fight.

O God, please help me. I don't know. Teach me, Lord. How do
you fight without hate? (Hare, 71-72)

As the play proceeds, we observe how the attempt by each
character to live out of his priestly identity leads to struggle and
conflict within himself, with God, with his fellow priests, and with
the community. It is a powerful portrayal of how personal identity

may rest on a very brittle foundation, of how it is protected, refused, even lost, such that the person is often shattered, and must begin once again to develop not only his priestly identity but his personal identity as well.

The fact that plays like *Racing Demon* can be written and performed to enthusiastic full houses, the fact that we have the topic of the struggle of redefining priestly identity as part of conferences and seminars throughout North America, and the fact that the popular press, no less than Catholic journals and newspapers, avidly discuss the state of Roman Catholic ministry and education for it should give us pause. The question has clearly become a public one, and the Church's efforts to answer it must be both subtle and honest. Not least of all it must be theologically sound. I now turn to a modest effort at setting the agenda for that theological discussion.

IV

This section brings the chapter to its purpose of providing a sketch of those elements necessary for relating theological education to a theological understanding of ministerial identity in the Roman Catholic tradition. This is not an essay of the sort which starts from scriptural texts, traces the history of a notion, and then attempts contemporary applications. As I have indicated in the introductory chapter, I depend upon the historical and analytical work others have done and which I will not repeat at length here. Nor do I begin with a transcendental anthropology as the foundation for a theology of Christian ministry, since my purpose is not to make an apologetic case for its credibility, but to explore notions that redescribe its functioning and are essential guiding notions for the work of theological education. I will consider ministerial identity as a determination of Christian identity, and that will require consideration of the notions of discipleship, charism, and ordination. It will prepare for the next chapter on the notions of authority and tradition.

It would seem self-evident that any particular ministerial identity is a modification of an already-established Christian identity. One does not proceed to priestly or other ministerial responsibilities and duties in the Church except after the process of attaining adulthood among the faithful, subject therefore to all the factors which give specificity to discipleship within a local Church community. This presumes an entrance into the community which consists of the sacraments of initiation, the gradual incorporation and activation of those sacraments through living the Christian way of life appropriate to the stages of human development, and participation in the life-preserving sacraments of Eucharist, Reconciliation, and Healing. Discovering that this common discipleship may contain within it both a call and the possibility of answer to a further sacrament of special function or status, namely marriage, deaconate, presbyterate, or episcopacy, is a slow and complex process. This is obvious in the manner of selection, education, and sacramental initiation of, for example, the presbyter. The individual submits to a personal and communal scrutiny to discover the presence of both the call to ministry and the aptitude to fulfill its duties. Individuals who may not have benefited from all the resources for growth in faith generally undergo a period of preparatory development before entering into the formal process of ministerial education. And within that world, scrutiny continues as growth continues, until the recommendation of appropriate persons brings the candidate for ministry into the sacramental moment of recognition and confirmation, or into a liturgical but not sacramental acknowledgement by the community, or into an appointment by some official act.

I am quite aware of the very awkwardness of this final phrase of the last sentence. It is my effort to face a challenge inevitable when discussing the notion of ministerial identity at present in the Roman tradition. We have become used to the limitation of ministry, in its technical sense, to the three "orders" of priest and bishop, deacon being revived more recently, and to minor orders which exist but seem ineffectual, with some other orders having being suppressed. The terminology of "extraordinary minister" has been adopted to account for new practices, but it has severe inner logical and theological contradictions. To identify differing modes of acknowledgement of ministry in the tradition is an attempt to note that the service rendered is indeed all ministry and that the present categories which emphasize the sacramental recognition of ministry may in fact be too limiting to the reality of ministry. Thus, for example, the notion of "the grace of office" is a useful one to indicate the Christian confidence in the adherence of the Spirit to human decisions and actions, but it must somehow be broadened (as is the case in religious communities which speak of the grace of office of the superior or head of a community) beyond the limitation of office to sacramentally-established membership in an order. Thus the grace of office, as the grace appropriate to an order or stratum of the Church, is the grace that is the charism which names the ministry of the Church. It is the prior grounding which makes the rule for the ever adapting manifestation in cultures and ages. The challenge for theology is to search for those unconditioned rules which are at work in this new broadening, properly understood as a retrieval, of the diversity of ministry. Because the doctrinal rules form a coherent whole which regulates the life and speech of the community organically, as it were, the apparent shift, change, invention or abandonment of one rule or other will be mirrored by and authorized by similar changes or reassertions in other intrinsically-related rules. Despite the confusion and controversy which this process engenders, the theological educator is in an advantageous position to observe the struggle of individuals as they actualize their sense of vocation by participation in the formation of a new identity, and look to the local church to name, confirm, and support that call and identity.

My quasi-phenomenological beginning requires exploration of two notions: ministerial identity as dependent upon Christian identity on the one hand, and ministerial identity as it is marked by a public commissioning, with a sacramental character. As to the first, I take it that the well-spring of being a Christian is being a disciple, a follower of Christ risen and a participant in the divine life through the indwelling of the Holy Spirit. This takes shape in the three equiprimordial moments of worship, witness, and teaching which are themselves a unity in human action with the gift of grace, the healing and elevation of human nature itself so that it may become the instrument of grace. One could at length search the scriptures for the warrants for this brief encapsulation of Christian identity in the stories of both Old and New Testaments, and follow out the implications into the first centuries that saw the formation of liturgy, common life, Church structure, and the self-descriptions which are the beginning of a theological tradition.

History records the lives of certain prominent individuals within the community whose witness, teaching, and participation in the worship of the community were thought essential to the self-description of the Church and who were recognized to be prime examples of who a disciple is. Lost to our scrutiny is the development in the first years of the existence of Christianity from individual lives and circumstances, through reflection on them, the establishment of customs and habits, to the routines of organization in the community which documents like the *Didache*, the *Apostolic Tradition*, and various sacramentaries give evidence of. It is surely the same passage that we understand the Scriptures themselves to have undergone, from individual stories, through habitual renditions, to written accounts, and thus to the moment of recognition of specific texts as the normative articulation, the Word of God which is the faithful presence of God. Though it cannot be denied that the hidden, unarticulated life of the many is lost in shadows and that those lives should be retrieved, however possible, for a more complete description of the Church, the significance of the visible and recorded structures and roles which developed discipleship into a tradition with social organization and sacramental ministry, both sinful and holy, must be carefully studied.

It might be wise to recall, however, that the Christian preoccupation with recovering the earliest shape and functioning of the community of disciples is not for antiquarian or purist reasons. There is no Christian purpose in a simple repetition of a pristine primordial moment of Christian existence. What we retain as normative from that formative period of the Church is the Scripture text, with its focus on recounting the essential core of belief, namely God's acts in Christ reshaping human life and all creation, and the living complex of the community which hands on to each successive age its structures, roles, attitudes, and all the rest which makes up a human sinful community saved by and at the service of God. The dynamic at work in those early years, so Christians believe, is no different than that at work now. It is the same Spirit, the same charisms and sacraments which mediate the Spirit, the Risen Lord, through which we live, and move, and have our being. Just as the search for the historical Jesus is a sadly mistaken one when made the touchstone for Christian authenticity, so a search for the purest moment of ministry among the first disciples is a misguided and ultimately unhelpful search. A contestation between assertions about the visible and accounted-for ministries and the invisible and neglected ones might well take account of the fact that the situation is and will continue to be the same: discipleship is not essentially a matter of being noticed, accepted, or praised. In fact, discipleship is fundamentally not of our own making or choosing, but is in the being chosen and in willing obedience and service.

I would hasten to add, however, that the considerable efforts of biblical scholars and church historians to retrieve a more nuanced understanding of the social conditions of the early Church is only beginning to have an impact on the reassessment of widespread theological notions about priesthood and all other forms of ministry. As the matrix of relationships is unearthed, the task remains to consider how, in an analogical fashion, the same risen Lord and his Holy Spirit is animating the contemporary Church, despite and perhaps as a challenge to our settled ways of conceiving and enacting ministry. The delicacy of discerning that presence and its charismatic foundations requires spiritual insight as well as scholarly acumen. It should not be surprising that the forms of official ministry in the Church undergo change and revision as does Christian identity itself, not as to its sure foundation but as to its engagement with contemporary culture and the sometimes sinful, sometimes ignorant, though ultimately unfaltering preferences for some embodiments of it rather than others.

One way in which to define more accurately the identity of those called to public and sacramental ministry is to distinguish them from those whose discipleship is marked by its intensity, dedication, unfailing fidelity—in short, its character as exemplary and illuminative of the essentials of worship, witness, or teaching. Saints and Christian heroes, like the rest of us, find their identity through the worship of Christ and the witness and teaching that flow from worship for its partial fulfillment here on earth as we await the coming age of final fulfillment. Perhaps saints and heroes are always easier to recognize by the very dramatic and intense manifestation in their lives of the presence of God's grace. The utter transformation of human frailty through their conformity to the life of Christ in his suffering or miracle-working or efficacious teaching is so striking that believer and unbeliever alike easily recognize and name their holiness. Saints are recognized, sometimes easily because of the distinctiveness of their lives, and sometimes only after their earthly life is over when they become better known by the Church at large. However, they are not chosen by the community to become saints nor are they given saintliness through the "laying on of hands," the sacramental sign of being instruments of God's efficacious presence in human affairs. Rather, they make visibly manifest the gratuitous and often troubling presence of God's special gifts and the rigor of the logic of discipleship. Nonetheless, in a very real sense they do have an institutional role, as do heroes in any culture. They are both comfort and accusation, epitome and exaggeration, animators and substitutes in the context of the desires and abilities of ordinary believers to become special, complete, fulfilled.

Not so with the call to ministry, to service of the community in its inner life and outward mission. Many priests and ministers are ordinary, if not pedestrian, in their discipleship, and like saints as well, they know themselves to be sinners. The nearly twenty-centuries-long procession of official ministers in the Church consists of unknown, even historically insignificant individuals. Their identity in large measure, unless they happened also to be saints or great scholars or political figures, was taken up into their sacramental identity, showing forth to the community and the world the presence, fidelity, and identity of God rather than themselves.

A second contrast which will help locate the particular identity of the official minister in the Church results from a consideration of those activities which establish the identity of the minister beyond the possession of a charismatic gift from God through the community's recognition, confirmation, and sacramental conferral of identity. Throughout the biblical text, and in the Pauline literature in particular, we are reminded that gifts given by the Spirit are not for the aggrandizement of the individual, but have their purpose for and within the community, being met by companion and complementary gifts. Inasmuch as such gifts are at the service of God's saving acts within the community, their exercise can aptly be called ministry. I tend to think that a contemporary challenge in the Roman tradition is the fostering of the gift of recognizing the presence of spiritual charisms which might contribute to aptitude for leadership in ministry, as well as the gift of the good implementation of such discernment. These are the necessary companion gifts to the call to ministry; without them, too many lights will remain under bushel baskets and never make it to the lampstand. This is particularly important for those who have become accustomed to only looking for the charismatic foundations of ministry in certain kinds of individuals.

As to the community's sacramental conferral of identity through ordination, in that act the community is not chiefly concerned with identifying the charismatic *per se* but in bringing to completion a process of discovery and education of those who will be apt to receive a sacramental grace which will accompany them, function in and through them, as the symbol of God's fidelity and the Christian people's response of obedience. The language of "reception of grace" must be paralleled by language which indicates the assumption of a place in the community with duties and rights, and a language which indicates the Christian hope and confidence in God's gracious coincidence with this new identity. As is the case with Christian marriage, so with ordained ministry, those who find themselves called by God and the community to receive these sacraments are fulfilling human personal talents in the individual, as well as specific social needs for roles in the worship, teaching, and witness of the Church, and may also be the recipients of special charismatic gifts. This seems especially to be the case in those called to ordained ministry within a specific religious community, one which endeavors to preserve the contribution to the Church of its founder's particular charism by recognizing and educating that same gift in many different circumstances. The whole community must pray, preach, teach, and conduct themselves in daily affairs according to the Lord's commandments. But God gives special gifts of praying, preaching, teaching and witnessing such that the human need for leadership and wisdom in the community is met with divine graciousness and provision. Just as the community helps young men and women to discover the possibility of Christian marriage, calls God's grace upon them in a sacramental action, and then accompanies them through the tasks of realizing that role, so the community ought to help men and women to recognize the possibility of sacramental ministry, provide the sacramental assurance, and accompany them through the task of exercising such a gift and its responsibilities.

In sum, it might be said that the identity of the minister is founded in and flows from the common identity shared by all Christians, is recognized in and through a charismatic gift which itself enables service in the community, and is commissioned or conferred sacramentally. While currently deaconal, presbyteral, and episcopal ordination are the three forms such sacramental activity takes, there is and should be a broader range of formal recognition and conferral of ministerial identity. The intellectual and social comfort and stability that a settled practice offers may have to undergo the discomfort and unsettled times in which new forms and practices are discovered or retrieved. This is, I think, particularly evident to those who engage in theological education. The typical preoccupation in the present Roman tradition with the identity of the priest has much to do with their number and their closeness to the work of the local church. While intending to make no proposals in the matter, I have consciously constructed this essay so as to be as broad as possible in the consideration of education for ministry, including potentially every sort of ministry I observe at work in the tradition as I know it. No matter what the result of the current search for a new, yet faithful manifestation of the Church's ministry, this essay is in search of a theological, ultimately doctrinal, understanding of the formal preparation for it.

There is a *theological* reason why there must be *education* for ministry precisely as a Christian activity. On the one hand, if service and leadership in the Church were solely a function of charismatic gifts, then it would seem nonsensical to engage in any form of education for ministry. Either the gift is given or it is not, either a natural talent is perfected by grace or it is not. The community's responsibility and task would be to discern the presence of that gift, give thanks for it, and allow it to function to the glory of God and the benefit of the Church. On the other hand, if service and leadership were conceived as simply the inevitable human activities that any group requires if it is to be an organized, efficient, and self-maintaining community, then there would be some form of education, but it need not be strictly theological or ecclesial. Rather, good training in various skills and arts so as to fulfill the needs of the group would make the best sense.

Ordained ministry can be conceived as neither simply one nor the other. It is not reducible to charismatic activity, nor is it merely a human convenience required by the social, public, and historical character of the Church. The process we call theological education is poised between the recognition of a call, a vocation from God, which is in a real sense charismatic, and the conferral of a sacrament which confirms that gift and inaugurates its exercise as the efficacious presence of God's fidelity and power. The sacraments of order, then, say more about God than they do about the individual, by which I mean that the conferral of identity links the human individual with a divine promise, a continuance of the "sacraments" which are Christ's saving acts, themselves pointing to Christ's identity beyond himself in both God transcendent and God immanent in the world. As the moment between call and sacrament, theological education cannot either provide the vocation or confer ordination. It takes those who are provided by God and the Church, and prepares them for the service and leadership of the community.

As such, theological education is not different than any other form of education, namely it is a process of inculturation which cannot do the impossible but must work realistically with the natural capacities the human person presents, whether as an infant educated in the home, or a young adult in university or technical school. In particular, like any form of professional education, theological education fosters and develops the special talents which are the differentiating character of the profession, handing on the tradition, yet also being changed as students become teachers and practitioners, altering its course by their own inventiveness. As specifically Christian and theological, education for ministry is at the service of the vocational, charismatic beginning. And it looks to the moment of ordination usually at the end of the initial educational process, or as is the case increasingly in the Roman tradition, also to the various kinds of public recognition of official ministry which are not sealed with ordination but nonetheless have official status in the Church. Theological education exercises a responsibility to present well-formed candidates to be recipients of the "grace of office."

It is in light of these two factors that the characteristics explored in the first part of this essay can be understood as moments of the identity of the minister. Being professional, practical, and devoted are not simply charisms of the Holy Spirit, but acquired abilities which theological education strives to develop in candidates for ministry. On the other hand, they are not merely human qualities, recognizable in the would-be leader or servant, or made advisable by the latest theories about group dynamics, community organization, or social psychology. They must be rooted in a recognition of the actual charismatic gifts which are potentially part of Christian discipleship, and which are the rich soil in which a vocation to official ministry in the Church can grow. As I have already noted elsewhere, this foundation in specific charisms is particularly evident in religious communities which focus their ministry, ordained and otherwise, in keeping with their often saintly founder's special spiritual gifts.

Education at the service of the formation of ministerial identity can be grounded theologically, not simply because of the kind of knowledge it pursues, but because of the very identity of those its prepares for service in the Church. The next chapter will consider the theological reasons why such education also prepares individuals to exercise ministerial authority in the preservation and forwarding of the Christian tradition.

5. Authority in Ministry and the Great Tradition

IF THE ISSUE OF THE IDENTITY OF MINISTERS WITHIN THE ROMAN Catholic tradition is a matter of concern and confusion for many in every area of Church membership, then the issue of authority receives as much, if not more, attention. My purpose, as in the previous chapter, is not to provide a full systematic theological discussion of authority, but to suggest by the barest of outlines a set of minimal rules of discourse on the subject, for the purpose of locating the theological basis of another important task of theological education. Preparing individuals to exercise authority in the Church as an essential ministerial activity is dependent upon the formation of their identity through the various elements of the professional education they participate in before ordination or appointment to an office or role. Both identity and authority find their place in the broad concept of tradition, and its function as the fabric of Church life. This chapter will conclude with a section specifically on the concept of tradition as a comprehensive notion within which to place theological education itself. This last section will therefore be a transition to the next part of this essay, concerning pedagogy, faculty, and curriculum, which are themselves indispensable vehicles of the living tradition.

I

Two preliminary remarks are needed to establish the context for my discussion of the authority of ministry and the minister. The first concerns the suspicion of authority as a notion still available for the organization of Church life and its theology; the second concerns the specific present-day preoccupation with matters of authority in the Roman tradition. As to the first concern, then, it is important to allude to an essential item in the background to Edward Farley's proposals for revising theological education, namely his claim that the "house of authority," within which Christians have lived and theology has been constructed, has collapsed irretrievably. (Farley, 1982, 3-168) He is not discussing the respect or lack of it for ecclesiastical authorities, though what he has to say about methodological issues could be used to illuminate the crisis of authority in various traditions. Rather, using the metaphor of Christians inhabiting a house, he diagnoses the interdependence of Scripture, dogma, and church as constituting a vicious circle of mutually-supporting authorities, which he suggests has been the basic shape of "classical" Christianity since its beginning. The European Enlightenment and the rise of historical, critical consciousness marks the end of the viability of the living arrangements of Christians within the house they had built. Authority must give way to evidence. Farley carefully distinguishes experience from evidence, the former mediating but not constituting the latter. "Faith experience" is not a field of evidence, then, but neither is the transcendent reference of faith, "God." (Farley, 1982, 177) Rather there are ecclesial, universal, and concrete fields of evidence, studied by historical and biblical theology, philosophical and systematic theology, and practical theology, respectively. This transformation of traditional *loci* of authority and traditional areas of study within theology requires a new genre for theology in keeping with the new paradigm, i.e., theology as ecclesial reflection, being historical, critical, practical thinking. Whether one has to make such large and definitive claims about the total collapse of a single previous paradigm, projecting some forms of Christian life and its theology back 20 centuries, and whether the European Enlightenment deserves the kind of authority it is given, are all questions which a thorough study of this and similar theories would require.

I allude to this theoretical discussion because Farley himself has tried to show that the sea change he has described has quite definite ramifications upon theological education in terms of a restructuring of curriculum, pedagogy, and faculty composition. As with most methodological proposals, the problem always remains as to how radical revisions pass from proposals on the ideal level to implementation in practicalities. Life seems to admit of incremental change of a slow and seemingly indeterminant sort. Even if we grant that Farley is right, that a complete rethinking of theology, of

Church life itself, is required in the post-Enlightenment world, there remains the practical matter of the gradual transformation of present forms of authority into new ones, both in theology and Church life. I would not be so quick as Farley is to locate the perduring confidence in the house of authority as being due to a "superficial glance about the Christian world" or consign evidence of this confidence mainly to "the persistence of Catholic and Protestant folk religion." (Farley, 1982, 166) In some hands, the possibly elitist tones that such judgments might betray, and the dangers of an overly subtle intellectualization of theology and church life it might engender, would not ultimately help the revision of theological education and its efforts to wrest both the study of theology and the restricted use of theology from the hands of a limited elite, namely the clergy. I have a definite doctrinal preference for a stronger sense of the presence of the Holy Spirit in the Church at large. While this is particularly advantageous in allowing for a correction of an idolatrous isolation of authority and for an encouragement of attention to disturbingly new manifestations of God's presence, it also necessitates attention to those conserving elements in Church life which might as easily be dismissed as being old-fashioned, as others are dismissed as being inconveniently novel.

A full evaluation of Farley's analysis and proposal belongs in a book on the history and methods of theology and their relation to the present situation of Christianity. In discussing practicality as a characteristic of the minister, I found his notion of theology as habit a valuable retrieval, but proposed a qualification of it. In considering the issue of authority, the same qualification concerning the object of theological habits and a further qualification about the perdurance of the house of authority as a legitimate notion need to be articulated, if ever so briefly. I am not convinced of the correctness of equating the whole of the past history of Christian theology with the particular characterization Farley offers in his metaphor of the "house of authority," and so I am not as eager to find a substitute for it. On his account, I would therefore be classed with those who, like Rahner and Barth, accept the challenge of post-authority modernity but maintain certain elements of the former house of authority, tradition especially. Farley finds this unacceptable, and requires the construction of an entirely new means for theological construction which transposes the old vehicles of authority and means of argument into a new paradigm which uses the vocabulary and concepts of phenomenology.

To the extent that Catholic thought has gone beyond mere polemic and in some degree adopted the agenda of modern philosophy, science, and culture, it too has experienced the challenges resulting from the divestment of authority consequent to the Enlightenment, and the ensuing collapse of that complex set of attitudes, mores, texts, usages, and modes of communication peculiar to modernity. There is no doubt that the adoption of some of the agenda of liberal Protestant thought, chiefly its style of biblical exegesis, its reliance upon modern subject-oriented philosophy, its apologetic concerns, and to some degree its accommodationist preferences, was essential to the efforts within Roman Catholicism to escape the dominance of forms of Church life and thought (some integralist, some obscurantist) which had hold of theology, liturgy, morality, and Church structure itself in the decades prior to the Second Vatican Council. However, the *ressourcement* which marked the period formative of the Council did not solely depend upon this particular preference in systematic theology, and much of its work entailed a return beyond the modern house of authority to a reappropriation of an older and more profound authoritative tradition. Thus, for example, the work of Karl Rahner could be read principally for its anthropological, foundationalist, and apologetic themes, yet it contains important efforts at a retrieval rooted more deeply than the 18th and 19th century, even if it is not methodologically committed to biblical and liturgical elements.

What counts as "authority" in theology, however, cannot be treated as an issue isolated from the crisis of authority in the structural life of the Roman tradition, nor can the responsibility of theological education for teaching authoritatively and forming individuals in the exercise of authority be treated separately from either theological or structural problems. These three aspects of authority become inextricably confused as issues of scholarship, discipline, and education cross over and are resident, as it were, in the same individual or group. The solutions to the problems or confusions as they are typically proposed are antithetical: on the one hand, freedom, on the other obedience. As an Enlightenment response, freedom of thought, individual autonomy, and inventiveness based upon "experience" are all of a piece when dealing with authority in the three areas. The emphasis on freedom can be named a response, or even a corrective, when one casts the prior state of affairs as obscurantist, repressive, and ideological. There are more problems with the "house of authority" than its being illogical according to Enlightenment norms of rationality. Once the new state of affairs based upon the exercise of freedom gets underway, it is a dialectical response which ultimately combines criticism with freedom of thought, cooperation with individual autonomy, and practical wisdom with experimental ferment. I doubt that I need to specify, for those in the Roman Catholic tradition, examples of each of these. Our tradition at large, particularly in North America, has ample instances, though it is salutary for those who live most of the time in the aeries of theological education to return to pastoral fields to experience other forms of the contestation of rigidity, freedom, and Christian common sense at work.

This displacement of established authority by critical free thinking is, of course, a move from one form of authority to another, but is, more profoundly, only one part of a move from one comprehensive notion of Christianity to another. Understanding it thoroughly requires a historical knowledge of its origin, astuteness in discovering its modes of existence in the Catholic world, and judgments about its various uses and abuses. However, since authority is only one element of a complex whole, it cannot be considered in isolation from the other changes in Christianity's self-conception and the enactment of its convictions. A principle of interpretation which gathers up the full range of changes and accounts for them in an architectonic fashion is essential. Such vastly different proposals as those of Farley and Lindbeck admit of only the simplest of comparisons. However, it is of interest to me that both search for a new paradigm beyond both dogmatic assertiveness and experiential expressiveness in a recovery of Christian belief and practice in its communal, social, and linguistic characteristics. The shift of paradigms which Lindbeck proposes seems to be a more helpful structure within which to consider the problems of authority in the Roman tradition which cut across scholarship, disciplinary order, and education, if they are considered dialectically and are applied to the actual recent history of the tradition.

In Lindbeck's first metaphor for understanding the nature of Christianity and its doctrines, the stability of a predominantly cognitive religion and the propositional embodiment of doctrine requiring intellectual appropriation has its most apt setting in life in a settled, smoothly operating, and hierarchical ecclesiastical structure. That is not to say that it may not try to maintain itself within other social situations, of course. The sort of theological scholarship and ministerial training appropriate to this embodiment of Christian belief are instanced in the North American seminaries of the 20th century prior to Vatican II, in which the oath against modernism, the thorough adoption of scholastic thought, the image of the model priest, the typical discipline of the seminary, and even the requirement to teach in Latin with official text books were all consistent manifestations of the sort of authority which was taken for granted. A description of this sort of seminary can be found in Chapters Ten, Eleven, and Twelve of White's *The Diocesan Seminary in the United States.* (White, 209-292) Those chapters will also give evidence of contrary realizations and efforts such as those of John Hogan, who questioned the hegemony of scholastic thought and teaching in Latin, and John Smith, who suggested that the study of the Bible should have priority in the seminary curriculum.

Similarly, following Lindbeck's second metaphor, the inventive though somewhat individualistic character of religion and doctrine conceived as expressive of an internal, self-authenticating moment functions best, it would seem, in a society structured upon inviolate rights and freedoms, loosely cohesive through agreed-upon conventions which do not impede personal assertiveness. When applied to the seminary situation and set in dialectical opposition to the first model's notion of scholarship and education, one can see the great values and benefits *methodologically* in this model's contrasting openness to a larger world of public scholarship, ecumenism, and the consequent insertion of the seminary into the broader world of professional training in North America. There would be many instances to confirm the value of this "moment" of change in the transformation of the Catholic seminary through its successful implementation of Vatican II reforms, the acquiring of public accreditation, the involvement of its faculty in the broader academic world, and a more pervasive concern for pastoral and apologetic needs. Though the term "authority" may often function in a pejorative sense in this antithetical moment, there is no doubt that "authorities" are appealed to and operative, chiefly under the rubric of "experience."

Finally, in Lindbeck's third metaphor, religion can be construed as a culture and its symbol systems, doctrine as the articulation of the rules of that culture and its traditions, as events which have become normative patterns for successive historical embodiments. It finds a home in a Church structure which is neither authoritarian nor laissez-faire, laissez-aller. It would prefer to avoid a reification of both integralist and accommodationist extremes, pursuing neither a dull and deadly maintenance of the positive elements of Christianity on the one hand, nor a fertile but unstable dependence upon its affinity with natural religiosity on the other hand. I find it helpful to consider this third moment, in an admittedly Hegelian fashion, as able to be a synthesis of some important elements of the two prior moments, not denying or forsaking their particular contributions to a fuller understanding of

Christian life, but offering both a theoretical and practical understanding of them which allows one to pass beyond the impasse of a mere repetition of previous controversy.

As will be come clear in the next chapter on pedagogy, this use of Lindbeck's schema is for the purpose of clarifying the issue of authority by removing it from the simple opposition of established authority's claims versus the lively inventiveness based upon an appeal to experience. Both claims, when seen as part of a larger construal of all the elements and activities of Christianity, can be seen to have a limited validity, and to be, to my mind, part of a more inclusive construal which can both relativize yet preserve them. Roman Catholic theological education for ministry could profit from attention to Lindbeck's three metaphors as a tool for understanding its recent history, the present oppositions it experiences and teaches, and as a prospect for how an institution, its faculty and curriculum might be refashioned. To entertain that possibility would be to combine an inner critique of theological education with the ecclesial and academic critique of authority which is underway. The seminary or school of theology is an institutional lightning rod for all three aspects, the educational, disciplinary, and scholarly.

The present situation for Catholic schools of theology is not really that much different than the situations of their predecessors in the last two hundred years which saw the contrasts of Lindbeck's first two metaphors in various forms. Scrutiny of every aspect of their functioning by various authorities often laid bare conflicting experience and interpretation expressed in a preference for differing rules of discipline. Efforts at scholarship, whether in the form of teaching itself, or research and writing, or preference for schools of thought, often led to conflicts parallel to those surrounding disciplinary matters. And it can hardly be said that concern for the pastoral and cultural appropriateness of theological education, what we might call today its inculturation, was absent in the North American Catholic seminary world in the last two centuries. Such concern was not always greeted with sympathy, or successfully translated into institutional form.

To end this first general comment, then, and pass to the next, I might summarize by saying the obvious: the conceptual clarification and critique of how authority is exercised within theological construction itself, insofar as it results in a different content for and manner of teaching theology, has results of singular importance in the education of ministers who then exercise authority and themselves teach new forms of it within the Church. The direction of change, of course, is also the opposite: if the theologians and methodologists pay attention to the changing face of Church life, they must take into account the appropriateness of what and how they teach, not simply to please the crowd but offer believers what they most deeply want, namely inventiveness that is faithful, traditioning which is part of the tradition. What most believers are concerned about, however, is not the conceptual clarity about authority which theologians can provide, but a living witness of authority which is inventive and faithful. This leads me to a remark about an aspect of ministerial authority somewhat neglected in the literature, but which is a moment of both controversy and continuity alongside changes in the use of authority in theological argument, and its exercise in the mission of the Church to the world.

Various recent authors on the subject of theological education have questioned the paradigm inherited from Schleiermacher and 19th-century developments in the shape of seminary or divinity school. Throughout this essay I have suggested both the value of this questioning and its particular pertinence to the Catholic situation. The retrieval of theological competence as the chief determinant of theological education, an all-embracing habit which is both faithful to the tradition yet critical within it, is salutary advice for Catholics as well as Protestants. It is not inaccurate to note, however, that Catholic preparation for ministry as its principle form of theological education did not digress that far from a focus on habits of theological competence as a goal of such education, even if at times the competence was rather perfunctory, its character as habit intellectualist or confined to the amassing of information, and its theological content retrograde, and its pastoral usefulness minimal. Most importantly, the Catholic notion of theological habit did not lose the teleology or specification of that habit in its object who is the living God, revealed in Christ, faithfully immanent in the Church through the gifts of the Holy Spirit. Nor did most other Christian denominations, of course. Thus the teleology of theological learning could be consistent with the teleology of the educational process itself, that is, the formation of individuals with a vocation who will be granted grace for sacramental and official ministries at the service of God and the Church.

This coincidence should be further explained, because it is a source of the specification of the kind of authority the Christian minister exercises. By contrast to the Catholic situation, let me quote Edward Farley's summation of the nature of the task of ministerial leadership in the Church:

Simply put, that task is the mobilization of the ecclesial community to just those things, to theological understanding at the
service of the believer's ministries. To put it differently, the
church leader, lay or ordained, works to enable the church's
ministries and the theological understanding(s) which they require. (Farley, 1983, 176)

The accomplishment of these two tasks is a very great challenge to
Roman Catholic ministry in the present. Diversification, delegation, and
even the invention of new forms of the traditional ministerial service in
the Roman tradition is not only necessary but desirable. Educating leaders who can bring this about is an urgent necessity. Of equal and con-
tributing importance is the provision of far greater education for the
faithful so that their own autonomous judgment in the context of
service will be an informed and subtle one, not overly reliant upon
external authorities nor susceptible to an adoption of nontheological
principles of action and interpretation because of a lack of theological
learning. Leadership which fosters collaborative and adult witness must
also foster sound and even sophisticated theological teaching among the
faithful. But the Roman tradition has a third vital task for its leadership,
which it shares with all Christian traditions, but which tends to remain
hidden in the recent literature on the revision of theological education.

Essentially to be found in ordained ministry, but present nonetheless in other forms of official ministry according to their capacities, is
the identity and function of the leader in the community when it is at
worship, the moment of Christian life which grounds witness and teaching. As the one who is to preside at, animate, and be the chief human
symbol of the community's liturgical action, the lay or ordained minister exercises an authority in addition to administration and teaching
within the Church. Simultaneously, the one who leads in worship an-
nounces the authority of God, is the chief witness and teacher of God's
fidelity within the act of worship itself. In a tradition with a strong
sense of the sacramental or mediated character of God's revelation, the
role of proclaiming authoritatively through Word and Sacrament the
fidelity of God to the world requires as careful attention within the
educational process as does the companion roles of teacher and enabler
of the faithful. In fact, I would venture to suggest that attention to the
logic of being a leader in worship might be salutary for any tradition as
an addition to the logic of enlivening multiple ministries and ensuring
adequate theological learning among the faithful. I am not suggesting,
obviously, a preoccupation with rubrics and liturgical choreography,

anymore than I would suggest that education for teaching and witness are matters of style or technique alone. Attention to education for leadership in worship would perhaps be a salutary redirection of much of the energy presently absorbed in the arguments about authority in the Roman tradition, not simply to displace valuable discussion about the redress of abuses and the renovation of structures, but to initiate a discussion of a form of leadership foundational to all others.

Only after completing this entire study did I read Jackson Carroll's *As One With Authority*. It engages the complex relationship of authority with identity and tradition in categories somewhat different from those of this first section; however, I find his discussion altogether compatible with my basic convictions. First, his conception of the basis of authority in God's acts and its two-fold manifestation in both representation of the sacred and professional expertise has been related to my remarks on the relation of profession and vocation in Chapter Two. In the present context, I would like to note agreement with his placement of the issue of authority in the context of ecclesiology, and mention that the three-fold functioning of the Church as a community of meaning, belonging, and empowerment is a felicitous naming of the life of the community and the tasks of leadership. As sociological categories they are illuminative of the religious categories of worship, teaching, and enabling which my reflections employ. It would seem that the three dynamics of the Church as a human community contribute to, and are shaped in turn, by the specification of them which specific Christian content and intent provides. A fuller investigation of Carroll's latest work would no doubt prove helpful.

II

A particularly valuable result of considering the liturgical leadership of the minister as foundational to teaching and animation is its own grounding in the same fundamental principle which can be applied to the discovery of the essential character of ministerial identity. Just as priestly identity, for example, is a modification of the same identity shared by all Christians, so priestly authority derives from the same ground of all Christian life, namely, faith itself which admits of only one authority, one Lord. Jesus' sense of his own authority is grounded in obedience to the one who sent him and service to those to whom he was sent. Jesus' life, then, can be understood as grounded in the worship which is his own love of the God we cannot see, with whom he is one, and as issuing in the teaching and enabling of his disciples which constitute his mission as savior.

This worship, teaching, and enabling are not merely exemplary at a distance, but have their fullest manifestation in his very life, death, and rising which remain present to the Church. A full account of Jesus' authority would require attention to the many instances in the Gospels in which disciples, unbelievers, spirits, and nature itself acknowledge his Lordship. In John's account of the washing of the feet, Jesus himself is presented giving the paradigmatic example of what Christian authority is: it is gained and exercised in imitation of Christ, in humble and rather ordinary service through which participation in his salvific death and rising comes about. It is quite evident throughout the New Testament that Christ's authority is a paradoxical reversal in which mastery, superiority, power, and every such characteristic are transformed by service and suffering. Nietzsche was quite right when he criticized Christianity for its preoccupation with what he called a slave mentality, with suffering and submission. From the perspective of the will to power, of the natural life of the instincts, of a transcendentless world, Christian authority makes no sense whatsoever. Christ crucified, the servant who must suffer and so enter into his glory, has always had to be explained, over and over, as Christ himself patiently did for the disciples on the way to Emmaus. Ultimately, only God's acts have the authority to establish Christian authority. I am quite intentionally employing the person of Jesus and the minister's (Christian's) relationship to him as the focus here, in contrast, for example to O'Meara's choice of "the reign of God." (O'Meara, 26-46) I do not think they would be necessarily incompatible, but commitment and service to a person rather than a notion seems more appropriate to the general conception of ministry I am employing.

Though elements of Church order are found in the Gospels, it is the rest of the New Testament which gives explicit testimony of the struggle to establish and enact the personal and structural elements of Christian life as it grew beyond those who initially followed Christ in his earthly life and became the first witnesses of his resurrection. It became necessary not simply to establish habits and social structures poised between culture and faith in Christ, but to present a theological understanding of that development beyond the inauguration of the Kingdom of God by Christ into its shape and form as the Church. The very act of perpetuating the community of disciples through preaching and baptism is itself an act of authority, grasped in faith as the fulfillment of the mission of Jesus now given to the disciples as their own.

Their authority, as shown in Acts for example, is the authority of the name of the risen Jesus, of the power of the Holy Spirit at work through them. The sometimes daring activities of the earliest Church and the incipient efforts at ensuring fidelity are referred back to Jesus, authorized by faith in him. Paul, the authoritative leader about whom and from whom we hear far more than Peter, teaches by edification and clarification, gives an account of his own personal witness as encouragement and example for others, and offers words of worship, of thanksgiving and petition throughout his writings. In the instructions to Timothy and Titus, the Pauline literature does not hesitate to encourage the appropriate use of authority by these two individuals and others in leadership, to ensure fidelity in worship, preaching, teaching, administration, and pastoral responsibilities. This is a mere table of contents, as it were, for a study of what O'Meara calls "primal ministry." (O'Meara, 76-94) It is not ignorant of the complexities involved in relating text to context, the dangers of received interpretations which are ideological or simply ill-informed, and more specifically the controversy over the significance of the Pastoral Epistles in matters of determining the development of ministry in the first decades of the Church.

In sum, it can be said that the exercise of authority which I am presuming to be identical with a vigorous and conscientious Christian life is a matter of authenticity. These persons have authority because they are authentic teachers and witnesses, their actions and words being cooperative yet transparent means for the power of God to work in the world. Theologically, the possibility of this instrumentality can be understood by reference to the enfleshment of the Word and the outpouring of the Spirit as the revelation of the actuality of divine agency in human efforts. The need for such authenticity is the common requirement for any Christian to have effective authority. As I have already discussed above concerning Christian identity as specified through charism or the laying on of hands in a sacramental action, any further exercise of specific kinds of authority is rooted in God's further initiative and the community's recognition of it, through the insightfulness that is likewise a gift from God. Thus service done for the community which flows from various charismatic gifts is judged for its authenticity, and accredited authority inasmuch as it truly manifests the presence of God and is received in the community for its own good. Paul is at pains to clarify just how these gifts are ordered towards unity, peace, and edification by the one Spirit and Lord who grants them. It is vital that they be scrutinized for their grounding in the unity that is the Body of Christ, and their consistency with the truth of sound teaching. The Pastoral Epistles in particular are concerned to limn the role of those whose particular gift "was given you by prophetic utterance when the elders laid their hands upon you." (1 Tim 4:14) That gift is not spoken of at length in terms of authority *per se*, but by reference to a variety of duties to be done for the welfare of the community: preaching, convincing, rebuking, exhorting, teaching, correcting, praying. There are things *not* to be done as well: one is to avoid vain discussions and senseless controversies, personal immorality and impropriety. The laying on of hands both recognizes and confers an identity and a corresponding authority whose focus, it is constantly repeated, is the truth of the message to be proclaimed and lived. It is theologically important that the second letter to Timothy sums up the authority of the minister with the verse: "As for you, always be steady, endure suffering, do the work of an evangelist, fulfill your ministry." (2 Tim 4:5) These letters, like the rest of the New Testament, do not give a formula for Church organization, but rather sketchy portraits of individuals, and an account of their progress into ministry and leadership.

It should be noted as a corollary that if this minimalist account of Christian authority is basically correct, then the Christian notion of authority as equiprimordial with the identity of the Christian is not at all the notion of authority which the Enlightenment repudiates nor the one which it proposes in championing autonomous reason. I take this insight to be the one which Farley presents in his discussion of the hermeneutic paradigms inherited from the Enlightenment, the fragility of knowledge, and the critical retrieval of tradition as essential to the scholarship of the university itself. While I might not follow him in the application of the terminology of "Christian mythos," in his hesitation about "belief in a doctrine," nor in a solution based upon a theory of "elemental modes of interpretation," the general consequences of his analysis are appropriate not only to relocating theological study in the university but are illuminative for the reconceiving of ministerial education as well. (Farley, 1988, chps. 1, 2, 8) Similarly, Hough/Cobb's criticism of the consequences of the Enlightenment, both outside and within the Church, prepares the ground for a retrieval of Christian authority. (Hough/Cobb, 31-43)

A second corollary concerns the kinds of authority I have not been discussing. Inasmuch as theological education itself attempts to prepare individuals to enter into the established order of the Church, within which such individuals will have both identity and authority, it will tend to prepare individuals for what is already operative and recognized. There can be little doubt that in a period of rapid and uncertain changes in the face of urgent needs such as the Roman tradition is presently undergoing, it would be insufficient to educate simply for the *status quo*. That undoubtedly must be done, but done in a fashion which takes into account the following four requirements as well.

First, an emphasis on the deepest and most essential Christian habits which make for authentic identity and authority will ensure a preparedness not only to exercise already operative roles, but to assess and adopt those attitudes and activities which may seem new by comparison to the established ones, but which may actually be compatible with or even more apt manifestations of the deepest requirements of Christian ministry. Second, the importance of developing the ability for critical thinking, for both speculative and practical wisdom, cannot be underestimated. A failure of institutional will to maintain the highest of standards for scholarly and pastoral competence would be to endanger the integrity of our human contribution to the divine economy. It will be the ministers in the field, so to speak, who will change the face of ministry itself, consequent upon or despite official directives and decisions, or the lack thereof. One only need look to the change in Roman Catholic liturgy to see how the best intentioned documents and decisions fare at the hands of competent and incompetent alike. What the liturgy has become is what the everyday celebration of it has become. Third, just as other professions and disciplines see the need for continuing education of their members, so the need for life-long education of ordained and lay ministers cannot be satisfied by haphazard moments of further education, much less by casting the burden upon spiritual renewal alone. Fourth, as Roman Catholic schools of theology diversify in both the composition of their student bodies, faculties, and program content, standard notions of preparation for ministerial identity and authority will undergo significant challenge in the normal life of the school, and they run the risk of being maintained for reasons of security alone, or dispensed with for pragmatic reasons. Neither result is appropriate to the kind of social responsibility that such institutions have. Though it is not my concern here to argue about or justify any particular forms of ministry, I am suggesting that the renewal of theological education in the Roman Catholic Church cannot be either educationally sound or deeply theological unless it is willing to accept its unique responsibility as a vital moment in the traditioning of the tradition, both for good and for ill effect. I will return to this point in the next section on tradition.

Only through proposing an anachronism could one claim to find more than the remotest hints in the New Testament of a kind of theological education for those uses of authority which are hierarchical, sacramental, or charismatic. The early forms of such service, the criteria for judging the presence of a call to such work, and the normative picture of what is expected of those who exercise charismatic gifts and hierarchical offices will continue to be clarified through careful study by disciplines both theological and otherwise. This is so not only for the primitive Church, but for much of the first millennium and beyond. It is striking that there is such a lack of explicit history and reflection on the actual forms of education within Christian traditions, especially Roman Catholicism. However, a caution as was given above needs to be iterated here, namely that searching for original forms of the exercise of authority is not based upon antiquarian or purist curiosity, but upon the belief that the same Spirit is at work now as then in guiding the Church as a whole. Nonetheless, the historical and interpretive work of retrieving the progression of forms, and an interpretation of them in their ecclesiastical and secular cultural contexts, remains illuminative. Having voiced these cautions, however, we can read several remarks in the Pastoral Epistles which point to the basic content of the preparation through which early ministers, bishops and deacons were introduced to their specific service to the community. The limitation of ministry to these kinds of service, with the resulting neglect or eclipse of others, has had significant results for the self-conception and functioning of the Church, and deserves the kind of reconsideration which many are now proposing. My point in considering them is not to insist upon these forms of ministry, but to be curious about what can be learned from the scant evidence of the preparation of individuals to engage in them. These remarks will constitute the point of passage to the final section of this chapter on tradition.

Education can be recognized through the various means of instruction, whether formal or informal, that are presented as normative for the development of the habits thought necessary for a particular way of life. In the New Testament, a special place is clearly given to the study of the scriptures, "the sacred writings which are able to instruct you for salvation through faith in Christ Jesus." (2 Tim 3:15) I need not rehearse here the movement from the study of the Old Testament, to the proclamation of the New Covenant, to the traditions and writings which eventuate in the New Testament. The various short formulaic passages, the hymns, and creed-like constructions within the New Testament together form a bridge toward the later development of actual creeds, doctrinal formulae and the wealth of theological writings which themselves make use of the whole of the Scriptures in a normative fashion. Thus the leaders in the community have a responsibility to adhere to "the pattern of sound words" (2 Tim 1:13) and "good doctrine," (1 Tim 4:6) and to guide the community by these.

Though knowledge of these truths comes obviously by teaching, through companionship with those who have also learned them, it should not be overlooked that the Christian family (cf. 2 Tim 1) was recognized as an important vehicle for acquaintance with and training in the sacred writings and in sound doctrine. It may indeed have been a very fragile and small subculture, but the Christian way of life was recognized as essentially a *tradition*, a careful handing on of "what has been entrusted" (1 Tim 6:20) to the faithful. Personal appropriation of doctrines and mores through a great variety of means is also essential to the schooling in the faith that is the context into which further gifts may be given by God, then recognized by the community and given formal status. The explicit evidence may be slim, distinctly proportionate to the culture of the time and the state of the earliest Church, but elements of what might be called education, as a necessary foundation for ministry of all kinds, especially sacramentally established service, can be discerned.

III

I have already introduced the term *tradition*, and my remarks about it will be at the service, once again, of a brief statement of principles. The institutions, their members, and the activities they engage in, which are the "stuff" of the abstract notion "theological education," constitute one of the most important parts of the Christian tradition. It might even be helpful to consider tradition itself as the process of education, somewhat as Maria Harris has in proposing that the Church should be understood to have a vocation to education as an essential element of its dedication to service. (Harris, 1989, 23-72) As a summation of the previous remarks on identity and authority and as a preparation for the final part of this essay, I wish to explore the unique responsibility for the tradition which falls upon persons and institutions involved in theological education for ministry. This will require some preliminary remarks of a broad nature as background to a single suggestion for further consideration.

The history of the notion of tradition can be traced to its origins in and before the New Testament itself, and has been the object of considerable study in the Roman tradition since the 19th century. The path of investigation in the more comprehensive studies, such as those by Congar, Mackey, and Geiselmann, combines historical, philosophical, and theological analysis. The historical studies move in typical fashion from scriptural evidence through patristic usage, medieval systematization, and reformation controversy, to modern developments, especially in the 19th century and since Vatican II. The theological issues range over the principle relations of Scripture to tradition and of apostolic to ecclesial tradition; among forms of tradition including magisterial authority, and distinctions such as active and objective tradition; and into the grounding of all such relations, forms, and distinctions in a theology of the Holy Spirit and the Church. The theological consensus asserts the utter primacy of Scripture over tradition, as is reflected in all the documents of the Second Vatican Council. It does not go so far as to assert the power of the Word as utterly independent of traditioning and its human structures, particularly the Church, but it also avoids a two-source theory of revelation.

The content and means of formal education within and for the sake of the tradition is not among the topics typically discussed in historical and theological works on tradition. For example, in a section entitled "Religious Tradition as a Universal Human Phenomenon," (Geiselmann, 84-97) Geiselmann proposes six laws for tradition: there is no religious tradition without (1) ritual, (2) myths, (3) fixed formulas, and (4) authority; (5) its forms and structures are incorporated into the tradition of revelation; and (6) continuity and actuality are the two opposing determinations of religious tradition. Much of the discussion in this section of Geiselmann's work is implicitly about education, and it is tempting to add a seventh law to the list of six laws of religious tradition which he proposes, namely the inevitability and importance of procedures and institutions of education in any tradition, particularly a religious one. Much of his discussion refers to elements of formal education, but he does not engage in an explicit consideration of it. Another work on tradition by Congar, however, does contain two sets of remarks which approach more explicit reference to matters of education.

The first concerns the liturgy, a topic I have suggested as an important focus of both ministerial identity and authority. (Congar, 354-375; 427-451). Congar explicitly calls the liturgy an "educative milieu" (428), a "tuition in the life of holiness, a kind of spiritual matrix in which Christians are formed." (358) He considers the liturgy "a privileged custodian and dispenser of Tradition" (354) and one of its chief "monuments" (427) since it celebrates, contains, and transmits the essential elements of the mystery of Christian faith. Such a notion may indeed be typical of Roman Catholicism, in company with Orthodox Christianity, and somewhat foreign to certain strains of Protestant Christianity. However, it is also at odds within the Roman tradition with the tendency to wish for and even prefer a kind of manual of Christian life which would codify and settle issues of every kind, especially in rules and ideas which appeal to the intellect. Liturgy, on the contrary, portrays and conveys the complexity of the Christian life and its mystery through multiple means. Congar continues by interpreting tradition as a means and mode of communication, with liturgy at its heart, explicitly in terms of education. I quote at length a paragraph which captures the tenure of his discussion, emphasizing the comprehensive and personal character of the education he is speaking of:

> Tradition's role is the role played by any milieu in forming deep attitudes and spontaneous reactions to situations according to a certain characteristic spirit, a certain group-ethic governing the actions one has been trained to perform, the goals, the main points of interest and the hopes of the group. All this shapes the "customs" of the group, its overall tendency, and it is with this that one faces up to the world. If revelation has been given to a people as such—under the Gospel, a spiritual people—it is only normal that this people should have a spirit or genius of its own, and itself should constitute a milieu. (Congar, 369)

This and its surrounding paragraphs seem compatible with the cultural-linguistic metaphor of religion and doctrine which Lindbeck proposes. As with criticism of that model, so also here, it is important to add a dialectical relation with propositional and experiential elements which would address the potentially uncritical and anesthetizing character of cultures and their habits. Whatever cautions and qualifications are required, nonetheless I find it illuminating to search for the theological principle at work in a reconsideration of theological education, particularly for ministry, in a theology of tradition and traditioning, itself rooted in the liturgy. Such a move is recommended by the documents of the Second Vatican Council themselves, especially those on revelation, priesthood, and laity, though the themes are hardly lacking from the rest of the documents. The unequivocal insistence on the centrality and foundational character of the study of the Scriptures for the life of the Church and of the formation of its ministers has yet to be fully implemented in the Roman tradition. This insistence is not a counter indication of the importance of tradition. On the contrary, as Congar and others consistently show in their study of it, renewing the theology of tradition is a first and important consequence of the Roman tradition's reappropriation of the dynamics of the Word in every aspect of its life. When placed within this larger context, the special contribution of Roman Catholic reflection on the revision of theological education for ministry might profitably focus upon its longstanding conviction that the identity and authority of its ministers is at the service not only of critical thinking and pastoral enabling, but of sacramental worship. As Congar and many others involved with the liturgical renewal suggest, that worship is the summit and source of Christian life. In a passage which is quite striking for Catholic ears, the document on revelation begins its twenty-first paragraph with the sentence:

> The church has always venerated the divine Scriptures just as she venerates the body of the Lord, since from the table of both the word of God and of the body of Christ she unceasingly receives and offers to the faithful the bread of life, especially in the liturgy. (Abbott, 125)

The second set of remarks by Congar to which I wish to give attention concerns the status of ministry itself in the tradition, and represents in miniature the basic problems of a theology of tradition. In a chapter of dialogue with contemporary Protestant thought, (Congar, 482-491) he considers whether it can properly be said that ministry itself is a gift of grace and the work of the Holy Spirit, such that it is a prolongation of the forms of ministry established by Christ himself. Since the original publication of these pages in 1963, dialogues between several traditions have explicitly addressed the ecumenical issues involved in relating the unique presence of God in the Word of Scripture and the instrumental activity of human persons in ministry. The significance of this problem to my present concerns is the centrality to the Roman tradition's conception of ministry, with the prominence it gives to ordained ministry, of the reality of that ministry as the vehicle of God's presence, not at odds with the Scriptures but dependent upon them. If it were the case that only the Scriptures, as the Word of God, were the infallible vehicle of the work of the Holy Spirit in any age, then the task of the minister would indeed be twofold, as I noted Farley has suggested, namely the very broad tasks of interpreting the Word and enabling the witness it entails. And these tasks can go forward if the minister is educated in the vision and discernment, in good judgment, whether as capacities, activities, or products, as Wood has suggested. To be quite clear: it does not seem to me necessary or desirable to set aside these two important facets of preparation for ministry, and Catholics can appropriate much of what Farley and Wood, among others, have suggested as remedial for theological education. However, the Roman tradition has a particular need to investigate the way in which sacramental worship and the ministries associated with it have become identified with certain hierarchical and ecclesiastical structures, thereby complicating the effort to discover the identity and authority of ministry in that tradition.

My discussion of tradition is at its end. A vital caveat must be added lest these theological remarks, and those on identity and authority, fail to be better than ideological wishful thinking. The actual identity, authority, and traditioning of the Church's ministers are subject to the claims of sinfulness as they are to the claims of redemption in Christ. That is not to say they are merely human, but rather all too human. In a post-critical period, especially as the critical stance has been formalized through social and psychological suspicion, theology and theological education might tend to hand over to other sciences the task of alerting us to our ideologies, and submitting our students to the therapies they prescribe, especially psychological and sociopolitical ones. Most radically, one might suggest that the entire Christian thing, so to speak, has to be first translated and purified from outside itself, based upon a notion that tradition itself, and all the positive elements of Christianity obscure rather than convey the truth. Barring extremes, all this is no doubt to the good, potentially and for qualified purposes. It would be unfortunate, however, if the critical power of the tradition itself, and of theology in its deepest principles, were overlooked as the first and essential means of critique. Guarding and guiding can, of course, be at the service of sin as much as of grace. And, at the heart of traditioning itself, is a subtle and not easily defined sense which, as many Christians believe, is evidence of the presence of the Holy Spirit guiding and guarding. Learning to distinguish the presence of that Spirit is a complex task, and ultimately that is the business of theological preparation for ministry in a very special way. I now turn to some aspects of the embodiment of that task.

Part III

Implementation

6. Pedagogy

THE THREE CHAPTERS OF THIS SECTION DEAL WITH TOPICS THAT ARE inseparable. Pedagogy, curriculum, faculty development, and institutional profile are areas of consideration which provide perspectives on the same complex reality, and to discuss one is to implicate the others. Many tensions and misunderstandings within a school of theology would be avoided if the various constituencies, namely faculty, students, staff, administrators, and governing boards, attended to the impact of their activities in one sector or about one aspect of the educational enterprise on other sectors and aspects. This is not only the obvious managerial concern of deans and presidents charged with the oversight of the enterprise. It is based upon the conviction that like a living entity, or well-tuned instrument, the harmony of parts is essential to the well-being and effectiveness of the whole. As with previous chapters, so also in this section I have endeavored to seek theological reasons for my remarks which will be consistent with the Catholic embodiment of theological education.

The middle section of this essay concluded with remarks about theological education as an essential moment of what is called tradition, properly understood as the complex activity of "traditioning," of handing on, forming, educating. Rather than discussing tradition conceptually in all its many forms, the following chapters offer reflections on three concrete vehicles of the Christian tradition: the persons who constitute the faculties of theological institutions, their activities as teachers, and the curriculum they implement. Other factors in this activity of tradition require similar consideration: governing boards, financial matters, geographic and cultural locales, physical resources, and many other such details.

Two notes of caution and a confession of limitations are necessary before proceeding. As with the two previous sections, I present the remarks of this part knowing that they border on fields of study which have their own scholarly experts, histories of development, and technical literatures. As with Part I, where historical and social analysis will act as an expansion and corrective, and as with Part II where theological reflection will challenge and develop my remarks, so in this section the vast literature of educational theory and practice will support and improve my efforts. The second caution consists of a reminder that in matters of pedagogy, curriculum, and institutional operations, achieving a balanced harmony is an artistic activity. General schemas and rules are helpful, but adaptation to particular circumstances and finesse in application are vital. To dare to discuss education in any form is to engage in reflection on an enterprise which is the whole of a culture in miniature. Little wonder that it is so difficult to do.

The remarks in this chapter on pedagogy are divided into four parts. First, I will consider what it is that makes teaching in a school of theology different by asking: 1) what is the context of our teaching? 2) who is it that is interested in issues of pedagogy in the school of theology? 3) who are the students? and 4) how are individuals prepared for teaching? Second, I will consider four models of teaching and their interrelations, each dependent of necessity on notions of how human learning takes place and what a religion like Christianity is. Thirdly, by uniting the specificities of situation with the choice of model for teaching in a school of theology, I will offer a description of some key factors in the work of preparation for ministry, with the last factor, the teaching of adults, being discussed at greatest length as my fourth set of remarks. In this last section I will present not so much a theory as a cluster of descriptions in which others, I hope, will recognize their own questions about teaching in a school of theology.

I

What may seem to be a merely terminological distinction will begin my first section on "what makes us different." I have been using the term *school of theology* or *theologate* to name the institution we are reflecting about, but it might also be called a *seminary* or a *house of studies*, or even a *divinity school,* and in some cases possibly it is part of a *program* that is carried out in a *department of theology.* Catholic schools may be "freestanding," in distinction to "university related," religious rather than diocesan, not to mention something as simple as small, medium, or large when calculating the size of faculty and student bodies. Whatever one may think of the efforts of guaranteeing uniformity in theological education for ministry through a variety of Vatican and National Conference documents and directives, plurality of situations is the rule of the day: a regional seminary with a dual program in Spanish and English *is not* a religious order's school of theology in a federation with Protestant divinity schools and a public university, which again *is not* a diocesan seminary in a rural setting. My point is a simple one: contexts differ.

There is a lack of uniform contexts within which preparation for ministry takes place. In order to be competent initiators of the uninitiated into competency and wisdom in their vocation, educators had best first take a good look around to find out where they are. They cannot simply be parachuted into a school of theology without adequate knowledge of the context into which they are going. It would be foolhearty to presume that principles of pedagogy can be transferred from one situation to another within theological education, anymore than you can transfer such principles wholesale from one form of teaching to another. The need to reassess the context must occur even from year to year in the same school, where the teacher with finesse spends time directly and by intuition assessing individuals and groups as to their background, talents and potential difficulties, in order to adjust course materials and procedures accordingly.

Second, it is not only teachers that are concerned with such problems. Most obviously, a school of theology also has administrators, notably a dean, who is charged with the educational health and welfare of faculty and students alike. Deanal concern with pedagogy includes maintenance of standards by which to assess potential for teaching when hiring new faculty, orientation of new faculty to the concrete situation, measurement of effectiveness in the classroom, prescription of remedies for problematic situations, and the general enhancement of the teaching environment for both new and long-term faculty. And there are others in the theologate world with equal interests in pedagogy: the field education directors and supervisors who do not function primarily in the classroom, the library staff which oversees a vital resource and locale for teaching and learning, those charged with the vocational formation of students, and spiritual directors who might even consider their own work a kind of teaching or who, at least, want to know just what goes on in the classroom and field placement that so affects the lives of their charges. If contexts differ, then within contexts further contexts differ, and there are different exigencies for different groups when discussing pedagogy.

And then there are the students themselves. Are they only candidates for ordination? Are they members of a mixed school which is part religious, part lay, part diocesan, part men and part women? More important than affiliation, state of life, or gender, what of the diversity of ages in the classroom, and especially the diversity of backgrounds? How many students come with little or no Catholic ethos which, in years past, gave a foundation of habits of life, knowledge of doctrine and principle, even habits of prayer and public worship which set students well on the way to a professional graduate education and made the school's work easier, or so we like to claim, gazing back at the halcyon days of the '50s and '60s. Teachers now, if they wish to be responsible, must contend with an initial assessment of the *status studentis* as much as the *status quaestionis*.

A final remark about differing contexts concerns the background and preparation for membership on the faculty of the teachers and administrators of our schools. Discussion of pedagogy is at best an afterthought, and at worst is avoided entirely, both in the kind of academic preparation the majority undergo to become teachers or administrators. Nonetheless, would I be constructing an entirely fanciful world if I imagined that most members of a faculty have a judgment about whether other members are effective teachers or not, and that most teachers would be a bit uneasy if the dean asked to visit their classroom and observe them at work with the students? Issues of pedagogy arise to consciousness in a faculty when the assessment of teaching effectiveness is part of the regular evaluation of faculty at an institution, governed by principles which are clear and corporately owned.

Other details might be added to the description of contexts and differences as a preparation for a discussion of metaphors for teaching in the theologate. If complex diversity of context, faculty and student profile and background is an accurate description of the situation, then the choice of a metaphor for what the teacher does, and what *good* teaching might be, must be in conversation with the actual situation. Whether it is a discussion of curriculum or faculty development, the situation would be the same. I do not think it is possible to legislate what the pedagogy, curriculum, or faculty development of a given institution should be. Like Aristotle's observation about ethical principles, which "hold for the most part," so also when discussing principles of pedagogy, or the development of curriculum, general rules will authorize various forms of enactment which will bear only a family resemblance from place to place.

A general caution must be first expressed about the need for a metaphor or model at all. Why not simply treat teaching in its own right, not by comparison with anything else? Like any complex set of human activities which admit of a goal or general purpose, some effort at conceptually unifying disparate but related activities generally lead to the use of a notion which is applied analogically to them all. In the case of education, that metaphor is most obviously borrowed from a theory of human nature, of human knowing in particular, or from a theory of society or culture. In the case of education within a given religion, it will also be determined by the self-redescription of the religion's members, their sense of what their belief and practices are about. As will be obvious below, the metaphors are not necessarily exclusive, but can be combined in varying ways, for varying purposes. The primary point of comparison which completes the phrase "teaching is like . . ." is ultimately not offered simply as a description, but also as a prescription intended to encourage the ordering and evaluation of the activities of teaching in terms of a preferred goal.

While metaphors or models have become popular as a means for ordering things, they can be problematic. They don't always easily fit concrete circumstances because they wash over the nuances and details that are crucial to contexts; or people end up arguing about the models rather than about the actual situations; and, models can be put forward nondialectically, that is, not as historical embodiments but as more or less equally viable means of explanation or enactment. I will propose the following models or metaphors for teaching as essentially interrelated, as value-laden, and as best understood in concrete contexts, being inevitably modified when describing any concrete situation. Like the governing metaphor of a poem, the instance of an art is the living embodiment of it.

With these actual and logical limitations, I will begin to link metaphors to contexts. Vital to doing so are the notions of what a religion like Roman Catholic Christianity is and what ministry is within it, two notions inevitably at work within the choice of a controlling metaphor for good teaching. As in previous chapters, I will employ the schema of metaphors Lindbeck has proposed.

II

In the discussion of metaphors or models which follows, as I have already indicated in the introductory chapter, I have used a variety of sources which provide general descriptions of the same or similar configurations of teaching and learning. The conflation of various schemata is my own invention, guided by the concerns of theological education in particular.

In holding together the great variety of activities which comprise teaching and learning in a school of theology, or any graduate professional school, certain metaphors seem obviously inadequate. For example, a strictly *behavioral metaphor* is clearly unable to hold together the sort of activities which are essential to the preparation of persons for ministry. Hypnosis may or may not succeed in helping one to stop smoking, aversive conditioning may aid in dealing with irrational fears or self-destructive behavior, and desensitization can indeed make it easier for individuals to cope with paralysing situations, but hearing confessions, leading the assembly in prayer, and consoling the dying do not result from the routinization of responses. Of course, there is no doubt that learning biblical languages requires a certain amount of rote learning, memorization, simple repetition, and that even other areas of ministerial studies might be aided by acquaintance through routine. Thus, a behavior-focused metaphor does have an essential insight, namely, that human functioning is dependent upon habits, even minimally conscious ones, and teaching that achieves its end is teaching that forms habits. However, the guiding metaphor must be sought elsewhere.

A variation on this metaphor more appropriate to theological education would take training as the focus. The acquisition of skills and technique is indispensable to any profession. However, the surface correctness may lack an intentional, reflective origin. As Aristotle observed about good actions, there is an important human difference between doing the right thing out of habit, and intending and knowing why one does it. Virtues are habits, but they are rooted in intellectual virtues ultimately. In the case of theological education, we must consider the possibility that outward performance of actions might belie inward disbelief, mistrust, or antipathy to the behavior. One might learn to "perform" on cue, but actually do so in a merely routinized way. The school of theology as "boot camp" for ministry has very limited appeal.

Nevertheless, let me reflect on a potential oddity in the school of theology: do some students, and perhaps teachers and administrators as well, perceive the situation or actually function in it *as if* training were of the essence of good education for ministry? Such situations are rare, one would hope, but I take note of the following description by Katerina Schuth:

> At more progressive theologates where traditional students are in the minority and at more conservative theologates where liberal students are in the minority, such students acknowledged that they tend to keep their views to themselves until after ordination. The words of one seminarian speak for more than a few students: "The message is to play the role until you are ordained, and then you can really express what you believe." (Schuth, 119)

Or, the institution might consider its clientele, so to speak, dioceses and their bishops, clergy and laity who await the graduates of that institution. What do they principally want? At the most crass, though realistic, end of the spectrum, the answer is "bodies." They want practitioners of ministry to fill ever-increasing vacancies, though everyone concerned would admit that training cannot achieve the principle objective of education for ministry, namely preparation of a deeply-committed professional who has finesse and intuition at the basis of his or her skills and techniques.

The clientele knows very well that the mere acquisition of basic skills does not make a good minister of religion, of whatever kind, and priests who can "do the basics" can be ruinous of the spiritual life of a parish. Identifying the multiplication of Masses on a Sunday with vital parish life, perceiving the laity as unable to worship if a priest is not present, and similar attitudes, could have a magical or entrepreneurial notion of Christianity beneath them, and could certainly foster a situation in which *training* becomes the focus of education for ministry. My point is a simple one: even if a training metaphor of education is *prima facie* inapt for education for ministry, there are demands and tendencies which presuppose it, if not encourage it, and this cannot be overlooked.

There are important ways in which training and behavior modification can exercise a valuable, even indispensable, influence on the total educational project. Particularly with the development of the "total institution" which the seminary became in the late 19th century, theological education took advantage of the control of individuals and their formation through such obvious means as a timetable of events for the day, restriction of movement, and the structure of the building itself, its locale, and the auxiliary services it provided. For example, the experience of an ordered day, divided between study, class, public and private prayer, with a minimum of time provided for personal needs and recreation reflects a system of values, but also reinforces that system. Similarly, as no women were encountered on a daily basis, other than women religious who functioned in service roles in the seminary, the seminarian was reinforced in certain attitudes and habits of relating to women which also were founded on a set of values and, in turn, fostered those values. Such a "hidden curriculum" is not unlike the "rule" of the monastic way of life or the strictures of military training. Much could be said about the advantages of such ascetical discipline, especially for the sake of a scholarly and prayerful life, and for a life conceived of as in opposition to or at least purposefully different from a prevailing culture. If the Church wants to preserve a monastic ideal for the minister, and strengthen the distance between the minister and the faithful, then behavior modification is essential along the lines of the traditional seminary of the 19th and early 20th centuries. It is not evident that such an attempt is warranted theologically or culturally, and pedagogically it will be exceptionally difficult in institutions with a majority of adult learners and persons not proceeding to ordained ministry. To return to previous chapters for a moment, it must be asked whether training produces the kind of identity and capacity for the exercise of authority appropriate to Christian ministry.

If the teaching of skills and techniques are more apt for Fido and the fetching of sticks than for human education, then adoption of a metaphor more appropriate for human beings should obviously focus on knowledge, the conscious and reflective transfer of information between teacher and students. Human behavior is rational behavior, based upon knowledge, and ministry as an ecclesial vocation and a public profession is dependent upon a body of knowledge. The Church wants intelligent clergy, and good teaching is teaching that ensures the intellectual development of the student, whether it has a modest goal of ensuring basic knowledge of Christian doctrine or an elevated goal of intellectual perspicuity and critical judgment. Gathering and storing information is an essential moment of this intellectual development.

In a variety of forms such goals are accomplished by what is called the *banking metaphor* of education. Store up the knowledge and use it when, where, and how it is necessary. If the former metaphor emphasizes skills with little thought, this one might lose sight of the skills in its emphasis on data and ideas. If the goal of theological education is to possess a body of knowledge, then good teaching is dependent upon the teacher's knowing the information, being able to convey it and to test for the student's comprehension and retention. Greater sophistication will include a testing for the ability to be constructive with the information gained, to apply it appropriately to situations. Of course, intelligent clergy can be inept clergy. Most teachers in schools of theology do indeed teach a good portion of their classes with the intention of conveying information, and send students off to libraries to gain yet more information. However, few of them would simply identify teaching in such a school with the acquisition of knowledge pure and simple.

But what about committees, and diocesan leaders, and the faithful at large, who expect "Father" to be a fountain of knowledge, or, better still these days, a repository of orthodoxy? In some areas, individual members of a congregation seem to know quite well just what Father ought to know, and apply the same criteria to others who take on ministerial roles. And there are situations in which students in classrooms know exactly what the professor ought to say and convey, before they are even introduced to the complexities of a subject.

Contemporary candidates for ministry, already formed by present higher educational institutions, may themselves prefer the simplicity and security of the banking metaphor, being eager to complete what they experience as an already lengthy and perhaps unsatisfactory process of education. They may show no intellectual curiosity or passion beyond getting what is necessary to do a good job and to contend with challenging and unstable pastoral situations. Students' lack of basic knowledge and their personal needs for security may militate against anything but the gathering of information. In some cases they come with such little Catholic ethos that professional education lapses into adult catechesis. Or the evident desire for settled and sure knowledge in a world of change brings out corresponding efforts by professors to satisfy the desire for certitude and clarity. Much of the excitement which surrounds preoccupations with orthodoxy and apodictic claims in Christianity, and Roman Catholicism particularly, is dependent upon a notion of religion as a body of knowledge which must remain intact. Good teaching, good learning, and therefore good pastoring are sometimes understood as passing on, memorizing, repeating just that body of knowledge without much interpretation. Granted that it is useful knowledge, even saving knowledge, but first and foremost it is knowledge.

The next metaphor I want to consider has ancient philosophical roots, but within Christianity can be understood as a reaction against the banking metaphor and the notion of religion associated with it. I will call it the metaphor of self-expression. It takes the rather slippery notion "experience" as its basis. It has an affinity with Platonic and Schleiermachian theories, joining a theory of knowing and learning with a particular notion of Christianity. The preoccupation with experience as the basis of theological education, and the resulting changes it requires in teaching activity carries with it an emphasis on appropriation and personalization of theology which is best understood as a reply, in dialectical fashion, to the banking metaphor and the intellectualist notion of Christianity.

It originates in a corporate experience of alienation. As teachers and students alike became aware of their discontinuity with the Catholic culture which the 1950s in particular embodied, the cumulative alienation from contemporary culture hit home. As Robert Wuthnow observes, the configuration of religious groups was effected by broad culture changes, particularly in education. New religious movements, liberalization of confessional statements, innovative social experimentation, and a high degree of strain were among the characteristics of this period in which new divisions began to emerge in North American religion. (Wuthnow, ch. 7) A keynote of the period was the turn to experience, the large-scale commitment to a rereading of the text, of the narrative of our common life as Catholics, and it had for most of us an unsettling effect, as well it should have.

At worst the result was the "write-your-own-Gospel" exercises, the "unfreeze-your-unconscious-archetypes" advice, the "construct-your-own-doctrine" assignments. Do I caricature? Well, perhaps. Surely Roman Catholic seminaries never went that far. Our legacy of theology as a cognitive enterprise is stronger than the belief in its being a practical or an affective one, a naively-democratic one, let alone a freely-invented one. But there is sufficient evidence that students and teachers alike pursued a variation of this metaphor of teaching and learning in the post-conciliar years. Its best part is the honest search for relevance which marks the reflective moment when educators ask themselves, are we really doing a good job? Are we really preparing these men and women for the Church of the 21st century? Its worst part is the "what-will-the-market-bear" approach to teaching, which indirectly educates students to do the same thing in their ministries. In other terminology this is an excessive apologetic or even accommodationist approach to theology and ministry, and the pedagogy corresponding to it.

The extent to which this metaphor is required by the contemporary Church can be gauged by the way in which some members of a theological faculty exert a subtle and sometimes overt influence on the style and intent of its teaching. The accommodationists in the faculty prize their own ability to do a variety of things which make them popular at times, if not in fact successful as teachers, precisely because of their commitment to accommodating Christian doctrine and practice to "the contemporary understanding of . . . ," or who may be influenced, consciously or unconsciously, by the need to provide "what the market will bear," however that may be justified. What is essential to good teaching in this case is translation, putting the tried and true into a new guise so as to have it understood, adopted, made relevant or practical or simply acceptable. Unlike the training or banking metaphors, the art of teaching according to the metaphor of self-expression does not consist in having the patience to insist on just the right exercises over and over again, nor having the assurance to insist upon the details of the matter, but rather being tolerant and encouraging of inventiveness.

II

So far I have suggested that the first item of the agenda when pedagogy is discussed in the school of theology is the specification of the diversity and particularity of context. A reflective appropriation of these details is indispensable. Second, there should be clarity about the metaphor, the imaginative construct that is chiefly operative when teaching is going forward. Third, it seems wise to tease out the two notions of what it means to learn and what Roman Catholic Christianity is as a religion—notions or heuristic devices which will inevitably underlie the discussion and potentially confuse it, if they are not made clear. The three metaphors I have proposed so far may not be entirely satisfactory for the pedagogy of education for ministry, but they can be illuminative of the way in which one teaches. Consider these metaphors as characterizing both the *vehicle* or *embodiment* of the subject matter of preparation for ministry and the *content* of Christianity. Is teaching a matter of training, conveyance of ideas, or encouragement of self-expression? Is Christianity a matter of skills, or ideas, or experiences?

Whether engaged in consciously or not, teaching involves assessing the situation, having objectives, eliciting trust, constructing the metaphor within which learning can take place, performing various exercises, assessing the results, and beginning again. Having high expectations for one's students is perhaps among the most important assets of a teacher. The content of those expectations, the heuristic which they embody, gathers up in an intuitive way the notions of identity, authority, and tradition of the individual faculty members and the group as a whole. Whatever the historical causes for the origin and continuance of the three metaphors I have limned so far, each has its expectations, and clarity about those expectations is indispensable to success in teaching and for its improvement. A judgment must be made, however, as to the varying degrees in which skills, knowledge, or the expression of "my experience" are part of the goal of a theological preparation for ministry in the Roman Catholic Church at the end of the 20th century. While each of these ends has a role to play in the composite effect, I suggest that a further, integrating goal is paramount, appropriate to the diversity of contexts, respectful of skills, knowledge, and experience, yet capable of confronting the pitfalls these bring with them, and appropriate to the nature of the education which is education for ministry in the Roman tradition.

The metaphor I am proposing is based on the analogy of teaching as parenting, that is, an activity which has the goal, focus, practices, and expectations of forming a person. Good teaching, the art of good teaching, is as complex and troublesome as rearing children, and has much in common with it. Parenting on the small scale is the effort at integrating a child into the family, of teaching it basic skills, providing basic information, encouraging inventiveness, and fostering the mysterious differences among one's offspring. On the large scale, parenting is the effort to introduce one's child to the culture at large, and ultimately to the variety of cultures whose appropriation is the sign of a truly civilized and educated person. In fact, that is precisely how one becomes a person. For better or for worse, in ways both obvious and subtle, the complex reality that is a culture determines what we can and cannot say, the limits within which our inventiveness can challenge and alter the culture itself.

To become adept at one's culture is the task of both indirect and direct education.

Obviously, teaching in a school of theology is *not* parenting in the literal sense. The usefulness of the metaphor is in its preference for an understanding of Christianity as principally a social, cultural reality, and education within it as comparable to the rudiments of education in any human society as it takes place under the aegis of persons who have a relationship of oversight which goes beyond contractual responsibility. The term *mentoring* will be considered briefly in the next chapter on faculty, and in as much as it shares some of the same characteristics as parenting, while avoiding other connotations, it might be a near substitute in what follows. As Parker Palmer has suggested, various aspects of *friendship* might well be used in constructing another metaphor for teaching, and parenting would include a special kind of friendship, ultimately, among its goals. I am aware of the inherent limitations of parenting as a metaphor, and take my own initial caveat seriously: analogies only work for the most part, and correctives from other allied metaphors like mentoring and friendship are welcomed.

Among its advantages, however, is the way in which the metaphor of parenting subordinates the acquisition of skills, knowledge, and accommodating inventiveness to a larger project. If you want to train an athlete, the procedures are straightforward, the results can be easily observed and tested. Being a *good trainer* requires techniques, and the appropriate pedagogy would be the art and practice of such *effective techniques*. Or, if you want to pass on information, the question of pedagogy becomes a secondary matter; you can get the information into the students more quickly, more easily, more accurately with all sorts of devices and techniques, and you can devise tests to make sure it was ingested and properly stored. Your central issue will be whether you are giving them the correct information, and those who oversee you will probably be concerned with the correctness of the information, and they will need some coaxing to spend the money on the frills. Being a good *purveyor of information* will chiefly focus on the *quantity and quality of the information*. Principles of pedagogy might tend to collapse into questions of good scholarship and how to get students to use those same principles.

It would be naïve of me not to append an aside here on the issue of the "information revolution" and the "information overload" that computer technology has and will continue to bring about for our students, and for ourselves. What is already amazing is the rapidity with which the simplest of research tasks can be undertaken, and the speed and accuracy of the transfer of information. This is particularly so in teaching language skills, and in basic matters of research and the production of written materials. If anything, these advances in technology require a concerted effort on the part of schools of theology, particularly because of their chronic underfunding, to be alert and shrewd innovators in this area. The effects of technology, not to mention television, have already begun to alter students' expectations in every level of education, and our teaching will suddenly become not simply outmoded, but actually ineffective. It is striking, however, that the preoccupation with computerization can simply end up reinforcing the training and banking metaphors of learning. Let me reiterate the judgment that these metaphors of what it is to teach and learn are, and will remain, fundamentally inadequate to what theological education for ministry aims to accomplish. Only by limiting that education can such metaphors be the dominant one.

Training and information acquisition were probably never taken as oppositional to the more comprehensive metaphor of parenting, at least not really so in the teaching of theology as preparation for ministry. In a settled post World War II and pre-Vatican II world, the demands of parenting students were simply differently conceived, were more settled, and consequently less visible. The focus could be more easily on information gathering, transfer, and retrieval. A world of textbooks, students accustomed to sitting in classrooms, scholarship which consisted in a constant mining of the tradition, composed a context in which it was easy to assess the adequacy of teaching and learning. The art of good teaching was much more closely related to the art and discipline of good scholarship and to the ease with which loyalty to the tradition could be enacted.

The challenge that a move to the self-expression metaphor of teaching and learning provided was rooted in the challenge of the Catholic Church at large, if not Christianity as a whole, to encounter the demands of the emergence of the new state of human society in the last third of the 20th century. In Roman Catholicism it was also the need to address intellectual and affective challenges which had been avoided in the previous century, and in the United States it was perhaps the delayed, or repeated, encounter with that Americanism which Pope Leo XIII had condemned. Here is not the place to detail just what this shift in cultures, particularly in Western Europe and

North America, is about, or to evaluate the official response to it. It might be wise to note that this entire discussion is about pedagogy in the theologate in North America particularly. My caveats about contextualization would make me hesitate to insist upon a transfer of principles to other parts of the world. However, the universalist tendencies of both the banking metaphor and the self-expressing metaphor have companion tendencies in the metaphor of parenting, if one surreptitiously begins to think in terms of a normative culture, self-contradictory as that may be. Evidence of this would be the insistence upon uniformity of practice and thought, rather than unity of diverse embodiments.

At least three activities specifying the parenting metaphor should be noted. First, there is the ability to be in conversation with the tradition of which one is a part. This activity takes shape through the education that brings about the good teacher. We have to be taught ourselves how to have the conversation with tradition, and to develop the tools for acquisition, criticism and inventiveness. Certain characteristics of a teacher undoubtedly come from generally developed talents: to be quick-minded, attractive, humorous, energetic always helps a great deal. Other teaching habits are acquired through specialized education. Just as parents tend to perpetuate spontaneously the shape of childrearing that they experienced by repetition or opposition, so teachers carry forward attitudes and contents which were the stuff of their own initiation into their discipline, field, or area of study. Teachers in higher education are all quite aware that pedagogy is not something that they are taught directly in our formal education, but that it is something that is the hidden curriculum of multiple years in school. It might be interesting to imagine, at a meeting of one's faculty, just who the principle individuals are who stand behind each member present as their educational ancestors, not only as to scholarly preferences but as to style of teaching as well. The conversation with the tradition depends upon a lineage of persons as much as of texts.

Second, there is the ability to be enthusiastic for that inheritance which constitutes the tradition. Not a naive enthusiasm, of course, but a critical one. Teachers who are angry with, uncomfortable with, deeply at odds with the tradition cannot teach it; they can parody it, find fault with it, but not in any real sense teach it. Conversely, the uncritical teaching of the tradition is equally poor teaching. It results from a deep and deadly misunderstanding of what the tradition is. Both stances require the insight that individuals do not carry or protect the tradition, but that it carries them as both teachers and students. Teaching requires the establishment of an atmosphere of initial trust—trust of the teacher by the student, of the student by the teacher, and, for both, a basic trust in the worthwhileness of the tradition itself, of the process of handing on, of the family, the culture into which the student is being initiated.

Finally, a critical enthusiasm for the tradition requires the ability to interpret it, to bring the past forward to engage the present while projecting the future. This is going beyond training in skills and acquisition of knowledge, to the inventiveness which does not reduce either skills or knowledge to expression of the present state of my mind or feelings, but precisely engages that present state with the skills and knowledge to project me into my own, and our corporate, future.

So far I have emphasized the positive aspects of the parenting metaphor. We are all aware, however, that parenting is partially, if not inevitably, dysfunctional. None of us have had perfect parents, and we are becoming increasingly aware that not a few of us had quite problematic parents. This realization is not unhelpful to my suggestion. Teaching construed as parenting admits of dysfunction and the formation of dysfunctional priests and ministers. It would be intriguing to form parallels between natural parenting and academic parenting in order to clarify the latter's pitfalls. Three comments will highlight some specific areas of concern for further consideration, dependent on differing situations.

First, concerning the matter of regression discussed in the chapter on identity, the overall effect of the program of studies must be to carry the students through all the stages of development necessary to the shaping of their new identity. Patience with the phases that students pass through, as well as insightfulness as to what might be preventing learning, is most helpful, especially in situations where the hothouse effect of a self-contained institution can intensify and exaggerate moments of change, or where the majority of students are second-career adults. Transference of a sort can occur in these situations, as a teacher reacts to a student's struggle with identity formation in terms of his or her own incomplete negotiation of a particular stage of development. Second, for Roman Catholics the education of women for positions of ministerial responsibility is fraught with dysfunctions, if for no other reason than because of our lack of familiarity with it. This particular dysfunction often simply goes unnoticed because of the lack of consciousness in the Roman tradition about the issues involved. It should be noted, however, that in many places it is precisely, and appropriately, in the context of theological education that conscientization and the development of new habits are taking place in the Roman tradition. This matter deserves an essay of its own, with an anecdotal basis and a systematic analysis. Third, I will simply note that the thematics of ecumenism, other religions, atheism, and general cultural analysis might go unattended because of congenital blind spots in a particular faculty. It is obvious that determining how a faculty is dysfunctional will depend upon certain corporate decisions about what is proper and needed for adequate theological education and by assessing just how the graduates of a particular institution exhibit systemic dysfunctions in their ministry.

III

The parenting metaphor requires some adjustments and specification if it is to be useful as a guide to thinking about pedagogy in the theological school. I will now turn to some brief remarks about four such factors, with a reminder that specific details are very much dependent upon the actual situation and resources of a given school. These factors are: first, the corporate character of effective teaching; second, the dependence of teaching on cultures at large and the cultures of the present-day Church; third, the demands of the particular subject matter, theology; and fourth, the fact that ministerial education involves teaching adults.

First, the use and enhancement of the corporate character of teaching is indispensable in theological parenting. It is one of the greatest assets of Christian schools of ministry. Studying and teaching theology in a professional school have as their foundation a focus and intensity of purpose which, for good or ill effect, pervades the life of the school. As the expression of vocational commitment, it is partly vehicle, partly content, partly assumption and motivation. Though it may not be articulated often, a sense of the corporate character of such work is akin to the family loyalty which parents both presume and foster.

However, at the graduate professional level, this aspect of theologate life does not necessarily shape our actual teaching. By the phrase "corporate character" I mean to imply that it is not sufficient to be aware of and in charge of what goes on in my course or my classroom without being aware of and in some sense responsible to and for what goes on in the rest of the program and its curriculum. Good teaching will increasingly require overcoming the artificial boundaries of departments and classrooms, of courses and units of study, which have been inherited from graduate education in general. This retrieval is essential to the maintenance of the teaching of theology as the teaching of a discipline.

The practical manifestations of the corporate character could take on a variety of forms: teaching as a team, crafting the common agenda together with others, sometimes even with one other professor in the actual teaching of a course, being able to refer not only to one's own teaching efforts but also to those of others on the faculty, corporately owning the curriculum of a given program. Overcoming the individualization of teaching, the fragmentation of curriculum, and the isolation of faculty members is an important item on the agenda of renewing the art of good teaching. Much has been written recently about the need to integrate field education with the work of classroom and library. Is it not first and foremost an integration of the teachers and their teaching that is needed? The corporate and disciplinary character of ministry itself needs to be lived out by the faculty preparing men and women for ministry.

To sum up: training an athlete is best done by one person with one strict regimen; communication of information can be done, and will increasingly be done, without direct personal effort of a teacher; and the eliciting of inner spiritual moments or tales of external interactions is best done by a silent partner. The learning and teaching of a discipline or profession thrives on the manifestation and experience of its corporate character. The intention of the Council of Trent in legislating the establishment of seminaries as closely associated with bishop, cathedral, and diocese is a manifestation in larger social structures of this insight as applied to education for the local Church.

Second, in making the parenting metaphor pertinent to education for ministry, it is important to take note that preparation for ministry requires a dialogue between faith and culture in which the inevitable dependence on both secular and ecclesiastical culture requires a balance between acceptance and critique. This factor is a recognition of the character of teaching as a social practice, as part of a social tradition. Our teaching is as much an encounter with culture at large as it is with individual students. This may well require a certain amount of propaedeutic work, of deconstruction and deformation, before the formative teaching can occur.

Graduate theological education presumes a relatively elevated level of reflection on culture, though in some cases we can no longer presume that our students have a capacity for clear and reasoned argument, are acquainted with the cultural history of Western civilization, have some facility with more than one language, or are well versed in the history of Western philosophy, to name but a few hoped-for prerequisites. Nor can it be presumed that a significant degree of personal and spiritual growth and sophistication constitutes the ground for the development of the spirituality and form of life appropriate to a professional minister in the Church. More radically, we might ask whether this wish list is realistic, whether it could be used concretely in admissions procedures, and what it indicates about investments in a normative account of culture and Christianity. One cannot teach well unless the parenting is proportionate to the kind of student encountered, and unless one is aware of the presuppositions about the students and their *sitz-im-leben*. One might end up teaching students who aren't really there.

It is important to assess how much of the teaching in a given situation should be devoted to the deformation of students, the discovery of presuppositions and modes of thought, prejudices and acquired habits which actually prevent learning. I am not talking about personal bad habits, or particular intellectual lacunae, or the lack of skills. Unlike the principal analogue for my model of parenting, our work comes after the most structurally significant personal and religious formation has been completed. Students may be nodding in assent to what is said in the classroom, or may go through the paces in a supervised pastoral placement, but does either effort bring about a change and growth in habits of thought and action? This is not to suggest that students are ill-willed or teachers are inept. Rather, I am suggesting that teaching as parenting cannot simply be "business as usual." Year by year there must be a constant assessment of what is actually heard by students when they are taught, of whether the "exercises" they are given are actually apt to their situation.

To be practical, I pose the following questions to myself and my colleagues who teach in a school of theology: do we teach in such a manner as to aid students in discovering the principles of both secular and religious culture with which they already operate, so that they can be critical of them and be made receptive to the correction or development of those habits, and do we support and encourage them in what may be a somewhat unsettling enterprise?

The ultimate aim of such teaching is to enable our students to become their own teachers. I would like to call this factor influencing our pedagogy the pastoral dimension of our teaching: like the good pastor, we strive to have a comprehensive concern for our students, aware that any single intervention must be within a nuanced sense of the whole person. An important pastoral attitude is taught to future ministers through the very manner of the teaching they experience which prepares them to be lifelong learners, to be, as it were, their own parents.

Third, the demands of the particular subject matter, theology, the *fides quaerens intellectum* of the Church, of the Roman tradition itself and particularly its ecumenical character, are essential factors in adapting the parenting metaphor to ministerial education. Forming persons to be intuitive and intelligent ministers in the Church requires a subtle blend of teaching the faith itself, without lapsing into preaching and catechesis, with teaching critical and innovative thinking without abandoning the normativity of revelation, its graciousness and foundation in mystery. Good teaching of Christian theology must convey its rootedness in the gift of faith and its need for critical thought, presented as much in the *way* it is taught as by *what* is taught. A double passion motivates and shapes our teaching: a love of the God whom we know, and a love for the knowing of that God. In keeping with the parenting metaphor, it would not be out of place to add a third passion necessary for those teaching within a school of theology: a deep love and respect for the people of God themselves, and for those bearing the grace of God who have come from and will return to the community to live out their vocation to ministry.

I have singled out the ecumenical character of the intellectual searching of faith in the present day, because I am convinced that it is of singular importance as a specification of pedagogy in the theologate. There is an urgency in the preparation of ecumenically-minded ministers who have not simply gathered information about other traditions nor acquired skills for dealing with members of other traditions, but have developed habits of thought and worship which are rudimentarily ecumenical. As I have indicated from the beginning, the specificity of this factor of my metaphor of parenting will depend very much on the particularities of the context. It requires teaching in such a way that students can appreciate what it means to "be at home" in other Christian traditions.

Fourth, and finally, to appropriate the consequences of the fact that schools of theology are teaching adults is essential to an appropriate use of the parenting metaphor. Because this is a generally neglected matter, I will devote the final set of remarks of this chapter to exploring it.

IV

The facts and statistics about the age and stage of life development of those who pursue education for ministry show that it is adult learners who increasingly constitute the student body at theological institutions. This is not new to the extent that students, in the past, came to theological education as adults, but did so generally in a steady flow of educational experience from elementary, secondary, and post-secondary to seminary education. The degree to which post-secondary education is not part of the controlled situation of preparation for ministry, and further, the degree to which other life experience intervenes before preparation for ministry takes place, is the degree to which we are dealing with properly so-called adult learners. This is not, per se, a disadvantage, but it does present a challenge. Whether they are psychologically adults or not is, of course, another question. The troubles of enforced delayed adolescence among seminarians, particularly those of religious orders, is a real problem which I do not wish to avoid, but can only mention here as yet another factor to take into consideration.

I want to sketch out three areas of investigation, beginning with the question: are theological students treated as adult learners? Though dealing with an adult is clearly different than dealing with a child or adolescent for the most part, removing obstacles to learning and enhancing the situation for learning is not so much different as more crucial. This might stand as a very general principle at the head of the list, encompassing all the rest. Adult theology students need a variety of positive things to ensure learning, primarily the creation of a community of learning and teaching which is set apart from their usual social situations. It consists of a physical locale, a psychological space, and a spiritual ambience. These are indispensable aids to learning and teaching, and we should not underestimate their hidden effects, both good and bad. Essential to good teaching is atmosphere, the intangible something *in which* I teach, and all the members of an institution must take some responsibility for establishing and maintaining that atmosphere.

Adults already have a developed self-concept which will enhance or hinder their learning, especially if teachers project and react to a contradictory notion of the individual they themselves have invented. The manner of teaching, the attitudes which carry the message, and the particular aspects of the subject matter which are chosen to be emphasized will subtly relate to the construction of an image and a set of feelings about one's students, to what Lewis Brandt calls a *personification*. (Brandt, chapter 8). Quite often we are required to reassure students of their basic worth as persons when they begin to experience difficulties in digesting the subject matter. Or, when we give off signals of hostility towards or disregard for the person of the learner, we might endanger the entire process. This should not be thought of as pampering adults, any more than adjusting one's teaching to frightened, confused, cranky, or especially energetic children is thought of as a compromise of the teacher's task.

Similar remarks could be made about more specific elements of the adult learner's self-concept. First, there is the importance of past experience as a resource for the adult learner, though it ought not to be confused with the principle of experience as a source of theological construction. The content of the experience is not the norm for theological instruction, but neglect of its formative influence in the past and its emotional power in the present, for ill or for good, would have the teacher run the risk of neglecting a formidable ally or foe. Second, adult learning will be aided or hindered significantly by the motives and emotions involved in the initial intent to undertake theological education. When obstacles are experienced in teaching, what is encountered may not be intellectual inabilities, but personal difficulties relating to appropriation of a vocation's demands, opposition to imposed values, anxiety about loss of the already-established sense of self, distress at appearing incompetent in the public forum, a desire, desperate or otherwise, for some sense of success in the new status of student. The establishment of an environment which tolerates experimentation, exploration, moments of a tentative unstructuring of the self for the sake of change may be quite a challenge for a school in which adherence to expectations both academic and ecclesiastical have a high priority. How teaching effectiveness is evaluated should take into account these and other specific characteristics which make the adult learner different from the child or adolescent.

A second question is: are teaching methods adjusted to adult learners? Of central importance is the factor of time. On the one hand, integration of new information and skills will require varying amounts of time for different students, and the transformation of already-established habits takes considerably more time and energy than other types of learning. On the other hand, adults don't like to have their time wasted. A hidden pragmatism may underlie some of their appeals to the criteria of relevance in their studies and some of their lack of tolerance for new ideas, diversity of opinion, and uncertainty of various kinds. Though it is important to aid students in evaluating themselves and to foster an openmindedness to new possibilities, it is also inevitable that students will undergo evaluation by academic or ecclesiastical authorities and must be helped to contend with such evaluation as adults. Theological institutions might learn something from the inventiveness in the business world which is constantly evaluating and developing its employees.

A third question concerns how members of a faculty project themselves as teachers of adults. Teachers with negative self-concepts or low self-esteem will be less effective with adults, in part because they may be threatened by their interaction with students who are their peers, at least in some aspects of life. The adult learner can attend both consciously and subconsciously to much more than just what is being directly said and implied. Enthusiasm or boredom, respect or scorn, inquisitiveness or rigidity in regard to the discipline of theology can be conveyed by the person of the teacher as much as by what is taught. Respect for learning and teaching as the conveyance of emotion and commitment is vital to the effectiveness of teaching theology to adults. What is helpful in understanding this factor is some familiarity with theories of the developmental process of learning and the variety of cognitive and learning styles. Ultimately it is a matter of allowing the adult learner to participate as a partner in the determination of how the educational process will take place. In teaching adults, it is important to achieve a balance between collaboration and authoritative direction.

V

These remarks on pedagogy in the theologate have presupposed that the issues of pedagogy, curriculum and faculty development are inextricable from one another and are context-bound. Good teaching in the theologate requires a retrieval and revision of the notion of a comprehensive preparation for ministry as the exercise of a discipline. I have subordinated various models of teaching and learning to parenting as a metaphor for good teaching, which itself relies heavily on a commitment to collaboration as the vehicle and the subject matter of professional preparation for ministry. A realistic appraisal of good teaching depends upon the insight that what is attempted in the school of theology is just the initiation into a lifelong activity of learning and adaptation for the priest and lay minister.

Parker J. Palmer, in his provocative work on the spirituality of education, uses the metaphor of friendship for illuminating the task of teaching:

> The teacher, who knows the subject well, must introduce it to students in the way one would introduce a friend. The students must know why the teacher values the subject, how the subject has transformed the teacher's life. By the same token, the teacher must value the students as potential friends, be vulnerable to the ways students may transform the teacher's relationship with the subject as well as be transformed. (Palmer, 104)

7. Faculty

TO INCLUDE CHAPTERS ON MATTERS OF FACULTY, CURRICULUM and institutional welfare in an essay such as this is not so much foolhardy as it is an exercise in the unnecessary or even the impossible. Acquaintance with a variety of situations does yield knowledge of some essential similarities, but the nearly infinite regress into empirical details, complex personalities, and the momentum of the specific history of an institution belie the apparent simplicity and wishful thinking which theoretical accounts provide. Therefore, prudence might suggest letting the reader conclude to the obvious from Parts One and Two, thus leaving the exercise a speculative one. Certainly anyone with even a limited experience of working within a theological institution, and especially those who have tried their hand at administration, know the considerable difference between proposals for the development of faculty, curriculum, or institutional structures and the realities of individual situations with their human dynamics. Proposals for the renewal of theological education are dependent upon implementation through the daily incremental steps taken by individuals in concrete situations. My own, albeit limited, experience within the Roman tradition has taught me that beyond the most general rules and suggestions, the outsider must become an insider before being able to say, let alone do, anything helpful. That process requires much observation and attention to the stories which give an account of the complex fabric of an institution, its members, and program. I have found great benefit from doing precisely such observing and listening when I have been part of meetings of various kinds which provide the opportunity to encounter the many facets of other theological institutions. Such encounters provide for a salutary relativization of the problems of one's own institution, as well as insights into alternate solutions. It is not always as easy to observe and listen in one's own institution, whether because of pre-formed judgments, the legacy of emotions which tie the present situation to the past, or the routinization of response and disclosure which impedes communication. Wisdom lies somewhere between the principle of the empty head (knowing nothing about the situation provides objectivity) and the principle of the plunge (knowing only through immersion and first-hand experience).

By considering the matter of pedagogy first, I have consciously placed teaching as the first moment of the implementation of the theological principles of Part II, which themselves were considered as foundational to the achievement of the qualities in Part I. Passing on the tradition, engaging in the formation of identity and its corresponding authority, is the chief purpose of institutions providing theological education for ministry. The actual shape of the institution itself, the profile of its members, the requirements of its programs, and its other activities are at the service of this prior purpose and activity, though obviously they are all mutually-conditioning elements of a complex whole. Even within a given Christian tradition such as the Roman one, there are thematic differences from situation to situation. Beyond a common general plan, there are important variations among the Catholic institutions which prepare individuals for ministry, as Schuth's study amply shows and as is foreseen and even encouraged by the *Program of Priestly Formation* itself. Nonetheless one can, as it were, feel at home in a variety of Catholic institutions because there is a convergence of similarities, of typical individuals, problems, and basic understandings. When attempting to learn from observing Protestant situations, then, one must be patient with the different ethos and its somewhat differing principles. It would be too limited a criticism to discuss the curriculum that Hough and Cobb have offered, for example, on the grounds that it does not take the Roman tradition into account. It is obvious at first glance that it is not in the spirit of Catholic theological education, of its *ratio studiorum,* its theological rationale or its ecclesial ethos. This in part reflects the present state of ecumenical exchange on the level of academic and professional theology, but it also points to divergences in pedagogy, faculty membership, curriculum, and institutional character which cannot be isolated from the larger ecclesial differences.

It is therefore with caution and a sense of realism that I present this chapter of reflections upon matters pertaining to faculty and the next on curriculum. My discussion of teaching was admittedly a proposal as well as an analysis of possibilities. This chapter's discussion will not rehearse the details of historical, statistical, or personal observations and analysis of North American theological schools. Throughout this work I have referred to the currently available materials which provide such information. Instead, my remarks on faculty and curriculum will consist of drawing conclusions from the remarks on pedagogy, isolating a few typical challenges, and offering no solutions whatsoever. As in the first part of this book, so also here I will try to profit from the chiefly Protestant literature already discussing these issues, making analogous remarks appropriate for the Catholic situation. Though the three elements form an organic whole, such that to discuss one is inevitably to broach the others, having discussed pedagogy, I shall proceed from faculty to curriculum, based upon the conviction that the soul of the enterprise resides in its members, whose functionally objective focus is the material embodiments of the tradition, and at whose service are the institutional structures and functions.

I

Faculty and students, actual individuals, are the living reality of what has been discussed so far. They are themselves the vital ingredients of the tradition itself. Whether as teacher, student, researcher, advisor, administrator, or in any of the other various roles in the school of theology, each individual who takes on this work of traditioning is "the servant of the Word of God" who works "in the horizon of faith in the Word of Our Lord and Savior" with "an outlook of loyalty to the Church and her Magisterium." (*Norms*, 89) The students and candidates for ministry "should feel co-responsible for their own theological formation," (*Norms*, 89) their ultimate goal being to enact in their own ministry the habits learned from those exercising the ministry of formation and teaching. The document from which these phrases are taken, "The Theological Formation of Future Priests," authored by the Sacred Congregation for Catholic Education in 1976, continues in paragraph 131 to characterize the sort of activity the interchange between teachers and students is:

> In fact it is a case not merely of imparting knowledge but of giving a tradition in faith. In this matter of Christian tradition, contact with the master is indispensable, since he is also bearing witness to the faith which has illuminated and transformed his life.

> His teaching thus becomes the discourse of a believing and pray-
> ing theologian in whom there coincide an understanding of the
> mystery and intimate joining of it to his life. Theology cannot be
> taught and studied as if it were a secular subject before which one
> can remain neutral. (*Norms*, 90-91)

But teachers are not simply preachers, nor students simply the Church's congregation. And teachers are not the uncritical purveyors of an established, ahistorical interpretation of the Word of God, nor students mechanical imitators. The implications of these qualifications I have already discussed in my remarks on pedagogy, and in the initial discussion of the scholarly and intellectual integrity of theological education as a whole.

It should be noted for purposes other than polemic that the reference to the "master" as "he" reflects the assumed limitation of theological teaching to clerics, and therefore to male faculty members. Factually this is no longer the case. Not all faculty which share in the ministerial formation of students are male clerics nor are all Catholics either, obviously so in ecumenical consortia. This presents both challenge and benefit, as those charged with the oversight of a program attempt to ensure that the Roman tradition is indeed passed on but that three elements of breadth are also included. First, the experience of teachers from other traditions not only guarantees a first-hand appropriation of those traditions' embodiment of Christian life, but the witness and wisdom of a "believing and praying theologian" from another tradition can be a rich, illuminating part of any theological education. Second, a diversity of persons, male and female, religious, lay, and clerical who teach and direct students provides tangible insight into the diversity of Christian vocations and the compatibility of both theological reflection and ministerial commitment with the variety of forms of discipleship. Third, a diversity of styles of theological teaching and research, though difficult to distinguish, are an added richness of diversified faculties.

The actual implementation of the principles just cited will be in accordance with guidelines and procedures for recruitment, appointment, and evaluation particular to each school. In the Roman tradition, especially since the Second Vatican Council, there is no lack of such guidelines, which, at their best, are advocates of balance between scholarship and practicality, tradition and innovation, plurality and unity, intellectual and spiritual demands, and similar dialectical pairs. Administrators, admissions officers, and search committee members can tell their stories about trying to abide by the guidelines, as made particular in a school's policies, and observers offer reflections and criticism on the present state of affairs. The recent literature on theological education does not take the membership of such institutions as a major focus of its study. Curriculum, the nature of theology, and the relation of the study of theology to the university are the more regular topics, and the reader is left to imagine what this might mean about changes in the kind of faculty member which ought to be fostered. Perhaps this mode of indirection is evidence of the same hesitation I prefaced this chapter with, and a respect for the integrity of differing traditions and their institutions. The search for criteria of appropriateness must be matched by truly prudent and pragmatic decisions in the actual situation. Because situations differ so much as to mission statement and resources, implementation is highly particularized.

While it is intriguing to wonder how one would go about constructing the profile of the exemplary faculty, the inevitably idealistic result does not recommend itself. Constructing new theological methods (or curricula) does seem to recommend itself, since ideas about ideas tend to mask their abstractness with heuristic appeal. It would seem positively impolite in print to advocate certain doctoral programs as productive of good new teachers, or to describe the actual person and work of an exemplary teacher whom others might then emulate. Proposing new procedures or program outlines offers indirect norms for faculty: if this sort of theology is to be done, this sort of program to be offered, then you need teachers appropriately prepared. One is left to draw the conclusions for ourselves. The "objective" appeal of methodology leaves the "subjective" business of building a faculty to administrators and committees. As in the case of pedagogy and curriculum, academics tend to be more willing and much better at discussing ideas and methodologies than forging the profile of a prospective faculty member, exposing their classroom and office activities for evaluation, or negotiating about courses and their sequencing. I think it would be an intriguing exercise to ask the members of a faculty to do just that, to portray verbally the kind of person who should be the next addition to their membership. This is especially important when new members and their education are often predetermined by factors and persons beyond the seminary faculty itself. Forging a conscious and corporate awareness of the profile of a competent faculty member would be an exercise bridging the abstractness of methodology and the empirical residue of particular situations. In other words, it would be an exercise in prudential wisdom. The following general remarks about theological faculties (as were those on pedagogy) might be thought of as an invitation to engage in a conversation on the matter within one's own faculty. As I forewarned, they offer no solutions to problems.

I

Four general areas concerning the establishment of a profile for a theological faculty can be set in conversation with the preceding chapter's remarks on pedagogy. The first two issues shape a faculty's identity because of its students: reflective appropriation of what notion a faculty has as an overarching designation of their relationship with students (mentoring, parenting, modeling among other possibilities); and the harmony produced out of the plurality and diversity necessary within a faculty's membership if it is to carry out its corporate task. The second two issues shape a faculty's identity because of its accountability to academy, Church, and society at large: the conception of the nature and aims of theological inquiry operative within a faculty, particularly as it relates to the current state of the Church and the academy; and the sense the faculty has of the relation of its work to the contemporary issues of society and cultures. The materials I have chosen to comment on were part of a seminar on the question of excellence in theological faculties, sponsored by ATS and part of its Basic Issues Research program, funded by the Lilly Endowment. (*Theological Education*, 1990)

Though I chose the notion of parenting to sum up the many relations of faculty to students, the notion of "mentor," as proposed by Roy Sano, offers a compatible concept to characterize the work of the faculty. (Sano, 1990) The notion finds an analogous usage in the Roman tradition's sense of the importance of faculty members as models for the seminarian. It should not be thought of as a case of making virtue out of necessity, when contemporary faculties do that modeling by being composites of male and female members, of ordained and lay members, and, as is often the case in consortia, of Protestant and Catholic members. Such diversity and collaboration are obvious elements of the new sorts of modeling or mentoring necessary for adequate preparation for ministry in the Roman tradition.

Considerable attention has been given in recent years to formation of students in a technical sense, and specialized staff members have taken on oversight of spiritual, liturgical, and psychological development of the students. In some institutions these "formation faculties" constitute a distinct "mentoring" or "modeling" group and thus add yet another sort of diversity to an already divergent faculty. They carry on a longstanding tradition of incorporating personal, spiritual development in the overall curriculum. To a degree previously unknown, individuals may come away from their theological education well versed in spiritual direction, and one-on-one counselling, eager to continue reading the flourishing body of literature on the intricacies and dynamics of the interior life. The attraction is an obvious one for many reasons, the first and most pervasive being the cultural importance of a well-developed spirituality in an age so devoid of awareness of the transcendent. Second, given a predominance of introverted personalities among prospective candidates for ministry, a penchant for introspection and intensified self-awareness combines well with the natural attractiveness of spiritual development. Third, the need for attention to psychological maturity and the almost inevitable experience of some form of personal crisis during the years as a student of ministry, especially around the issue of ordination itself, can be effectively dealt with through the careful work of a competent spiritual advisor. However, a disjunction of the interior from the exterior with an undue isolation of the personal and private can permit a delay in the initiation of the proper integration needed. The result, that is to say the sort of ministerial character that is formed, may be of the traditionalist or the iconoclastic variety. Both are grounded in a conviction that one maintains an outward show long enough to complete one's education, and then one can express and act upon one's truest convictions. The vocational instability of either sort can be traced to the dissociation of inner conviction from outward activities, of spiritual life from pastoral and intellectual expertise. In considering a faculty's profile, then, it seems best to be cautious about limiting its parenting or mentoring activities to those assigned with the spiritual or personal development of the students.

Thus while the enhancement of the technical role of spiritual director or formator does focus certain essential aspects of theological preparation, the faculty as a whole cannot be exempt from the responsibility for teaching by example the virtues or "excellences" which the contemporary minister must develop. A too-sharp distinction between teaching and formation can lead to the isolation of the elements of a composite formation from one another, possibly in an antagonistic relationship. Learning to integrate intellectual, pastoral, and spiritual wisdom by observation of a diverse yet cooperative faculty, and often as part of a diverse student body whose members receive particularized attention, is an important goal of the hidden curriculum of theological institutions. Such teaching and learning within the institution is not, of course, a substitute for the hands-on learning and teaching of an internship or the early years of ministry under the guidance of a pastor who functions as the master guiding an apprentice. This sort of learning has already had considerable effect on candidates through their observation and participation in various kinds of Church life long before they entered formal education for ministry. Faculties, both academic and formational, must consider carefully how their efforts build upon or challenge already formed habits and ideas learned from the Church at large. Similarly, when internships occur between portions of the academic program, any effort by faculty consciously to integrate these two stages of learning can only reap benefit.

Finally, both faculty and mentoring pastors must be attentive for signs of the formative work of the Holy Spirit who also labors to shape the Church's ministers in their sacramental and spiritual lives. The application of an appropriate hermeneutic will ensure that neither of two extremes will occur in ministerial preparation, given such a belief in God's own agency. Those charged with such preparation must depend neither too much nor too little on the work of grace.

In our present age, it seems that an unhealthy disjunction of the study and practice of spirituality from the rest of the theological curriculum ironically fosters a suspicion of the specifically Christian transcendent dimension. As Sandra Schneiders has argued, spirituality needs to develop independent from its theological companions in order to pursue its own methods and goals (Schneiders, 1989), perhaps as an interesting hybrid of the philosophical, psychological, and religious. When set free from dogmatic or moral theology, however, it can inadvertently substitute these former norming studies with a secular discipline such as psychology or with a syncretism which vitiates its Christian usefulness. Or, in trying to do too much on its own, spirituality can falter under the weight of an unrealistic and confused agenda. The rest of the program of ministerial preparation equally suffers by dissociation from the spiritual traditions of the Church and the burgeoning discovery of spirituality as both an area of study and of practice. There is the need for a vision of the interconnectedness of spiritual, pastoral, and academic activities needed for education into professional, practical, and devotional maturity. My first observation, then, about the excellence or quality of a faculty in its technical and extended sense concerns its ability to engage in this broad sense of parenting or mentoring work, within which the various activities of teaching and learning are related through a hierarchy of goods to be pursued. The explicit statement of this hierarchy may well be found in curricula and mission documents, but needs the communicative and organizational finesse of deans and directors of programs.

There is a dark side to mentoring, of course, when exclusionist tendencies, even potentially oppressive tendencies, exercise a selectivity which *a priori* excludes certain types of individuals or at least ignores them. This is particularly so in the case of women and minority groups whose stereotypes encourage those who have invested in becoming leaders of the established order (i.e., teachers or administrators) to perpetuate the established patterns, most often unconsciously. I am not covertly discussing whether or not certain individuals or groups of individuals should or should not exercise varying types of ministry. Such discussion, and decision, is beyond the scope of this essay and of my person alone. The issue must be addressed, no doubt. However, what I wish quite overtly to say is that, once a great diversity of persons has been admitted into both faculty and student body, then a whole range of preestablished customs and attitudes which are the daily stuff of any particular institution must be questioned. This is not best done by grandiose plans about "future directions" which can degenerate into ideological preaching and position taking, though the vivid portrayal of opposing opinions has its merit on occasion. I tend to think it is best served by competent administration and the sensitive attention to the small details of helping individuals to feel at home and actually be at home in a given institution. As predicted above, seeking general rules for faculty, curriculum, and institutional renewal will result in the statement of such commonplaces as this, because knowing more detail about how to enact such rules depends very much upon the actual situation of each school. I take as primary the task of education and its goals (namely the retrieval, criticism, and passing on of the tradition) as the "higher good" to which all others are subordinated. Thus the issues of social construction and intellectual principles shaping the character of theological institutions are best discussed in light of the overarching purpose of effective and trustworthy teaching. I would presume that these factors would be evaluated with the help of the kind of theological principles I limned in Part Two.

As to the second issue, namely diversity itself as essential for excellence in a faculty, Marjorie Suchocki is correct, in her search for "Theological Foundations of Ethnic and Gender Diversity in Faculties" (*Theological Education*, 1990), to propose the doctrine of God, the true nature of the Christian God, as the ultimate foundation of this as well as other aspects of theological education. However, an analysis of the history of trinitarian theology discloses a careful balancing between difference and unity, relations and community. The term "diversity" does not find a prominent part in that history, and its association in English with meanings such as unlikeness, distraction, difference, and even mischief (as in some 16th-century usage) tends not to recommend it. The centrifugal force of such a notion seems to lead more towards the disintegration of theological education than the strengthening of it. Rather than a definition of the inner life of God as principally diversity, the great tradition has maintained that a very specific kind of harmony constitutes God, namely a community of persons. The notion of harmony not only includes but requires as an element a multiplicity of parts which are organized into a collaborative, congruous, or cooperative whole. The notion of "community" expresses a kind of human harmony and is more expressive for me of the doctrinal insight derived from trinitarian theology which I would appeal to as essential for excellence in a faculty engaged in theological education. As well, it would be in keeping with the clue Suchocki takes from theological anthropology.

In the latter part of her remarks, Suchocki suggests that the use of a theory of dynamic evolutionary anthropology, whether it aims at an idealistic world community or a Teilhardian omega point, would allow theological education to embrace heterogeneity and a kind of optimism about diversity which presumes that an underlying identity and harmony are both possible and necessary. A judgment that educating tomorrow's Church leaders in a homogeneous seminary community will ill prepare them for leading the church in the modern world is at first sight obviously true, and in fact such utterly homogeneous Catholic situations now rarely exist in North America. Diversification of both faculty membership and student body composition has firmly taken hold. However, her judgment must be tested over against the experience of those who teach and study in settings which have particular forms of homogeneity, and for whom one of the pressing difficulties is still the lack of a rudimentary identity and harmony both of students and (sometimes) of faculty.

A distinction should be noted here. There is an important difference between the factual diversity which already exists and poses great challenges to the harmony and effectiveness of a theological faculty or student body, and a controlled and reasoned diversity which is instituted by deliberate decisions. Definite parameters establish the basic qualifications, whether for students or faculty members, and factors particular to each institution further specify the range of individuals who are acceptable. It should be remembered that in the Roman tradition a literally incredible diversity has already been introduced through the admission of candidates for lay ministry, especially women, into what had been an exclusively male, clerical world just three decades ago. Assimilating and consolidating that elementary diversity is still a major item on the agenda of Catholic reform.

Two other kinds of diversity already present concern the contexts out of which teachers and students come. The doctoral education of an increasing number of professors for theological institutions takes place within university departments which orient these men and women to a life of scholarship that is vitally pluralistic and ecumenical. The challenge which ensues is not, as Lamb has suggested, of some supposed danger to Catholic identity, but rather of incorporation of these new faculty members into established faculties and institutions. What will ensue, if the incorporation is successful, will be the reconfiguring of curriculum and teaching, and even institutional structure. The challenge is indeed the maintenance of Catholic identity throughout renovation, though not through some sort of restriction of the education of faculty in a controlled environment.

The context from which the students come is itself a source of another kind of factual diversity. Unlike the relatively homogeneous family and cultural background of seminary students 40 years ago, present-day students often begin studies somewhat at a remove from their families, with various personal and career experiences, from a wider range of ages, and not always acquainted with the basic elements of the Roman tradition. In some respects we have returned to the experience of the 19th century in North America, when the arrival of European cultures brought homogeneous but culturally quite divergent groups of candidates, causing changes in seminary life.

The challenge is still the same, however, to welcome and incorporate such students who constitute the new diversity that is fast becoming the norm. Both forms of diversity are ones we already struggle with in the Roman tradition, and all to the better. Some of these factual forms of diversity are the result of social and cultural changes not initiated by the Church, and others are the result of profound developments in the Roman tradition which are only beginning to be appreciated.

The actual pursuit of diversity, by way of recruiting or hiring individuals who represent specific groups in society or particular points of view, was not the intent of the theological and ecclesial renewal of seminary training set forth by the Second Vatican Council. Even as recently as 1965, then, the Roman tradition was still chiefly concerned with priestly training, with no direct suggestions about the training of bishops, with limited concern about the education of deacons, and hardly any notion of what was to be required for the education for lay ministry. Yet nonetheless, through the inauguration of that specific renewal and a reorientation of every aspect of Church life, choices which ultimately foster a diversity in ministry were made and activities set in motion which have brought the tradition to its present state. It should be no surprise that the work of the Holy Spirit represented by such a monumental event as a Council of the Church would enliven the entire Roman Catholic community in unexpected ways.

Many members of the Catholic faithful, at great cost to themselves, have begun the long and arduous task of achieving an adult knowledge of their faith, especially through study of the Bible, have engaged in programs of spiritual growth, and offered themselves for ministerial responsibilities. Others in increasing numbers have pursued doctoral studies and are taking their place in both university departments of theology and professional schools. Many institutions have not simply responded, but have promoted these developments. Perhaps somewhat unlike other traditions which have not experienced such a burst of enthusiasm from their members, the Roman tradition has incorporated considerable diversity in a short space of 25 years. For some, the changes are too slow, especially concerning the role of women, and they are becoming disheartened; for others, the divergence has been too quick, confusing, and to their minds heterodox, and they are disheartened too. It is not particularly helpful when many of the former group are the laity themselves, and the latter group are well-placed, often powerful individuals, whether lay or clerical. When a group opposing change is itself highly homogeneous and associated with claims to exclusive authority, it lays itself open to scrutiny for possible vested interests and ideologies, whereas divergent and unpowerful groups which discover common interests and principles are vital sources of potential change, provided that they forge an identity in harmony with the tradition they are in the process of handing on in a new configuration. Ultimately, of course, issues of ministry and education cannot simply be decided on the basis of social and political factors independent of theological considerations. Discerning the work of the Spirit from false prophets is a slow, careful, and sometimes trying task, but it is characteristic of that work that it fosters unity on the one hand and service on the other.

Suchocki is not insensitive to the potential dysfunction which diversity (and lack of rudimentary identity) might occasion. Her paper's final section, in presenting the need for a renewed theology of knowledge, seems to appreciate the priority of identity and particularity before levels of tolerance for diversity and consequent profit from such diversity can be reasonably expected. There is an ambiguity involved in championing diversity of viewpoints and communities, given the growing desire in many traditions to consolidate and reassert in a particularistic fashion the identity and uniqueness found there. In institutional terms, it might be helpful to contrast the experience of a federation of schools with a single multi-denominational school and both of these with the single denomination school. Diversity cannot be determined abstractly. Certain institutions of necessity must come to terms with forms of inner diversity which others do not have or cannot have. Tolerance and realism about the differences among traditions and their limitations are as important ecumenical sensitivities as are efforts at coordination and consolidation of traditions. Theological convictions about *how* we come to know God, as much as convictions about *whom* we know when we encounter the Christian God, are foundational to the toleration and fostering of diversity as an element of excellence in theological faculties.

The harmony which underlies this diversity is to be found in a certain commonality of life and belief which most often never comes to articulation or reflection in a theological faculty, except perhaps on those rare occasions of retreat from the business of the everyday. Often overlooked, but essential moments, are those of the corporate worship of the school and of the faculty by itself. Single denomination schools have a particular advantage here, though ecumenically diverse schools also find appropriate forms. Whereas much of the literature, when it comes to institutions and faculty, seeks harmony and credibility in methodology and scholarly accountability, such essential matters cannot be separated from the formative and foundational character of worship itself. Theology as reflection upon Christian life does indeed require a theory of religious knowledge, and the role of worship in that theory can only be neglected at great peril. Such is the legacy of the European Enlightenment. Lest the reader think I have lapsed into mere piety here, let me recall that acceptance of an agenda of renewal which places *theologia* at its core cannot retrieve this concept from the tradition without taking into account the context for the successful operation of such habits of the whole human person. The tradition of the Church confirms the harmony of habits of thought, speech, and action with habits of worship.

Though it cannot be adverted to here with more than a brief aside, the relation of worship to theological education is a particularly poignant problem in the Roman tradition of the present age. Worship, which should be unifying and reconciling in keeping with its own inner logic, functions as a counter-example of the mutuality and cooperation experienced elsewhere, especially in those theological institutions which have diverse student and faculty membership. The harmony of persons and activities which are ingredient in the corporate pedagogy of an institution risks losing an essential control over its own authenticity and credibility when worship becomes divisive, is experienced by any group as a hostile environment, or degenerates into being a forum for ideological concerns foreign to Christian belief's search for a radical integrity before God. That is not to say that harmony for harmony's sake is the goal, especially if it were achieved through the neglect of justified critique or the imposition of thoughtless conformity. Living with certain kinds of liturgical discomfort is not only realistic at present in the Roman tradition, but can be transformed into an important forum in which a faculty might further its mentoring by raising the consciousness of themselves and their students, even within the liturgy, to the presence of sinful structures within ministry itself, which is as thoroughly human a reality as it is a reality graced by God.

II

The second set of issues concerning the faculty gives attention ultimately to its relationships beyond the institution. A major theme of the recent literature, impinging quite directly on determining faculty excellence, is that of the relation of theological education to the academy and the Church. In the two major works of Farley, for example, and in the ATS Summer Seminar of 1989, the relation of seminary and divinity school to the university is discussed primarily in terms of theological methodology, its criteria and credibility, and its relation to other kinds of academic study. The dialogue of theology with other disciplines and studies in the university is no doubt an essential element of excellence in theological education, and the conceptual tools employed by the chief Protestant authors to lay out the problems and pose resolutions are not foreign to Catholic theologians, nor would they be thought straightforwardly wrongheaded. The simple fact is, however, that the relation of theological studies, both professional and otherwise, to the Catholic university has a very different history which raises somewhat different issues. As well, worldwide structures of accountability and the interpenetration of religious communities and institutions of higher learning relate accountability to academy and Church more closely and with challenges as difficult and as interesting as those of Protestant institutions. An analysis of the social determinants of contemporary theology and its institutions, such as that offered by a French Canadian sociologist Fernand Dumont, in his work *L'institution de la théologie,* is as important as an analysis of the history of ideas and the proposal of new methodologies.

As a Catholic observer of the recent literature on the subject, specifically in relation to education for ministry, I think it important to point out that the discussion was inaugurated and pursued principally as a contemporary search by mainline or establishment Protestantism to reconsider its effectiveness and credibility, partly to retrieve its heritage from beyond the remnants of liberalism, and thus to revisit the 19th-century debates which established the study of divinity as part of the modern university. For some time into this century, excellence in Catholic theology did not depend upon the complete adoption of the fourfold division of subject matter, the functionalist goals of theological education, and the scholarly accommodation to the reigning conception of modernity for criteria of meaning and truth. It is only comparatively recently that the Catholic curriculum began to imitate more fully their Protestant counterparts. Let me hasten to add that lack of attention to these requirements did not guarantee that Catholic theology and education for ministry was unqualifiedly successful, much lest apt, for the needs of the time. Forms of obscurantist scholasticism (propositionalism of sorts), naive biblical scholarship, and adversarial attitudes towards, or at least suspicion of, the modern human sciences prevented Catholics from being "excellent" in what they taught and how they formed their priests. Overcoming these limitations was the long labor of *ressourcement* in the early 20th century, and it was forwarded by distinguished scholars who took the best of the convictions of the modern university milieu and married them to the ecclesial concerns which far outreached the established ecclesiastical mood and politics in the Roman tradition. Thoroughgoing revision followed the directives of the Second Vatican Council, and continues today, though somewhat like the becalmed waters of ecumenism, we seem to be in a similar moment of unsuspecting calm before the next major set of stormy times will require the next round of adjustments to declining numbers, financial constraints, and the urgency of contemporary issues.

In particular, the anthropologically-centered character of a proposal like that of Farley, which judges the ecclesial basis and traditioning character of Christian theology as resistances to the essential restructuring of theology, is ultimately inspired by an accommodation to modernity, however much this revision of theological study might be critical of the received vision of the university ethos and its definition of truth. Thus, the retrieval of *theologia* and the reunification of the intellectual search appropriate to the academy are not necessarily to be achieved by an abandonment of the "house of authority" and a translation of theological study through historicity into hermeneutics. If the alternatives, namely ecclesially-based study which does accept a house of authority, is seen in Protestant terms as sectarianism or fundamentalism, it is little wonder that they are eschewed. To be accused of being "pre-critical" in one's use of scripture or the monuments and classics of tradition bears an immense weight of judgment which results in considerable social and political exclusion, ecclesiastically and otherwise. Strangely enough, the attractiveness of the "pre-critical" continues to sway large segments of North American Christianity, and Christians elsewhere as well. There is likewise a good deal of the "pre-critical" about students themselves, since often they come to ministerial education with a less than university-level understanding of their own religious heritage, and without having experienced the application of critical thinking to religious belief.

Excellence in Catholic scholarship as reflective of the norms assessing excellence in the faculty of a theological institution has not succumbed to sectarianism or fundamentalism, despite the ever present tendency to these forms of Christian life. In fact, Catholic faculties have never been more attuned to the wider world of scholarship and research, and the requirements of an intelligent and responsible ecumenism. A significant factor which has led to this enhancement of the best in the tradition has been the diversification of doctoral studies pursued by new faculty in university-related departments of theology and religious studies. The results can be observed not only in the actual work of such faculties, but in the hiring and promoting practices of Catholic institutions, especially as they are now scrutinized by public accreditation procedures.

It is factors other than a lack of conviction which endanger the academic excellence of specific institutions. Unintelligent and nervous interference from various sources, severe financial constraints, and the weariness of faculty members themselves who are faced with unrealistic workloads or unsympathetic environments—these are the sort of factors which militate against the best of intentions and convictions. The contemporary pressures on seminary faculty challenge even the most dedicated scholars and practitioners, some of whom ultimately find a more congenial atmosphere for their work elsewhere. The struggle for the Catholic institution will be to foster and retain its well-educated and inventive faculty members despite pressures to the contrary. Those pressures include well-intentioned but unfortunately ill-advised suggestions that diversity in the education of theologate faculty is to be avoided. (Lamb, O'Meara, 1990)

A fourth issue which raises questions about the character of excellence in a theological faculty concerns the sense the faculty has of the relation of its work to the contemporary issues of society and culture. If the issue of credibility in the academy encourages a study of theological procedures, credibility in the congregation and the market place encourages consideration of pastoral and apologetic effectiveness. The pressing concerns of society and culture do not, however, straightforwardly constitute the agenda of theological scholarship or education. A revision of methods and curricula simply to accommodate culturally-demanding problems is essentially wrongheaded, and would produce correspondingly inappropriate alterations in faculty membership. Similarly, though less obviously, a peculiar Catholic temptation at the moment would be to transform methods and curricula through the adoption of one or other "perspective." Theological education is not immune to the current struggle to find adequate ways in which to accommodate to the proliferation of perspectives and the resistance to commonality and tradition which marks contemporary North American society. The challenge is to resist the somewhat satisfying effects of actually accommodating to multiple perspectives for the sake of individual and group interests, and instead, to engage in the difficult task of naming and developing actual common principles more profound than individual and group rights.

Lest these remarks stray too far, I should note that there is indeed a line of connection from theoretical concerns about theological procedures and topics to actual choices of faculty members. Decisions about what is necessary for a curriculum to be complete, and about what constitutes adequate preparation for a teaching career, are essential ingredients in the decisions about whom to hire and tenure. Any hesitation in my remarks about adopting the revisions which Farley or Wood suggest, for example, based upon their reconsideration of theological procedures, has to do with a concern for the ecclesial dimension of such revision, which offers beneficial help and formative influence on the search for criteria of excellence in a theological faculty. While the attention to the status of theological education for its credibility within the university is proper, it must be held in dialectical tension with credibility within the Church.

III

I have noted four elements for consideration in assessing the excellence in a Catholic faculty: corporate activity as mentor or parent, harmonization of requisite diversity, credibility in the academy and Church, and incorporation of various perspectives as required by interest groups and the pressing issues of contemporary human suffering. Throughout this discussion I have considered those who teach and engage in formation or direction as a group. It seems futile to me to discuss the excellence of particular individuals, since criteria for each varies from discipline to discipline, field to field, however much there are general criteria for them all. Anyone who has engaged in a search committee's work of sifting through applications for faculty positions, or for funds for scholarly research, knows that the judgment of a knowledgeable member of the specific area of study is indispensable to making an informed judgment on the excellence of a given applicant. Equally important are the more intangible and intuitive guidelines needed for determining the profile of a new faculty member proportionate to the profile of the corporate person which is a theological faculty. The principle challenges for such a Catholic faculty are, in my judgment, the problems of unity and collaboration among scholars engaged in academically and ecclesially creditable work ultimately focused upon transmission of the great tradition of Christian belief in the formation of persons capable of ministry, both pastoral and academic.

This chapter ends where it began, with an observation about the factual details of the development of theologate faculties. Individual schools and dioceses have traditions of recruitment, education, and promotion of faculty members, most often from within the pool of members of religious communities or the local presbyterate. As that pool of possible teachers and scholars becomes smaller, and potentially lacks apt individuals for intensive graduate study, the established mechanisms for the maintenance of the network of schools in North America will change radically. The effects of this situation are already evident, as many seminaries have closed and are still closing, and the actual pool of competent doctoral graduates is made up of diverse individuals from many graduate programs. When faced with financial restraint, some institutions may well attempt to maintain themselves through the traditional patterns of hiring, depending upon religious and priests who do not require salaries on a level with public standards or the needs of self-sustaining individuals and families. As with the reduction in the number of elementary and high school institutions within the Roman tradition in North America, so it seems that this effort to maintain the usual patterns of hiring will soon be impossible.

More importantly, the very issues of appropriate pedagogy, diversity, competence and general excellence with regard to both Church and academy are at stake in establishing new traditions of developing faculties in theological schools. The problems of inept interference and financial constraints notwithstanding, the pressing matter which must be brought to the consciousness of board members and search committees alike is the need for discovering new ways to identify and foster new faculty members. The salutary advantage that is gained by enlarging the pool of possible candidates to include the great variety of individuals who have studied at the best of graduate institutions is accompanied by a challenge to discover the content and measure of two other characteristics essential to a competent faculty. The changing situation may ensure highly professional faculty, but the previous methods dependent upon religious and clerics as the pool could presume a degree of practicality and devotion based upon the ecclesial status of the individual. What is needed now is a conscientization which will enable schools to recognize the equally sophisticated practicality and devotion of candidates not from the traditional pools, and the inventiveness to foster such pastoral and spiritual maturity. The reader should not be surprised by the implication that the characteristics of the competent graduate of ministerial education are the same for the competent faculty member.

As I forewarned in the opening remarks of this chapter, the discussion of faculty has intertwined with observations about the students they teach, and about the curriculum which organizes their pedagogical efforts. Wonderment about what kind of students are or should be prepared for ministry was the beginning of this work; the shape of curriculum will now be its final chapter before a few concluding remarks.

8. Curriculum

THE DEVELOPMENT OF AN EXCELLENT FACULTY, ONE WELL-PREPARED to fulfill its responsibilities, requires the convergence of many factors and no small amount of good luck. Beyond general principles, it is impossible to specify just how to accomplish the goals of building up a competent and dedicated faculty. It takes conscious and continuous dedication by administrators and faculty members themselves to maintain the energy necessary to pursue faculty development since, like the maintenance of a historic building, there is a never-ending need for refurbishment and renovation, tasteful additions and sometimes serious structural repair, all the while attempting to preserve the structure's historic integrity. Given the rapid turnover in the administration of Catholic theological institutions, especially among academic deans, continuity and long-range planning is presently very difficult. In turning now to the matter of curriculum, we seem to have a much more tangible and accessible element of academic institutional life. One can set down in print, and in fact must do so, in catalogues or bulletins a specific outline of a curriculum for each program that prepares the Church's ministers. Such is a requirement of public accrediting bodies, but also of the churches as well. Curricular plans produce documentary evidence of adherence to and completion of a process. They are tangible records of ideas and intentions. Unlike impressionistic profiles of the qualities of ideal teachers or administrators, a curriculum allows argumentation over quantities of hours to be spent, credits to be given, temporal sequence, ratio of requirements and electives, timetables, not to mention course names and assignment of duties to specific teachers. But, like mission statements which catch up in brief form the vision and dynamic of an entire institution, a curriculum can be

167

read as a palette of colors and dictionary of shapes with which to project the kind of minister and ministry an institution is committed to.

A comparison of present-day Catholic curriculum with that of nearly a hundred years ago, as documented by White, shows a nuanced difference in appearance. The relative distribution of courses in areas of study is not the principle indicator of differences, and additions such as field education, theological reflection seminars, and courses on contemporary social issues are indeed new to the curriculum, but not entirely novel in their content or intent. What constitutes the real point of difference is how the faculty and students interact in the teaching/learning situation and what conception they have of the purpose and goal of the process. Two allied issues are how students conceive and act upon the relation of their study to their actual ministry, and how teachers conceive and act upon the relation of their research and writing to their actual teaching.

The recent discussion of curriculum as a major element in theological education has wisely inaugurated a far-reaching investigation of precisely these two issues, though the discussion is as abstracted and theoretical as the results should be practical and concrete. This remark is not intended as a criticism. As will become evident, what is more important in the matter of curriculum is establishing the architectonic rules which govern the particulars than attempting to prescribe the details which are best left to pragmatic decisions in actual situations. Revision of the curriculum begins with the evaluation of alternate depictions of the *whole* of a curriculum, and both their suitability to present needs and their rhetorical power to be persuasive. This requires a notion of the Church and of the academy, of the minister and the scholar, of the human person as agent, thinking and doing, and of God as an agent. As one or other of these factors take dominance, differing depictions of the enterprise of theological education result.

Three major investigations, those of Farley, Wood, and Hough/Cobb, generate their curricular suggestions out of a discussion of what constitutes the essence of Christianity and the ideal minister, of the procedures and criteria of theological method, and of a theory of knowledge appropriate to Christianity as a religion but also compatible with the methods and criteria of other sciences and disciplines. Once these notions are established, the procedures of theological study can be designated, though only Hough/Cobb goes so far as to propose an actual curriculum (and in two versions). I will briefly consider each of these three proposals as instances of alternate configurations of curriculum based upon theological, and possibly denominational or at least contextual, convictions which offer clues to options for the configuration of relations between teachers, students, course work and objectives, ministry and research. I think it is wise, and inevitable, that no concrete curriculum can be proposed, or imposed, as the result of such studies. Even the actual curriculum offered by Hough/Cobb is presented with a careful proviso that it need not be, nor might ever be, actually put to use. I will, however, note the usually brief remarks in each of these studies which relate their own proposals to the status quo. Since their work has generated considerable comment, I will not repeat here either a comprehensive study of their arguments or those of their critics.

I

In his first work on the subject, *Theologia: The Fragmentation and Unity of Theological Education*, Farley diagnosed the American (Protestant) situation as one in which the development of theology as a habit or capacity for wisdom and discipline has disappeared as the unifying rationale of the institutional preparation for ministry. This displacement is due to cultural and institutional factors, as well as developments in the theory and practice of theology itself, as focused in Schleiermacher and the encyclopedic movement of the 19th century. The resulting shape of theological study is dependent upon its division into the fourfold scheme (generally bible, history, systematics, and pastoralia, though with variations), with preparation for clerical leadership as its unifying purpose, and the severance of the theoretical from the practical as evidenced in the antagonism of the "academic" and the "pastoral," the former being considered elitist and irrelevant, the latter collapsing into various forms of functionalist competency. Farley's overarching judgment is that these factors contribute to the loss of *theological* understanding as the unity of theological study. His constructive proposal consists of a four-step movement: 1) thematization of the "faith-world"; 2) relativization of that world through a hermeneutics of suspicion; 3) an ensuing critique of that world construed as a tradition; and 4) a moment of second naiveté which reappropriates the moment of faith. The process is the traditional movement of faith seeking understanding in its modern, post-critical dress. It is an activity proper to all believers, and specialized in the church leader inasmuch as not only does the leader engage in the same theologically-interpretive activity within concrete situations within the Church, but the leader is also responsible for facilitating such interpretive activity among the faithful generally.

In his second work on the subject, *The Fragility of Knowledge: Theological Education in the Church & the University*, Farley develops at greater length the moments of this interpretive activity called theology. This time the placement of his proposal is after an assessment of the state of university education and the varieties of post-Enlightenment hermeneutics which dominate it. I leave aside here his efforts at legitimizing the study of religions, and within it the theological study of religions, within the university. His remarks in this first part bear quite directly on the judgments which establish his proposal for theological study, and therefore for curriculum, even though he does not propose any specific rendering of his theory into a program of study. I have already discussed this essential shift as Farley sees it, but it is important to repeat it here. In his own words:

> There is a shift when theology and the study of theology occur outside the authority paradigm. It is the shift from theology as a cluster of sciences based upon *a priori* authority to theology as historically-situated reflection and interpretation. The outcome of that shift is that the structure of theological study or pedagogy is recognized to be determined by basic modes of interpretation rather than by sciences. Instead of being a structure of sciences or of pedagogical areas created by the aims of clergy education, the structure of theology becomes a structure of basic modes of interpretation. (Farley, 1988, 128)

The orderly study of faith, then, occurs through five disciplined modes of interpretation (of tradition, truth, action, situation and vocation) which mutually condition one another, forming a complex whole of hermeneutical study, all of which cuts across the received boundaries of specialty fields, disciplines, and sciences as represented by the fourfold division and its institutional embodiment in departments. This is true for any form of theological education, clergy education being only one special instance of the general pattern. The elements of the structure are required by the nature of theology itself, conceived as a form of hermeneutics, and obviously cannot be displaced by a focus upon the acquisition of ministerial skills as the chief aim of clergy education. Moreover, clergy education need not, therefore, be isolated from other kinds of advanced

theological education since they all depend upon the same
hermeneutical activities. By comparison to this new proposal,
Farley finds the present situation in need of considerable revision:

> A post-baccalaureate three-year menu of introductory and sur-
> vey courses, eked out with courses that focus the interests of
> several specialty fields, is not sufficient to the needs of the
> leadership of a religious faith desperately imperiled in the con-
> temporary world. Theological study as advanced hermeneutic
> education requires a new institutionality of clergy education.
> If clergy education continues in its present institutional form—
> the three-year program of seminary studies, with roots in the
> early 19th century—the church needs to devise also a "major
> course" directed to a special type of church leader. (Farley,
> 1988, 178)

Of special interest to the Catholic observer is Farley's indication of three kinds of study propaedeutic to theological education:
historical-cultural, philosophic, and religious. These three represent
the basic background upon which advanced study ought to build.
Educators at the Master of Divinity level are increasingly aware of
the lack of general knowledge which students give evidence of, and
remedial education constantly encroaches upon the work at hand.
Catholic seminaries, in particular, have consistently maintained the
requirement of significant philosophical study prior to theological
study, though the quality of that preparatory study has been uneven.
Farley's remarks about the present situation as compared with his
proposal are applicable to the Catholic situation, but they do seem to
suggest that his proposal is more apt for advanced graduate study of
Christian theology, and to some degree overshoots the programs in
need of a new proposal.

Wood's analysis and proposal in *Vision and Discernment* begins, as did Farley's, with a focus on Schleiermacher's *Brief Outline
on the Study of Theology*, its origins and devolution into the present
situation. His exposition is particularly lucid and I will not repeat it
here, except to note his conclusion. The three- or fourfold pattern,
allied as it is to the procedures and social embodiments of secular
study guided by critical history, philosophy, and the human sciences
and unified by a teleology of preparing Church leadership, has a
powerful and persuasive hold upon institutions of theological learning. It forges an uneasy partnership between the providers of scholarly, academic knowledge of Christianity with those who can train in
pastoral expertise. He concludes his first chapter with an anticipa-

tory remark, suggesting that the threefold structure might have a more profound basis in the structure of the subject matter of theology itself, namely "Christian tradition, Christian witness, the church." This subject matter would "demand a three-level or three-dimensional scrutiny, in which it is examined first with respect to its origin, then with respect to its content, and finally with respect to its goal." (Wood, 19) Out of this notion of a threefold subject matter he will develop his definition of theology as critical inquiry and its three questions of authenticity, truth, and aptness.

The comprehensive definition of theological inquiry as a critical investigation of Christian witness hovers between two notions of why that witness is not self-evidently valid, one of which is secular, the other religious. At times Wood speaks of the critical inquiry in keeping with a notion of it as "an aspect of the continuing repentance to which the church and all its members are called," (Wood, 24) somewhat blurring the distinction between witness and theology. If the exercise of theological inquiry is a form of repentance, then it is a form of witness, engaged in to purify thought, word, and deed, "a venture of self-transformation in obedience to the Word of God in scripture." (Wood, 27) The religious assumption underlying this notion of "critical" is a complex one, including at least a doctrine of sin and of the inadequacy of all invented symbols for the transcendent.

Alternately, the secular notion of "critical inquiry" demands that theology through its three questions be responsible to the practice and requirements of "critical historical scholarship generally," of philosophical inquiry, and "the disciplines concerned with the understanding of human culture and behavior." (Wood, 44-48) What makes these forms of understanding "critical" is simply presumed, that is, that they "embody certain well-tested procedures, and are in turn embodied in institutional contexts and political settings which sustain them." (Wood, 60) They are the common practice and accepted forms of human rationality's own self-transforming agenda in face of natural ignorance and evil, and they are carried out in accordance with its own inherent teleology. Wood only briefly considers whether the principles and practice of the secular methods of inquiry might be inadequate to or even come in conflict with the tasks of Christian theology, particularly in the case of the use of philosophy within theology. (Wood, 45-47; 60-62)

What makes each aspect of this inquiry irreducibly Christian theology is the comprehensive aim of testing Christian witness according to its own criteria of consistency, truth, and fittingness. Wood concludes his proposal for the structure of theological inquiry by a discussion of systematic and moral theology. Systematization or coordination of the first three activities of historical, philosophical, and practical theology can take on the configurations of proclamatory, apologetic, or perspectival/contextual theologies, which in effect are forms of systematization giving the leading edge, so to speak, to historical, philosophical, or practical theology and their root questions respectively. Moral theology receives scant discussion, somewhat as an afterthought. This complex and nuanced proposal about theological inquiry is precisely that: a proposal for a deeper understanding of what goes on when theology is afoot. It might be useful for a faculty in the following way:

> If those involved in theological study are able to place their own efforts and concerns in relation to this account, and are helped by it at all to a clearer and more fruitful understanding of the theological enterprise or of particular aspects of it, it will have served its main purpose. (Wood, 41)

It is in his final chapter that he takes up the more concrete relationship of this analysis to curricular matters. Intervening is a chapter whose purpose is to set aside the noxious argument about the dichotomy of theory and practice as a wrongheaded debate, and to propose the adoption of a different sort of dialectic, that of vision and discernment. Vision, Wood suggests, aims at the comprehensive and overarching view of things, discernment at the uniqueness of the particulars which make up that larger landscape. They complement one another, each being in need of the other to obviate their inherent limitations, and both being essential to adequate theory and practice. As with the three questions making up theological inquiry, the areas of study they constitute, and the two further activities of systematic and moral theology, these two activities of vision and discernment cut across the established boundaries of curriculum and guild-oriented faculty divisions naming characteristics of the composite activity of theological work.

Wood does not see his notion of theology as critical inquiry to be ultimately at odds with three other historical construals of theological education: as formation in faith itself as a habit of grace, as handing on of the content of tradition, and as professional training for church leadership. His comprehensive sense of inquiry allows him to relate to and even to enclose these other notions of theological education within the nuanced set of activities he has already prescribed. As to the relation between his proposal and current curricula, he makes the following observation:

> It would help to begin by expanding our view of the place of "theology" in the theological curriculum. This does not mean increasing the number of courses required in systematic theology, or enhancing their prestige somehow. It means, instead, understanding the entire curriculum as really and truly a theological curriculum, that is, as a body of resources ordered to the cultivation in students of an aptitude for theological inquiry. (Wood, 94)

The third proposal for rethinking the curriculum which I wish to consider is that of Joseph Hough and John Cobb, *Christian Identity and Theological Education.* I have already given considerable attention to their work in the chapter on practicality as an essential characteristic of the minister. In order to ensure the cultivation of practicality as the chief determining characteristic of the minister, they must propose a new model of the minister and a new image of the Church, since they find the current need for revision in theological education to be occasioned by the same need for repentance that Wood called upon. The image of the Church is revised with a series of contemporary characteristics which are not altogether unreducible to the traditional four marks of unity, holiness, catholicity, and apostolicity. The resulting ideal holds together traditional activities of worship, prayer, and consolation with contemporary social and political action.

As to the character of the minister, they propose a new sort of person called "the practical theologian," who will combine two ideals: first, the practical Christian thinker, who is rooted in Christian identity and oriented to Christian practice; second, the reflective practitioner, who does not apply theory in practice as experts servicing clients do, but who reflects in action and enacts that reflection. This requires the formation of a Christian identity, through critical and revisionist remembrance of Christian origins and history, for the purpose of living out Christian beliefs and values with attention to the multiple perspectives required to address the pressing issues of contemporary society. I have already considered their history of models of the minister, and their images of the Church, offering modifications to both in keeping with actual Catholic history and practice.

Those changes are perhaps even more necessary in a proposal like that of Hough/Cobb because, if it is actually to generate a new view of curriculum focused upon practicality in actual Church life, then it must correspond to the actual ecclesial identities of various communities and their practices. I take it as self-evident that there is not simply one single Christian identity, in fact, and that a proposal based on such a presumption would be subject to the same criticism as is Farley's proposal about methods and subject matters, which Hough/Cobb itself considers excessively abstract and academic. If Hough/Cobb fails to address the actual Church while eschewing methodological considerations, then its proposal falls on barren ground, being inattentive to either church or academy.

If Hough/Cobb had not actually provided a curriculum outline, one might have been able to engage in a generous reading of their text which might have translated the rhetorical argument in a fashion that saves the urgency and righteadedness of their turn to the practical but would avoid the major difficulties which Ogden and Reynolds have articulately exposed. (Browning, chapters II and VII) However, the actual outline of courses, even in its revised form, shows a set of debilitating lacunae in their revised notion of *theologia* which are not, of course, unique to their proposal. The study done by Sherryl Kleinman of a midwest seminary dedicated to what she terms the humanistic role of the minister offers a glimpse of what the institutional shape of education for ministry might be if principles such as those offered by Hough/Cobb were combined with a thoroughgoing definition of religion as humanistic and the minister as roleless. Whether the curriculum would contain the usual courses or be entirely renamed and restructured is not the point. It is the egalitarian and humanistic ideology, no matter how it is taught, that inhibits the establishment of an identity and a basis for authority in the minister. What is ironic, then, is that the form and content of *theologia* in Hough/Cobb might well produce ministers who could not actually be practical, not because they are ill-versed in technique or in the recognition of issues, but because they would lack the capacity for critical Christian thought to specify their practicality as Christian.

These three proposals, Farley, Hough/Cobb, and Wood, represent the three depictions of theological education which Wood himself considers in his final chapter. First, Farley, albeit in modern dress, considers the subjective element primary, with "modes of understanding" as the leading item in construing the rest of the materials of the educational process. This preference for phenomenology might be attractive to some Catholics, and his concern for a more advanced study than the typical postbaccalaureate program would appeal to the more rigorous, if not elitist. In order to establish his new program of study, principally a new method of study, he must critique the academy and its scholars, offer a new vision of both, and then propose the new school of theology, its members, and their work seen through the prism of new subjective (though not subjectivist) procedures. Second, Hough/Cobb reacts to his proposal as abstract and formal, in retreat from the urgent issues of the day, and incorrect in its abandonment of preparation for church leadership as the organizing aim of seminary education. Their proposal, however revisionist, does take as the leading element the external tasks of ministry. They follow a path analogous to Farley's, though their critique is of the Church and its ministers, their corresponding ideals are of a new Church and new leaders within it, and the prism through which they see schools, faculty, students, and programs is a collection of issues and activities held loosely together by the general notions of identity, practice, and global context, what Reynolds calls "the trinity of concerns in terms of which the totality of seminary education is structured." (Browning, 1989, 95) Finally, Wood himself represents the third option, taking the objective element, the tradition in both active and passive senses, as the leading determinant. Though he sounds much like Farley, his choice of essential questions for theological inquiry is determined by the subject matter, "the Christian tradition, Christian witness, the church." (Wood, 19) By using the shift in paradigm for the meaning of a religion and its doctrines as proposed by Lindbeck, Wood is able to marry two essentials of theory and practice: doctrine is taught as formative of Christian life rather than as esoteric historical information, and ministerial responsibility is rooted in theological vision and discernment rather than psychological or social skills. With these notions of doctrine and responsibility, Wood can hold the three depictions of theological education together. He summarizes the relation of the subjectively and objectively oriented depictions as follows:

> . . . an education in theological inquiry is, in some sense, "formation," and "formation" involves learning to be critical; an education in theological inquiry implies the appropriation of tradition, and any adequate appropriation of tradition involves the use of theological judgment. (Wood, 93)

And as to the task-oriented construal, he observes:

> . . . theological education is not necessarily professional educa-
> tion for ministry, but the heart of proper professional education
> for ministry *is* theological education—meaning by "theological
> education" an education in theological inquiry. One may prop-
> erly seek and obtain a theological education without any inten-
> tion of preparing for church leadership of any sort; but one
> may not properly prepare for church leadership without acquir-
> ing theological competence. (Wood, 93)

Wood's proposal is, I suggest, somewhat of a bridge between those
of Farley and Hough/Cobb, addressing the limitations of both of
them.

Reorienting theological education involves redefining and regaining the study of Christian theology at its heart. As these three
studies propose, this can be accomplished by giving attention to the
requirements for accountability to Church, university and world.
Such realignments would obviously have effects on faculty membership and pedagogy, but have actually been focused on matters of
curriculum. Yet strangely enough, the proposals are not really about
curriculum directly. I can make this suggestion with fairness even
to Hough/Cobb since it puts forward a curriculum with hesitancy,
which is subsequently revised, and undoubtedly could still be revised yet again. The message of all three efforts is, rather, to encourage a rethinking of the scholarly and field educational activities
of the typical school of theology across the whole curriculum. As I
have already quoted Wood, it is to understand "the entire curriculum
as really and truly a theological curriculum." (Wood, 94) Actual
revisioning would come about as the individuals who teach and research reconceive their own activities and their relationships to one
another. New courses and a new configuration of departments or
divisions of study would come about consequent upon a thoroughgoing revision of educational practice itself, theological study being its
essence, however redefined. The real argument is about that redefining, not the realigning of courses. My judgment is that Wood
comes closest to being useful to the Roman tradition, and that the
task is more one of retrieval of inner Christian dynamics that tend to
be obscured by accommodation to present needs or translation into a
new idiom.

The regulations for an actual curriculum, as set down in the
Program of Priestly Formation in its third edition, offers two model
curricula giving minimum requirements as to course hours spent on

specific areas of study, each model showing different manners of configuring the traditional contents of ministerial preparation. There is no rigid imposition, but a recognition of inevitable nuances from school to school, each with its own internal history and educational emphases. In order for Farley, Hough/Cobb, and Wood to be applied to this curriculum, attention must be directed away from the rearrangement of courses and topic areas into matters more akin to rethinking pedagogy and discovering the rhetorical style necessary for effective ministry today. To worry about rearranging the remnants of the tract system of teaching theology would belie the inner changes that have already taken place and are still going on in the courses themselves. The current ferment in the discussion about the use of alternative methods in theology and about how to be effective as preachers of the word and servants of the sacraments shows no sign of an immanent resolution, nor should we expect one. The curriculum will be renewed in the Roman tradition, perhaps now in any tradition, not by a direct intervention but by the subtle changes that differences in pedagogy and faculty composition will inevitably cause.

III

From within a quite different scholarly expertise, Maria Harris considers the matter of curriculum as an essential element of the Church's comprehensive practice of education. She proposes a quite different schema of activities which are the broad basis for the construction of curriculum. They give structure not only for a course of studies within educational institutions, but within the Church as a whole, naming the regions of Church life within which activities of teaching and learning occur. Harris understands education to be an essential characteristic of Christian life itself, being an interplay of the multiple forms of world-making which name Christian discipleship. She avoids both a propositionalist or an experientialist distortion of Christianity (the integralist and modernist tendencies of which Van Beeck speaks), thereby broadening a discussion of education in the Church beyond schooling on the one hand, and self-actualization on the other. Considering curriculum in this comprehensive way places specialized preparation for ministry in continuity with the general education of the Church as a whole. It also helps to give perspective to the necessary, but somewhat confined, considerations of professional education in its relationship to the university or to social and political contexts.

The five areas of curriculum she proposes are denoted by reference to New Testament Greek terms for essential activities of discipleship: *leiturgia, kerygma, diakonia, didache,* and *koinonia*; that is, liturgy, proclamation, service, teaching, and community. As descriptive categories of activity in the Church, they would require an argument establishing their necessity and sufficiency as determining Christian life. If employed as a basis for reconceiving the aims of curricular change, they offer a quite different set of options than either the traditional departmental and specialty categories, or the phenomenological modes and other essentially philosophical categories, or topical and issue-determined categories. They recommend themselves not least for their value in offering a principle of unity which determines the shape of curriculum from within the Church instead. I also find them particularly companionable with the suggestion that the identity and authority of the priest or minister is established through their living embodiment of the tradition's activities, precisely the activities which Harris considers thematic of the whole of Church life as education.

Use of these five categories might provide further content for Wood's general subject matter of Church life and witness, but need not thereby overthrow the present division of studies so as to produce a drastic change in the naming and sequencing of courses. What they do provide is a set of ecclesial categories of a different phenomenological sort than the all-purpose categories which Farley offered (of tradition, truth, action, situation, vocation) and the corresponding categories Wood offered (of historical, philosophical, practical, discerning, and envisioning). Her effort to gather up the multifarious activities of Church life and, in naming them, propose them as the chief themes of Church education also provides an alternative to the images of the Church and the array of issues which Hough/Cobb proposed. As well, they have correlative biblical images, especially in the life of Jesus, and do offer a basis for a different phenomenology of theological knowledge. As potential criteria by which to determine how to educate students in the knowledge and habits necessary for leadership and sacramental mediation, ecclesial categories such as these provide a relevancy at once deeper than the issues of Hough/Cobb and more theology-specific than the modes of understanding of Farley.

When searching for the rationale for a theological curriculum, the variety of schemata offered by Wood, Hough/Cobb, and Harris can be helpful in forming a matrix for asking whether the necessary elements of a complete preparation are present in any given curriculum. Though a dangerous exercise, it is intriguing to compare the three conceptual groups:

Wood	Farley	Harris
history	*tradition*	*didache*
philosophy	*truth*	*kerygma*
practicalities	*action*	*diakonia*
discernment	*situation*	*koinonia*
vision	*vocation*	*leiturgia*

An adequate curriculum ensures that students have a thorough knowledge of the content of the tradition, are able to make a case for the truth and credibility of it, and can make that truth practical, especially through the service of leadership. They do so with facility in the local Church according to its specific needs, but in communion with the confessing, worshiping universal Church.

There are any number of practical details I have not adverted to concerning curriculum. There is the need of students to be assured that they are adequately prepared to meet the demands of ministry, and there are the limitations of the professor trained in doctoral programs in theology and religious studies attuned to the scholarly guilds, educated to be a practitioner of methods and procedures. There are issues such as sequencing and weighting of courses, and there are the established terrains of departments and individual professors. Revision of the curriculum depends upon the acceptance of far-ranging visions of the subject matter of theology and its methods, of the needs of the world, of the shape of ecclesial life, of the means of rendering belief credible, and finally on the good will of faculty members willing to question what they contribute to a program.

IV

One test case would involve the reconsideration of the purpose and character of the introductory course to theological study which initiates students to the entire program of preparation for ministry. This has been my own concern over the last 10 years of teaching in a school of theology, preparing a diverse group of students for ministry of various kinds. In the Roman tradition this has required a reconsideration of the area of theology called "fundamental" or "foundational" theology.

Francis Fiorenza's reconsideration of this area offers insight into basic issues necessary to the overall development of theological study. His concern with fundamental or foundational theology is not merely an interest in a curricular matter pertinent to one professor or one course, nor is it merely yet another attempt at proposing a new methodology for theology. While the language and focus of his discussion might seem esoteric in its vocabulary and argumentation, it does address a vital issue in the reconsideration of theological education for ministry, and in its very content is evidence of an important concern which should underlie the revisioning of curriculum.

As his historical study in *Foundational Theology* (Fiorenza, 1984, chapter 9) shows, this very small bit of the curriculum has a development which is very instructive of changes in the entire conception of theology, its curriculum and methodology, in the Roman Catholic tradition. To understand the 20th-century attempts at revision of this aspect of theological study, one must consider the reforms in priestly education established by the Council of Trent and the first efforts at a course with an essentially pastoral intent, employing positive theology to present the basic tenets of faith. As Catholic theology responded to the Enlightenment and its critique of revelation, foundational theology redefined its prolegomenal character to be more of an apologetic for the validity of faith itself, and therefore of theology and church structures. In the 19th century, as theology responded to the modern university, foundational theology attempted to establish the "scientific" character of theology as a whole, in a variety of forms, with differing contents.

The history of the revision of this doorway into theology offers a glimpse at the factors bringing about the gradual reshaping of the entire curriculum, especially as to the rationale for its structure and content. The course of foundational theology changed from a focus on positive theology, through its work as prolegomena, to its being apologetics, and now to its current guise according to various proposals. Fiorenza summarizes his own proposal for foundational theology through the following contrasts:

> A historicist and transcendental perspective has been replaced by a hermeneutical consciousness of the limitations of human understanding. An idealistic ideal of scientific endeavor with its search for unity and self-evident foundations has been re-

placed by a scientific ideal that relates norms of rationality to specific communities, concrete paradigms, and diverse practical criteria. The clear-cut distinction between theory and practice or between theory and application has been replaced by an awareness of their interrelationship. We have come to recognize the role of praxis upon the formation of theory and the relevance of application for understanding. (Fiorenza, 1984, 117-118)

In an admittedly terse fashion, I have also suggested considerations necessary for the introductory course in a theological curriculum of ministerial preparation. (Schner, G., 1985) I shall not repeat them here except to reiterate a conviction that the course of introduction is a microcosm of the changes in curriculum as a whole. It must reflect an awareness of the complex of elements and doctrines which compose theology and the enactment of faith in ministry, not simply according to the state of the Church in a given era, but as faithfully as possible according to the Great Tradition of theology and ministry across centuries and traditions. To introduce students to the study of theology as a whole, specifically as the core and motive power of preparation for ministry, requires clarity about all the sorts of things this essay has attempted to explore.

Part IV

The Future

9. Whither the Theological Institution?

A BOOK SUCH AS THIS IS MUCH LIKE THE BIOGRAPHY OF A LIVING person. It risks being out of date by the time it gets published, since a continuing revision of description and interpretation is inevitable when the story is about a living, changing entity. Such is the collection of theological institutions in North America which make up the now relatively small group of Roman Catholic schools of theology preparing individuals for ministry. To ask where they are going presumes several things: that they are indeed "on the move," that the movement is not haphazard, and that it is worthwhile knowing the answer to the question. In this concluding chapter, I return to the exploration of a question, as in Part I, and would encourage those who read this essay to ask that question about the institutions of theological education they know and are concerned about. The future of such institutions should not be decided by its members, the hierarchy, or the "experts" alone. As an essential item in the tradition itself, theological education needs the critique and support of the Church as a whole in all its parts, those who direct it, those who pass through it, those who depend upon its graduates.

As to the presuppositions of the question, it is easy to defend the first, namely that such institutions are in the midst of unsettled times. These pages are not the place for institutional gossip, though story telling is a prime means for discovering the truth of my assertions. Whether it be financial constraints, shrinking enrollments, ecclesiastical politics, or a self-imposed process of institutional review, theological schools and seminaries are passing through radical changes from dissolution to transformation. Some are undergoing expansion and modification because of generous support, diversification of their student bodies, and the enactment of new or revised mission statements. It has become a commonplace to note that it is not the occurrence of changes that is novel, but the rapidity with which they occur and the significance of their content.

There are several good warrants for the second presupposition, that the movement is not haphazard, both as to those factors promoting change which are initiated by the schools and those they undergo from outside forces. Some of the consistency of movement is ensured by the oversight of the episcopacy in its role as legislator for and governor of the process of preparation for ministry. Cooperation among the members of the administration of schools in geographical regions or within religious communities ensures a form of commonality "from below," as it were. Though much less directly influential in the process of change, there is considerable evidence among the faithful generally of a commonality of insight about ministry and its future which grasps the urgency and importance of the present changes taking place. That common intuition, however, does not necessarily result in concrete action or a simple uniformity of endeavors. There are many parallel movements, each with its rationale and emotional investments, and each with significant consequences for the Church. Few are as retrograde or heterodox as the prophets of doom would tell us; most are deeply concerned for a continuing enlivenment of the tradition through some form of conscious redirection of ministerial preparation beyond the received paradigm; and all are worthy of consideration at least because they reflect the real diversity of contemporary life in the Roman tradition.

Because the present situation requires consideration of several different kinds of theological institutions, their differing memberships and constituencies, and their correspondingly different ideals, the choice of the types of institution best suited to the future of ministry in the Roman tradition in North America requires continuing reflection on "where we are going." The commonality of general goals and the unity of principles for programs belies not only the actual diversity, but the potential for quite different futures. This brings me to the third presupposition, that it is worthwhile knowing the answer to the question of where we are going institutionally. Individual institutions or groups of them which try to formulate a plan for their own future will be engaged in projecting a vision and steps towards it which is composed of, at least, the factors which the preceding chapters have investigated. Such planning requires a consideration of nonnegotiable factors, empirical and ideal, as much as invention of new configurations. Self-preservation and development can only profit from awareness of analogous situations in other institutions.

This chapter will be brief. Even more so than with matters of pedagogy and curriculum, I do not propose any single ideal configuration for the theological institution. I will consider, however, two general caveats about the institution in which ministerial preparation takes place.

I

As in previous chapters, it is advantageous to profit from the already existing reflection on these matters, and two articles of James Gustafson recommend themselves here: "The Vocation of the Theological Educator" and "Priorities in Theological Education." In the first of these two articles, his reflections upon the last 30 years of literature since the Niebuhr-Williams-Gustafson study of the state of theological education in North America contain two themes which are of timely importance: the theological school as an intellectual center of Church life, and theology itself as sapiential knowledge. Both notions can be helpful guidelines for assessing which configuration of activities would be best for the Roman tradition. Moreover, I return through these articles to the overarching presumption I noted at the end of the introduction to this work, namely that the whole of theological education must be a scholarly and intellectual contribution to the life of the Church.

The second theme concerning theology as sapiential knowledge needs little development here. It has been rudimentary to much of what has been said already, as I indicated in the introductory chapter. Gustafson himself borrows Farley's notion of theology as a *habitus* and an unfolding of wisdom as the groundwork for developing, through a series of contrasts, a portrait of the person and character of the theological educator, and by extension, of the faculty as a whole. Inasmuch as the study and teaching of theology involve both cognitive discipline and an orientation of the soul through Christian faith, there is a displacement of attention from curriculum, courses, or teaching techniques to the importance of the recruitment and development of a faculty committed to the pursuit of theology as a *habitus,* the human unfolding of a God-given and God-focused wisdom.

There is a determining influence, then, of this second theme on Gustafson's first, the role of the school of theology as an intellectual center of the Church. Just as the retrieval of theological habits as the heart of the educational process and those involved with it require reconsideration of how theology is a particular kind of knowledge and practice, so to propose the school of theology as an intellectual center requires some reconsideration of what sort of "intellectual life" is appropriate to it. Disinterested research on the model of academic *Wissenshaft* is not the goal of theological scholarship. That is not to suggest, however, that honesty and intellectual rigor are incompatible with such scholarship. This point particularly needs to be reinforced for some who are confused about the intellectual life of Catholic schools, both inside and outside the tradition. Some confuse intellectual integrity with integralism, and others confuse intellectual rigor with forms of reductionism. (Van Beeck, 53-69) Assessing the scholarly conscience of the theologian, the intended audience of the results of theological research, and the principles of selection for such study would be excellent vehicles with which to assess the direction of an institution's development through reflection on the dynamism and effect of its intellectual life. Catholic faculties are hardly unaware of the traditioning and pastoring implications of all that they study, teach, and publish. I use those two words, "traditioning" and "pastoring" with an understood caution that they too often carry connotations and ideological agenda which must be exorcised before they can be well used. Gustafson himself cautions that such theological works must involve "some passion in their execution" yet not collapse "into homily or prophetic rhetoric. . . ." (Gustafson, 1987a, 58)

In a second article, Gustafson names a problem which Catholic theologates are increasingly experiencing as institutions: the proliferation of activities they undertake, either to ensure their financial viability, or more importantly to meet the varying demands of their locales and of their student population. (Gustafson, 1987b) Such changes result in, and require, careful reconsideration of the mission and administrative direction of the institution. (Schuth, 59-61) Gustafson's concern is whether, amid this often vital but confusing development, there is a concomitant loss of unity and purpose in the theological institution, and even perhaps the loss of its adherence to the unique purpose it should have, namely the education of persons with a sense of calling to ecclesial ministry in the churches.

This sense of purpose is similarly defined by Schuth. She observes:

> Theologates are "schools for the Church," with the primary mission of educating people for pastoral ministry. Theologate programs are not the same as non-ministerial theology programs at universities; their academic standards are often as high, but the acquisition of pastoral skills that is integral to theologate programs is absent from the strictly academic programs of universities. (Schuth, 59)

I do not dispute the factual character of the difference, but would caution the use of that difference as the defining characteristic. In this matter, Farley's analysis of the coincidence of a skills-oriented program and the loss of theology as the heart of the study of such a school is pertinent. As missions are redefined, a focus on pastoral skills will not provide an adequate center for the redefining of a theologate's mission and the ensuing practical decisions needed to continue developing an institution. Matters seem to have come full circle and returned us to the beginning of this essay. Careful thought about the professional, practical, and spiritual maturity of our students is the vehicle for discovering the intellectual integrity of our institutions, albeit an integrity which is normed by the rules governing the identity and authority of ministry itself within the Christian tradition.

For a school to define itself essentially by contrast to the university departments of theology is troublesome for several reasons. First, the common commitment to intellectual excellence should rather be confirmed and emphasized than undercut; second, the university-related departments need the pastoral, that is practical or ecclesial character of theologate studies to give them an essential element of their own identity and the necessary critical edge to engage the university at large. This comment echoes, I hope, Farley's concerns for the fragility of knowledge in the university. Third, the university departments of theology have an important set of experiences to reflect upon both for themselves and for the sake of the theologates, namely the struggles of lay and ordained students who engage in graduate theological education in order to become professors at professional schools. Greater interaction and collaboration between university advanced degree programs and professional programs not only would benefit both, but would ensure the maintenance of the intellectual integrity of both worlds of education. It should be quickly added that the third party to this discussion must ultimately be the congregations of the Church in all their particularity. If the relation of the school of theology as professional to the university as scholarly and research-oriented is complex, the dialogue with the congregation is as yet hardly initiated. Proposals have been made (Hopewell, Hough/Wheeler), but in the Roman tradition, while good will and desire might be on the rise, the means for even beginning effective conversations seem lacking.

In sum, my two caveats take note that any institution in its efforts to be at the center of the intellectual life of the Church must exercise a realistic limitation of its activities if it is to maintain its health and fulfill its mission and identity. The challenge to the present-day school of theology in the Roman tradition is twofold: to renew its identity and mission in ministerial education as a principle vehicle for the inventive traditioning of the Church, and to resist the fragmentation or trivialization of that educational purpose because of a sincere desire to serve the needs of the Church which might itself turn into a self-destructive effort to become the only educational institution within the tradition. Hidden in both challenges is the danger of an inward collapse of the institution upon itself, as it becomes neither inventive nor traditioning but merely self-sustaining.

This brief final chapter has come to an end. Before taking leave of my readers, without belaboring the obvious, I wish to reassert the preliminary and heuristic character of what has preceded. This essay has not described a "state of the art" institution, nor has it simply detailed established and unquestioned patterns of education, nor has it attempted to predict the future. It has posed questions for reflection and sought out a few basic rules which could determine the shape of the continuing revision of preparation for ministry and the institutions in which it takes place. Education for ministry in the Roman tradition is on the verge of yet greater changes, and I hope this essay will aid the process of clarification needed to bring them about.

Bibliography

Documents

Bishops' Committee on Priestly Life and Ministry, National Conference of Catholic Bishops. *A Shepherd's Care: Reflections on the Changing Role of Pastor.* Washington, D.C.: USCC Office of Publishing and Promotion Services, 1987.

The Documents of Vatican II. Ed. W. M. Abbott, S.J. New York: The America Press, 1966.

Norms for Priestly Formation. Washington, D.C.: United States Catholic Conference, 1982.

The Program of Priestly Formation. Washington, D.C.: United States Catholic Conference, 1982.

Books

Thomas Aquinas. *Summa Theologiae.* Ed. T. Gilby. London: Eyre and Spottiswoode, 1964, Vol I.

T. W. Blue. *The Teaching and Learning Process.* Washington, D. C.: National Education Association, 1984

L. Boff. *Church: Charism and Power.* Trans. J. W. Diercksmeier. New York: Crossroad, 1985.

L. W. Brandt. *Psychologists Caught.* Toronto: University of Toronto Press, 1982.

D. Browning. *Religious Thought and the Modern Psychologies.* Philadelphia: Fortress Press, 1987.

D. Brundage. *Adult Learning Principles and Their Applications to Programme Planning.* Toronto: Ministry of Education, 1980.

J. W. Carroll. *As One With Authority: Reflective Leadership in Ministry.* Louisville, Kentucky: Westminster/John Knox Press, 1991.

Y. Congar. *Tradition and Traditions.* Trans. M. Naseby and T. Rainborough. New York: Macmillan, 1967.

J. P. Dolan, et al. *Transforming Parish Ministry.* New York: Crossroad, 1990.

F. Dumont. *L'institution de théologie.* Montreal, Quebec: Editions Fides, 1987.

L. Duck. *Teaching with Charisma.* Boston: Allyn and Bacon, Inc., 1981.

The Education of the Practical Theologian: Responses to Joseph Hough and John Cobb's "Christian Identity and Theological Education." Ed. D. Browning, D. Polk, I. Evison. Atlanta, Georgia: Scholars Press, 1989.

E. Farley. *Ecclesial Reflection: An Anatomy of Theological Method.* Philadelphia: Fortress Press, 1982.

E. Farley. *The Fragility of Knowledge.* Philadelphia: Fortress Press, 1988.

E. Farley. *Theologia: The Fragmentation and Unity of Theological Education.* Philadelphia: Fortress Press, 1983.

F. Fiorenza. *Foundational Theology: Jesus and the Church.* New York: Crossroads, 1984.

J. R. Geiselmann. *The Meaning of Tradition.* Trans W. J. O'Hara. Montreal: Palm Publishers, 1966.

D. Hare. *Racing Demon.* London: Faber and Faber, 1990.

M. Harris. *Fashion Me A People.* Louisville, Kentucky: Westminster/John Knox Press, 1989.

E. Hill. *Ministry and Authority in the Catholic Church.* London: Geoffrey Chapman, 1988.

J. Hopewell. *Congregation.* Philadelphia: Fortress Press, 1987.

J. Hough and J. Cobb. *Christian Identity and Theological Education.* Chico, California: Scholars Press, 1985.

J. Hough and B. Wheeler, eds. *Beyond Clericalism: The Congregation as a Focus for Theological Education.* Chico, California: Scholars Press, 1988.

S. Kleinman. *Equals Before God,* Chicago: The University of Chicago Press, 1984.

G. Langford. *Education, Persons and Society: a Philosophical Enquiry.* London: Macmillan, 1985.

D. Lapp et al. *Teaching and Learning: Philosophical, Psychological and Curricular Applications.* New York: Macmillan Publishing Co., Inc, 1975.

G. Lindbeck. *The Nature of Doctrine.* Philadelphia: Fortress Press, 1984. (Lindbeck, 1984)

J. P. Mackey. *The Modern Theology of Tradition.* New York: Herder and Herder, 1963.

T. O'Meara. *Theology of Ministry.* New York: Paulist Press, 1983.

P. J. Palmer. *To Know As We Are Known.* San Francisco: Harper and Row, 1983.

J. Passmore. *The Philosophy of Teaching.* London: Duckworth and Co., 1980.

J. F. Ross. *Portraying Analogy.* Cambridge: Cambridge University Press, 1981.

M. M. Schaefer and J. F. Henderson. *The Catholic Priesthood: A Liturgically Based Theology of the Presbyteral Office. Canadian Studies in Liturgy,* vol. 4. Ottawa, Ontario: Canadian Conference of Catholic Bishops, 1990.

K. Schuth. *Reason for the Hope: The Futures of Roman Catholic Theologates.* Wilmington, Delaware: Michael Glazier, Inc., 1989.

G. Tavard. *A Theology for Ministry.* Wilmington, Delaware: Michael Glazier, 1983.

F. J. van Beeck, S.J. *God Encountered.* New York: Harper and Row, 1988.

J. White. *The Diocesan Seminary in the United States.* Notre Dame, Indiana: University of Notre Dame Press, 1989.

C. M. Wood. *Vision and Discernment: An Orientation in Theology.* Atlanta, Georgia: Scholars Press, 1985.

Robert Wuthnow. *The Restructuring of American Religion.* Princeton, N.J.: Princeton University Press, 1988.

Articles

J. Carroll. "The Professional Model of Ministry—Is It Worth Saving?" *Theological Education,* vol. XXI, no. 2, Spring 1985, 7-48.

R. Chopp. "Emerging Issues and Theological Education." *Theological Education,* vol. XXVI, no. 2, Spring 1990, 106-124.

E. J. Ciuba. "The Impact of Changing Ecclesiological and Christological Models on Roman Catholic Seminary Education." *Theological Education*, Autumn 1987, 57-72.

F. Fiorenza. "Theory and Practice: Theological Education as a Reconstructive, Hermeneutical, and Practical Task." *Theological Education*, supplement vol. XXII, 1990, 106-124.

J. Gustafson. "Priorities in Theological Education." *Theological Education*, supplement vol. XXIII, 1987, 69-87.

J. Gustafson. "The Vocation of the Theological Educator." *Theological Education*, supplement vol. XXIII, 1987, 53-68.

J. D. Hall. "Theological Education as Character Formation?" *Theological Education*, Vol. 24, Supplement 1, 1988, 53-79.

E. J. Kilmartin, S.J. "Lay Participation in the Apostolate of the Hierarchy." *Official Ministry in a New Age*. Ed. J.H. Provost. Washington, D.C.: Canon Law Society of America, 1981, 89-116.

M. Lamb. "Will There Be Catholic Theology in the United States?" *America*, May 26, 1990, 523-534.

G. Lindbeck. "The Church." *Keeping the Faith: Essays to Mark the Centenary of Lex Mundi*. Ed. G. Wainwright. Philadelphia: Fortress Press, 1988, 179-208. (Lindbeck, 1988a)

G. Lindbeck. "The Church's Mission to Post-Modern Culture." *Postmodern Theology*. Ed. F. B. Burnham. San Francisco: Harper and Row, 1989, 37-55. (Lindbeck, 1989a)

G. Lindbeck. "Scripture, Consensus, and Community." *Biblical Interpretation in Crisis*. Ed. R. D. Neuhaus. Grand Rapids, Michigan: W. Eerdmanns, 1989, 74-101. (Lindbeck, 1989b)

G. Lindbeck. "Spiritual Formation and Theological Education." *Theological Education*, Supplement I, 1988, 10-32. (Lindbeck, 1988b)

G. Lindbeck. "Working Paper on Aspect of University-Related Theological Education." Lindbeck, Deutsch, and Glazer. *University Divinity Schools: A Report on Ecclesiastically Independent Theological Education*. New York: The Rockefeller Foundation, 1976.

G. O'Collins. "Catholic Theology (1965-90)." *America*, February 3, 1990, 86-105.

T. O'Meara. "Doctoral Programs in Theology in U.S. Catholic Universities." *America*, February 3, 1990, 79-103.

R. Sano. "Theological Faculties As Mentors of Ministers for the Church." *Theological Education,* vol. XXVI, no. 2, Spring 1990, 11-34.

M. Suchocki. "Theological Foundations for Ethnic and Gender Diversity in Faculties or Excellence and the Motley Crew," *Theological Education,* vol. XXVI, no. 2, Spring 1990, 35-50.

S. Schneiders. "Spirituality in the Academy." *Theological Studies,* vol. 50, no. 4, 1989, 676-697.

G. P. Schner. "Formation: A Search for Rules." *The Way Supplement* 56, 1986, 71-84.

G. P. Schner. "Formation as a Unifying Concept of Theological Education." *Theological Education* vol. XXI, no. 2, Spring 1985, 94-113.

J. G. Schner. "The Failure of the Flight from Intimacy." *The Pius Riffel Lecture.* Toronto: Regis College, 1984.

R. Thiemann. "The Future of an Illusion: An Inquiry Into the Contrast Between Theological and Religious Studies." *Theological Education,* vol. XXVI, no. 2, Spring 1990, 66-85.

R. Wister, "The Teaching of Theology 1950-90: The American Catholic Experience." *America,* February 3, 1990, 88-109.